A 3-level grammar embodiment project: visualizing grammar and writing practice

Level **2**

Grammar ViSTA

 DARAKWON

Grammar ViSTA Level 2

지은이 김해자, 손의웅, 최현진
펴낸이 정규도
펴낸곳 (주)다락원

초판 1쇄 발행 2018년 4월 5일
초판 11쇄 발행 2023년 12월 14일

편집 이희경
디자인 조수정, 박은비, 김나경
일러스트 이경
영문 감수 Amy L. Redding, Michael A. Putlack

다락원 경기도 파주시 문발로 211
내용문의 (02)736-2031 내선 503
구입문의 (02)736-2031 내선 250~252
Fax (02)732-2037
출판등록 1977년 9월 16일 제 406-2008-000007호

ISBN 978-89-277-0826-1 54740
      978-89-277-0824-7 54740(set)

http://www.darakwon.co.kr
다락원 홈페이지를 방문하시면 상세한 출판정보와 함께
동영상강좌, MP3자료 등 다양한 어학 정보를 얻으실 수 있습니다.

Level **2**

Grammar
ViSTA

STRUCTURE

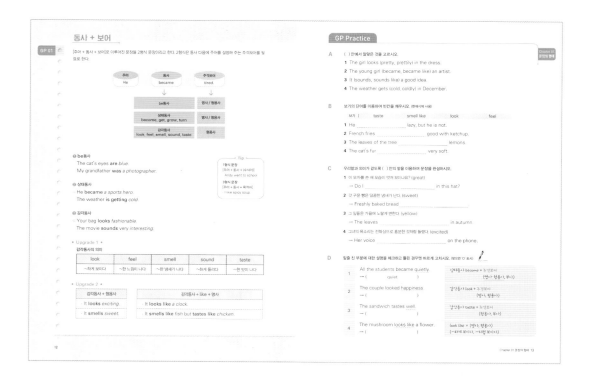

1 Grammar Point

• 문법패턴 도식화
총 177개의 핵심 문법을 도식화하여
시각적 학습 효과를 극대화시켰습니다.

• 대표 예문 선정
GP마다 대표 예문(☆)을 선정하여 문법 내용과
실전 예문을 동시에 학습할 수 있습니다.

• Tip과 Upgrade
주의해야 할 내용은 Tip으로,
심화 문법 내용은 Upgrade로 정리하였습니다.

2 GP Practice

• 선택형·단답형·서술형 문제
선택형, 단답형, 서술형 영작으로
단계적이고 반복적인 학습이 되도록 하였습니다.

• 오답 찾고 설명하기 문제
오답 찾기 방식으로 핵심 문법을 스스로 정리하고
자기 주도적 학습이 되도록 하였습니다.

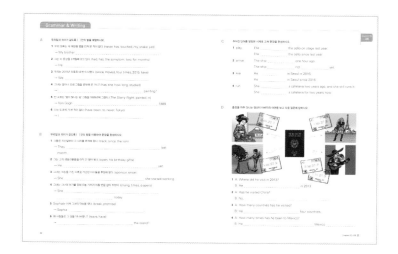

3 Grammar & Writing

- **단어 배열·문장 완성형 문제**

  학습한 문법 내용을 토대로 단어 배열 및
  문장 완성을 통해 실질적인 쓰기 연습이
  되도록 하였습니다.

- **구문 및 표현력 평가 문제**

  실생활을 소재로 한 대화나 삽화 문제를
  구성함으로써 수행평가에 필요한 구문 작성 능력과
  표현 능력을 키울 수 있도록 하였습니다.

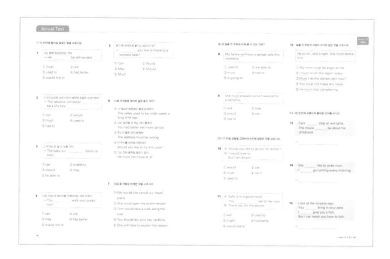

4 Actual Test

- **실전 문제**

  학습한 내용을 다양한 실전 문제를 통해서
  다시 한 번 정리할 수 있도록 하였습니다.

- **내신 대비 서술형 문제**

  최신 내신 유형을 반영한 문제로 구성하여
  서술형 내신을 완벽하게 대비할 수 있도록
  하였습니다.

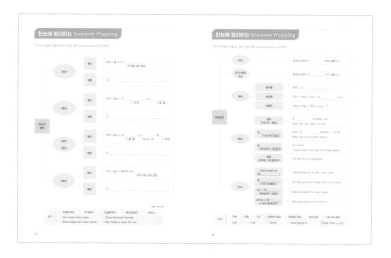

5 한눈에 정리하는 Grammar Mapping

- **문법 맵핑**

  학습한 문법 내용 전체를 한눈에 파악하고
  핵심개념을 맵핑 이미지로 다시 한 번
  정리할 수 있도록 하였습니다.

Workbook

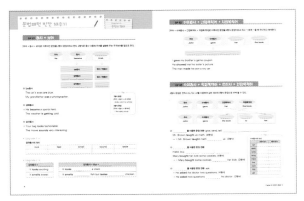

1 문법패턴 빈칸 채우기

- **노트 완성형 문제**

  노트 형태로 제시한 핵심 문법 사항의 빈칸을 채워 나가면서
  자기 주도적으로 학습할 수 있도록 하였습니다.

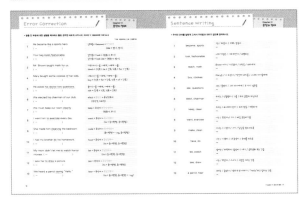

2 Workbook 연습문제

- **단계별 반복학습 문제**

  풍부하고 다양한 연습문제를 통해 문법과 쓰기 연습을
  극대화시켰습니다.

3 Error Correction & Sentence Writing

- **오답 찾고 설명하기 문제**

  학습한 문법 개념을 정확하게 이해하고 있는지
  시험해 볼 수 있는 자기 주도적 학습 방법입니다.

- **구문 영작 문제**

  학습한 문법 지식을 바탕으로 구문 단위로 영작을 능숙하게
  할 수 있는지 검증해 볼 수 있는 문제 유형입니다.

4 도전! 필수구문 156

- **대표 예문 영작 문제**

  GP마다 선정한 대표 예문을 통문장으로 영작하고
  암기할 수 있도록 구성하였습니다.

---

* 본 교재는 대등한 쓰임의 단어들의 경우 ( )나 /로 구분 표기합니다.
  (일반적 용도로도 사용)
  ex which (that): which 또는 that 사용 가능
       which / that: which 또는 that 사용 가능
* 본 교재는 문법 설명 파트에서 학습 요소의 강조를 위해 굵은 서체나
  이탤릭체를 사용합니다. (일반적 용도로도 사용)

Grammar ViSTA Contents

Chapter 01

문장의 형태   011

GP 01   동사 + 보어   012
GP 02   수여동사 + 간접목적어 + 직접목적어   014
GP 03   수여동사 + 직접목적어 + 전치사 + 간접목적어   014
GP 04   동사 + 목적어 + 목적격보어   016
GP 05   사역·지각동사 + 목적어 + 목적격보어   018
• Grammar & Writing   020
• Actual Test   022
• 한눈에 정리하는 Grammar Mapping   026

Chapter 02

시제   027

GP 06   현재완료   028
GP 07   과거와 현재완료   028
GP 08   현재완료 용법   030
• Grammar & Writing   032
• Actual Test   034
• 한눈에 정리하는 Grammar Mapping   038

Chapter 03

조동사   039

GP 09   can, may, will   040
GP 10   must, have to, should   042
GP 11   had better, used to, would like to   044
• Grammar & Writing   046
• Actual Test   048
• 한눈에 정리하는 Grammar Mapping   052

Chapter 04

수동태   053

GP 12   능동태와 수동태   054
GP 13   수동태의 시제   056
GP 14   수동태의 여러 형태   056
GP 15   동사구 수동태   058
GP 16   by 이외의 전치사를 쓰는 수동태   058
• Grammar & Writing   060
• Actual Test   062
• 한눈에 정리하는 Grammar Mapping   066

Contents

Chapter 05

to부정사 067

GP 17 to부정사의 명사적 쓰임 068
GP 18 to부정사의 형용사적 쓰임 070
GP 19 to부정사의 부사적 쓰임 072
GP 20 to부정사의 의미상 주어 074
GP 21 to부정사를 이용한 구문 074
- Grammar & Writing 076
- Actual Test 078
- 한눈에 정리하는 Grammar Mapping 082

Chapter 06

동명사 083

GP 22 동명사의 명사적 쓰임 084
GP 23 동명사의 관용적 쓰임 084
GP 24 동명사와 to부정사 086
- Grammar & Writing 088
- Actual Test 090
- 한눈에 정리하는 Grammar Mapping 094

Chapter 07

분사 095

GP 25 현재분사와 과거분사 096
GP 26 분사의 형용사적 쓰임 096
GP 27 감정을 나타내는 분사 098
GP 28 현재분사와 동명사 098
GP 29 분사구문 100
- Grammar & Writing 102
- Actual Test 104
- 한눈에 정리하는 Grammar Mapping 108

Chapter 08

대명사 109

GP 30 재귀대명사 110
GP 31 부정대명사 one, another, other 112
GP 32 one, another, other(s)의 표현 112
GP 33 부정대명사 all, both 114
GP 34 부정대명사 each, every 114
- Grammar & Writing 116
- Actual Test 118
- 한눈에 정리하는 Grammar Mapping 122

Contents

Chapter 09

비교표현   123

GP 35 원급, 비교급, 최상급   124

GP 36 원급을 이용한 표현   126

GP 37 비교급을 이용한 표현   126

GP 38 최상급을 이용한 표현   126

- Grammar & Writing   128
- Actual Test   130
- 한눈에 정리하는 Grammar Mapping   134

Chapter 10

접속사   135

GP 39 시간 접속사   136

GP 40 이유 접속사   136

GP 41 조건 접속사   138

GP 42 양보 접속사   138

GP 43 명령문 and / or   138

GP 44 접속사 that   140

GP 45 상관접속사   140

- Grammar & Writing   142
- Actual Test   144
- 한눈에 정리하는 Grammar Mapping   148

Chapter 11

관계사   149

GP 46 관계대명사의 역할과 종류   150

GP 47 주격 관계대명사 who, which, that   150

GP 48 목적격 관계대명사 who(m), which, that   150

GP 49 소유격 관계대명사 whose   152

GP 50 관계대명사 that   152

GP 51 관계대명사 생략   154

GP 52 관계대명사 what   154

GP 53 관계부사 when, where, why, how   156

- Grammar & Writing   158
- Actual Test   160
- 한눈에 정리하는 Grammar Mapping   164

Chapter 12

가정법   165

GP 54 가정법 과거   166

GP 55 단순 조건문과 가정법 과거   166

GP 56 I wish 가정법 과거   168

GP 57 as if 가정법 과거   168

- Grammar & Writing   170
- Actual Test   172
- 한눈에 정리하는 Grammar Mapping   176

문장의 형태

GP 01 동사 + 보어

GP 02 수여동사 + 간접목적어 + 직접목적어

GP 03 수여동사 + 직접목적어 + 전치사 + 간접목적어

GP 04 동사 + 목적어 + 목적격보어

GP 05 사역·지각동사 + 목적어 + 목적격보어

• Grammar & Writing

• Actual Test

• 한눈에 정리하는 Grammar Mapping

동사 + 보어

[주어 + 동사 + 보어]로 이루어진 문장을 2형식 문장이라고 한다. 2형식은 동사 다음에 주어를 설명해 주는 주격보어를 필요로 한다.

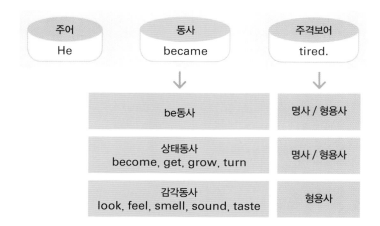

❶ be동사

The cat's eyes **are** *blue.*

My grandfather **was** *a photographer.*

❷ 상태동사

☆ He **became** *a sports hero.*

The weather **is getting** *cold.*

❸ 감각동사

☆ Your bag **looks** *fashionable.*

The movie **sounds** very *interesting.*

○ Tip ○

① 1형식 문장

[주어 + 동사 + (수식어)]

· Andy went to school.

② 3형식 문장

[주어 + 동사 + 목적어]

· I like spicy soup.

• Upgrade 1 •

감각동사의 의미

look	feel	smell	sound	taste
~하게 보이다	~한 느낌이 나다	~한 냄새가 나다	~하게 들리다	~한 맛이 나다

• Upgrade 2 •

감각동사 + 형용사	감각동사 + like + 명사
· It **looks** *exciting.*	· It **looks like** *a clock.*
· It **smells** *sweet.*	· It **smells like** *fish* but **tastes like** *chicken.*

GP Practice

A   ( ) 안에서 알맞은 것을 고르시오.

1 The girl looks (pretty, prettily) in the dress.

2 The young girl (became, became like) an artist.

3 It (sounds, sounds like) a good idea.

4 The weather gets (cold, coldly) in December.

B   보기의 단어를 이용하여 빈칸을 채우시오. (현재시제 사용)

보기 |	taste	smell like	look	feel

1 He _____ lazy, but he is not.

2 French fries _____ good with ketchup.

3 The leaves of the tree _____ lemons.

4 The cat's fur _____ very soft.

C   우리말과 의미가 같도록 ( ) 안의 말을 이용하여 문장을 완성하시오.

1 이 모자를 쓴 제 모습이 멋져 보이나요? (great)

　→ Do I _____ _____ in this hat?

2 갓 구운 빵은 달콤한 냄새가 난다. (sweet)

　→ Freshly baked bread_____ _____.

3 그 잎들은 가을에 노랗게 변한다. (yellow)

　→ The leaves _____ _____ in autumn.

4 그녀의 목소리는 전화상으로 흥분한 것처럼 들렸다. (excited)

　→ Her voice _____ _____ on the phone.

D   밑줄 친 부분에 대한 설명을 체크하고 틀린 경우엔 바르게 고치시오. (맞으면 'O' 표시)

1	All the students became <u>quietly</u>. → ( )	상태동사 become + 주격보어 (명사·형용사, 부사)
2	The couple looked <u>happiness</u>. → ( )	감각동사 look + 주격보어 (명사, 형용사)
3	The sandwich tastes <u>well</u>. → ( )	감각동사 taste + 주격보어 (형용사, 부사)
4	The mushroom <u>looks like</u> a flower. → ( )	look like + (명사, 형용사) (~하게 보이다, ~처럼 보이다)

수여동사 + 간접목적어 + 직접목적어

[주어 + 수여동사 + 간접목적어 + 직접목적어]로 이루어진 문장을 4형식 문장이라고 하고 '~에게 ~을 해 주다'라고 해석한다.

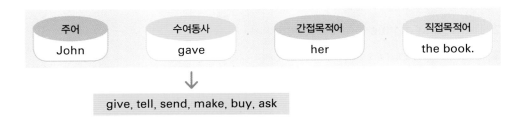

I **gave** *my brother* a game coupon.
He **showed** *me* his sister's picture.
The man **made** *his son* a toy car.

수여동사 + 직접목적어 + 전치사 + 간접목적어

4형식 문장은 전치사 to, for, of를 이용하여 같은 의미의 3형식 문장으로 바꿔 쓸 수 있다.

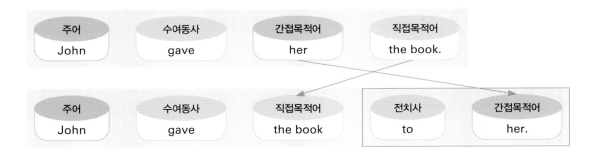

❶ **to를 이용한 문장 전환**: give, send, tell, bring, show, teach…
Mr. Brown **taught** *us* math. (4형식)
→ ☆ Mr. Brown **taught** math *to* *us*. (3형식)

❷ **for를 이용한 문장 전환**: make, buy, cook, find, get…
Mary **bought** *her kids* some cookies. (4형식)
→ ☆ Mary **bought** some cookies *for her kids*. (3형식)

❸ **of를 이용한 문장 전환**: ask…
☆ He **asked** *his doctor* two questions. (4형식)
→ He **asked** two questions *of his doctor*. (3형식)

Tip
수여동사의 의미

	3형식 동사	4형식 동사
tell	말하다	말해 주다
teach	가르치다	가르쳐 주다
write	쓰다	써 주다
bring	가져오다	가져다주다
make	만들다	만들어 주다
buy	사다	사 주다
cook	요리하다	요리해 주다
find	찾다	찾아 주다
get	얻다	구해 주다

GP Practice

A   ( ) 안에서 알맞은 것을 고르시오.

1 She sent (a text message me, me a text message).

2 Sally (gave, found) her umbrella to her brother.

3 Brenda bought a pencil (to, for) her classmate.

4 Don't (tell, ask) strange questions of the new student.

5 My mom brings a glass of milk (to, for) me every morning.

B   두 문장이 같은 의미를 갖도록 빈칸을 채우시오.

1 Molly gave me some useful advice.

→ Molly gave _____ _____ _____ _____ _____ .

2 She made the children a wooden seesaw.

→ She made _____ _____ _____ _____ .

3 He told me his secret by mistake.

→ He told _____ _____ _____ _____ by mistake.

C   우리말과 의미가 같도록 ( ) 안의 말을 이용하여 문장을 완성하시오.

1 그는 그의 엄마에게 은반지를 사 드렸다. (buy, a silver ring)

→ He _____ _____ _____ _____ _____ .

2 형은 일요일마다 나에게 중국어를 가르쳐 준다. (teaches, Chinese)

→ My brother _____ _____ _____ on Sundays.

3 Chris는 우리에게 재미있는 동영상을 보여 주었다. (show, a funny video clip)

→ Chris _____ _____ _____ _____ _____ .

D   밑줄 친 부분에 대한 설명을 체크하고 틀린 경우엔 바르게 고치시오. (맞으면 'O' 표시)

*직목: 직접목적어, 간목: 간접목적어

1	She sold <u>us her homemade pizza</u>. → ( )	팔다 (~를 ~에게, ~에게 ~를) sell + (간목 + 직목, 직목 + 간목)
2	She sold her homemade pizza <u>for us</u>. → ( )	팔다 (~를 ~에게, ~에게 ~를) sell + 직목 + (to, for) + 간목
3	He asked a question <u>in me</u> in class. → ( )	묻다 (~를 ~에게, ~에게 ~를) ask + 직목 + (of, in) + 간목
4	Could you find a seat <u>to me</u>? → ( )	찾다 (~를 ~에게, ~에게 ~를) find + 직목 + (to, for) + 간목

동사 + 목적어 + 목적격보어

[주어 + 동사 + 목적어 + 목적격보어]로 이루어진 문장을 5형식 문장이라고 한다. 5형식은 동작의 대상이 되는 목적어와 그 목적어를 설명하는 목적격보어를 필요로 한다.

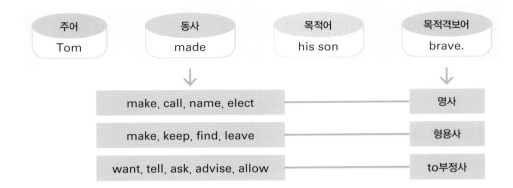

❶ 목적격보어로 명사를 쓰는 동사: make, call, name, elect…

People **called** him *a hero*. (그를 영웅이라고)

They **named** their daughter *Ann*.

☀ We **elected** him *chairman of our club*.

❷ 목적격보어로 형용사를 쓰는 동사: make, keep, find, leave…

Tom **made** me *happy*. (나를 행복하게)

☀ We must **keep** our room *clean*.

I **found** the sofa very *comfortable*.

❸ 목적격보어로 to부정사를 쓰는 동사: want, tell, ask, expect, advise, allow…

☀ I **want** him *to exercise every day*. (그가 매일 운동하기를)

She **asked** me *to buy her dinner*. (나에게 저녁을 사달라고)

He **allowed** his daughter *to watch TV*. (그의 딸이 TV 보는 것을)

• Upgrade •

4형식 문장 vs. 5형식 문장

4형식 문장	He **made** his son *a chair*.　　그의 아들에게 의자를 (his son ≠ a chair)
5형식 문장	He **made** his son *a doctor*.　　그의 아들을 의사로 (his son = a doctor)

GP Practice

A ( ) 안에서 알맞은 것을 고르시오.

1 The waiter asked us (sit, to sit) by the window.

2 Do you expect her (believe, to believe) you?

3 His books made (him a rich man, a rich man him).

4 Parents try to make their children (happy, happily).

B 자연스러운 문장이 되도록 다음 표현을 연결하시오.

1 Don't call me ・ ・ ⓐ fresh.

2 It keeps food ・ ・ ⓑ a baby.

3 I found history ・ ・ ⓒ very interesting.

4 The doctor advised him ・ ・ ⓓ to eat more meat.

C 우리말과 의미가 같도록 ( ) 안의 말을 배열하시오.

1 엄마는 내게 잔돈을 가지라고 말하셨다. (to, me, the change, keep, told)

→ My mom _____.

2 과학자들은 이 돌을 "Alien"이라고 부른다. (this, call, Alien, stone)

→ Scientists _____.

3 그녀는 내가 아침을 거르지 못하게 했다. (to, me, skip, allow, breakfast)

→ She didn't _____.

4 모자는 아기의 머리를 따뜻하게 유지시킨다. (warm, keeps, head, the baby's)

→ The hat _____.

D 밑줄 친 부분에 대한 설명을 체크하고 틀린 경우엔 바르게 고치시오. (맞으면 'O' 표시)

1	Soccer will make people <u>excitedly</u>. → ( )	make + 목적어 + 목적격보어 (형용사, 부사)
2	I wanted him <u>getting</u> the job. → ( )	want + 목적어 + 목적격보어 (to + 동사원형, 동사원형 + -ing)
3	A good night's sleep keeps us <u>health</u>. → ( )	keep + 목적어 + 목적격보어 (명사, 형용사)
4	The teacher told us <u>repeat</u> after him. → ( )	tell + 목적어 + 목적격보어 (동사원형, to + 동사원형)

사역·지각동사 + 목적어 + 목적격보어

GP 05

5형식 문장의 동사가 사역동사와 지각동사일 때는 목적격보어로 동사원형을 쓴다. 다만 지각동사는 [동사원형 + -ing]를 쓸 수도 있다.

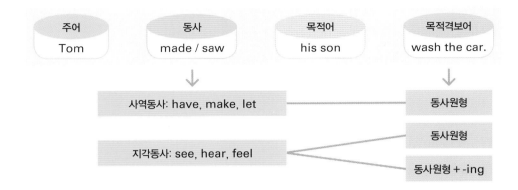

❶ **사역동사**: have, make, let…

☀ She **made** him *clean the bedroom*.

☀ I **had** my brother *do his homework*.

☀ My mom didn't **let** me *watch horror movies*.

❷ **지각동사**: see, watch, hear, listen to, feel, smell…

☀ I **saw** her *draw (drawing) a picture*.

☀ We **heard** a parrot *say (saying) hello*.

She **felt** something *crawl (crawling) on her back*.

> **Tip**
>
> 사역동사는 '~하게 하다, 시키다'의 의미로 남이 어떤 동작을 하게끔 하는 동사이다.
> 지각동사는 사람의 감각 기관을 통해 보고, 듣고, 느끼는 것을 나타내는 동사이다.

• Upgrade •

❶ get

get은 5형식 문장에서 '~하게 하다'의 의미로 쓰이고 목적격보어로 to부정사를 취한다.

He **got** us *to bring our own towels*.

(= He **had** us *bring our own towels*.)

❷ help

help는 5형식 문장에서 '~하는 것을 돕다'의 의미로 쓰이고 목적격보어로 to부정사나 동사원형 모두 취할 수 있다.

The teacher **helped** me *to choose a career*.

The teacher **helped** me *choose a career*.

GP Practice

A ( ) 안에서 알맞은 것을 고르시오.

1 He made the boys (keep, to keep) quiet in the library.

2 I heard my sister (playing, to play) the violin in her room.

3 The coach got the players (rest, to rest) in the shade.

4 She helped her young son (ride, rides) a bike.

B 보기의 단어를 이용하여 빈칸을 채우시오.

보기	arrive	burn	think	drive

1 My father always makes me _____ twice.

2 She didn't let me _____ her car.

3 People saw something _____ in the building.

4 The teacher got his students _____ on time.

C 우리말과 의미가 같도록 ( ) 안의 말을 이용하여 문장을 완성하시오.

1 나는 Judy가 어떤 남자와 말하는 것을 들었다. (listen to, talk)

→ I _____ _____ _____ _____ with a man.

2 그는 나에게 돈을 갚도록 했다. (have, pay back)

→ He _____ _____ _____ the money.

3 Kevin은 우리가 클럽에 가입하도록 해 줄 것이다. (let, join)

→ Kevin will _____ _____ _____ the club.

4 우리는 원숭이가 나무에 오르는 것을 보았다. (watch, climb)

→ We _____ _____ _____ a tree.

D 밑줄 친 부분에 대한 설명을 체크하고 틀린 경우엔 바르게 고치시오. (맞으면 'O' 표시)

*가능한 답은 모두 체크

1	The gift will make him <u>to feel</u> good. → ( )	make + 목적어 + 목적격보어 (to + 동사원형, 동사원형, 동사원형 + -ing)
2	I saw her <u>cutting</u> the paper. → ( )	see + 목적어 + 목적격보어 (to + 동사원형, 동사원형, 동사원형 + -ing)
3	She helped him <u>finding</u> a job. → ( )	help + 목적어 + 목적격보어 (to + 동사원형, 동사원형, 동사원형 + -ing)
4	He got the man <u>fix</u> the radio. → ( )	get + 목적어 + 목적격보어 (to + 동사원형, 동사원형, 동사원형 + -ing)

A 우리말과 의미가 같도록 ( ) 안의 말을 배열하시오.

1 그것은 놀라운 아이디어처럼 들린다. (an, idea, like, amazing, sounds)

→ That _____.

2 그 음악은 나를 편안하게 만든다. (me, relaxed, makes)

→ The music _____.

3 William은 그의 할머니에게 팔찌를 사드렸다. (a, his, bought, bracelet, grandmother)

→ William _____.

4 그녀는 나에게 음식을 잘 씹으라고 말했다. (to, me, the, well, food, chew, told)

→ She _____.

5 그녀는 손님에게 멋진 저녁을 요리해 주었다. (for, cooked, a nice dinner, her guest)

→ She _____.

6 엄마는 내가 직접 운동화를 빨도록 하셨다. (me, my, wash, made, sneakers)

→ Mom _____ by myself.

B 우리말과 의미가 같도록 ( ) 안의 말을 이용하여 문장을 완성하시오.

1 아버지는 나를 공주님이라고 부르신다. (call, a princess)

→ My dad _____ _____ _____ _____.

2 그 수프는 맛있는 냄새가 난다. (delicious)

→ The soup _____ _____.

3 나는 어제 내 자전거를 Mike에게 빌려 주었다. (lend)

→ I _____ _____ _____ _____ yesterday.

4 그녀는 그에게 이 나무 아래에 텐트를 치라고 부탁했다. (ask, set up)

→ She _____ _____ _____ _____ _____ a tent under this tree.

5 우리는 두 소년이 교실을 떠나는 것을 봤다. (see, leave)

→ We _____ _____ _____ _____ the classroom.

6 고모가 나에게 야구 경기 표 세 장을 주었다. (give)

→ My aunt _____ _____ _____ _____ to the baseball game.

7 그 미소 짓는 치과의사는 소년이 편안한 마음이 들도록 했다. (make, feel)

→ The smiling dentist _____ _____ _____ _____ at ease.

C 그림에 맞게 주어진 말을 이용하여 문장을 완성하시오.

dance on the stage

read her blog

shake suddenly

wear his new hat

1 I watched the girl _____ .

2 She expects us _____ .

3 Did you feel the building _____ ?

4 My brother let me _____ .

D 다음 대화를 읽고 흐름에 알맞게 ( ) 안의 말을 배열하시오.

Kate	Hi, Steven. You look busy. What are you doing?
Steven	Hi, Kate. I am planning my trip to Europe next week.
Kate	That's great. [1] A travel plan will (trip, your, make, exciting).
Steven	Yes, but I don't know where to visit first.
Kate	[2] I can (you, tips, some, give). Last year, I went there for 10 days.
Steven	Really?
Kate	Actually, I made a plan for the trip, and I still have it on my computer.
Steven	[3] Can you (to, it, me, send)?
Kate	Sure. [4] It will (to, you, help, travel) around Europe.

1 A travel plan will _____ .

2 I can _____ .

3 Can you _____ ?

4 It will _____ around Europe.

(1–5) 빈칸에 들어갈 알맞은 말을 고르시오.

1

Your plan sounds _____ to me.
Let's do it.

① well   ② greatly

③ nicely   ④ good

⑤ perfectly

2

He showed his new smartphone _____
his friends.

① to   ② at

③ of   ④ in

⑤ for

3

I expected her _____ on time.

① arrive   ② arrives

③ arrived   ④ to arrive

⑤ arriving

4

She bought a handmade bag _____ me.

① to   ② at

③ of   ④ in

⑤ for

5

Greg's joke made us _____.

① laugh   ② laughs

③ laughe   ④ to laugh

⑤ laughing

(6–7) 우리말을 영어로 바르게 옮긴 것을 <u>모두</u> 고르시오.

6

난 뭔가가 물 아래로 숨는 것을 봤어.

① I saw something hid underwater.

② I saw something hiding underwater.

③ I saw something to hide underwater.

④ I saw something hides underwater.

⑤ I saw something hide underwater.

7

Sam은 내게 귀중한 교훈을 가르쳐 줬어.

① Sam taught me a valuable lesson.

② Sam taught a valuable lesson me.

③ Sam taught a valuable lesson to me.

④ Sam taught a valuable lesson for me.

⑤ Sam taught a valuable lesson of me.

8 다음 밑줄 친 문장과 의미가 같은 것을 고르시오.

I don't think that <u>money will bring us
happiness</u>.

① money will bring happiness us

② money will bring us to happiness

③ money will bring happiness to us

④ money will bring happiness for us

⑤ money will bring happiness of us

(9–10) 빈칸에 들어갈 말을 바르게 짝지은 것을 고르시오.

9

> The burgers in the commercial look _____. But the real ones taste _____.

① delicious - different

② deliciously - differently

③ greatly - different

④ great - differently

⑤ deliciously - different

10

> · I want you _____ the floor.
> · The noise made Mrs. Jones _____.

① clean - mad

② to clean - mad

③ to clean - madly

④ clean - madly

⑤ cleaning - mad

11 문장의 형식이 나머지와 다른 것을 고르시오.

① I saw him drawing a tower.

② They found you humorous.

③ I heard someone call my name.

④ My uncle bought me a nice laptop.

⑤ Mom told me to bring an umbrella.

(12–15) 빈칸에 들어갈 수 없는 말을 고르시오.

12

> She will _____ angry if you are late.

① be   ② get

③ look   ④ look like

⑤ become

13

> My dad _____ Henry to drive me home.

① told   ② asked

③ had   ④ got

⑤ wanted

14

> John _____ a gift box to Mary.

① gave   ② sent

③ handed   ④ made

⑤ offered

15

> The teachers _____ the students practice speaking English.

① had   ② made

③ advised   ④ helped

⑤ watched

(16–19) 두 문장의 의미가 같도록 빈칸에 알맞은 말을 쓰시오.

16 My roommate lent me some money.

⇨ My roommate lent some money
_____ me.

17 I saw a stranger walk down the stairs.

⇨ I saw a stranger _____
down the stairs.

18 Susan got her son to set the table.

⇨ Susan had her son _____
the table.

19 He helped me solve the math questions.

⇨ He helped me _____
the math questions.

(20–21) 어법상 어색한 것을 고르시오.

20 ① I found his lesson helpful.
② It tastes like strawberries.
③ I heard a man shouting for help.
④ His jokes made me feeling better.
⑤ The police keep people safe.

21 ① His face turned red suddenly.
② The doctor advised me to drink
boiled water.
③ I will let you choose from the lunch
menu.
④ She told him to go to the bookstore.
⑤ He allowed Paul enter his room.

22 어법상 알맞은 문장이 몇 개인지 고르시오.

> ⓐ Why do you look upset?
> ⓑ I got him carried my bag.
> ⓒ Let me introduce myself to you.
> ⓓ Kevin told his story for us.
> ⓔ We expect you to pass the test.

① 1개   ② 2개
③ 3개   ④ 4개
⑤ 5개

(23–24) 우리말과 의미가 같도록 (　) 안의 말을 이용하여 문장을 완성시오.

23 나는 그 여자가 잔디 위에서 책을 읽고 있는 것을 봤다. (read)

⇨ I saw the woman _____ on the grass.

24 그는 내게 안전 규칙을 따르라고 말했어. (follow)

⇨ He told me _____ the safety rules.

(25–26) 우리말과 의미가 같도록 (　) 안의 말을 배열하시오.

25 그 연설자는 우리에게 미래를 위해 에너지를 절약해야 한다고 충고했다.
(to, us, save, advised, energy)

⇨ The speaker _____
_____ for the future.

26 그들은 종이접기가 매우 재미있다는 것을 알게 되었다.
(paper-folding, very, found, fun)

⇨ They _____
_____ .

27 다음 대화의 내용과 일치하도록 빈칸에 알맞은 말을 쓰시오.

Tyler: Mom, can I have one more pet?
Mom: No, two dogs are enough.

⇨ Tyler's mom won't _____ him have one more pet.

(28–29) 틀린 것이 있으면 고치고 이유를 설명하시오.

28 We wanted the teacher talking slowly.

고치기: _____ ⇨ _____

이유: 5형식 동사 want의 목적격보어는
(to + 동사원형, 동사원형 + -ing)

29 He cooked chicken soup to Matilda.

고치기: _____ ⇨ _____

이유: (3형식, 4형식) 동사로 쓰인 cook 뒤의 어순은
[직접목적어 + (to, for, of) + 간접목적어]

30 다음 조건을 이용하여 알맞게 영작하시오.

이 소설은 내가 자연에 대해서 생각하게 만든다.
조건 1: make, think about, novel
조건 2: 7단어, 5형식 문장

⇨ _____
_____ .

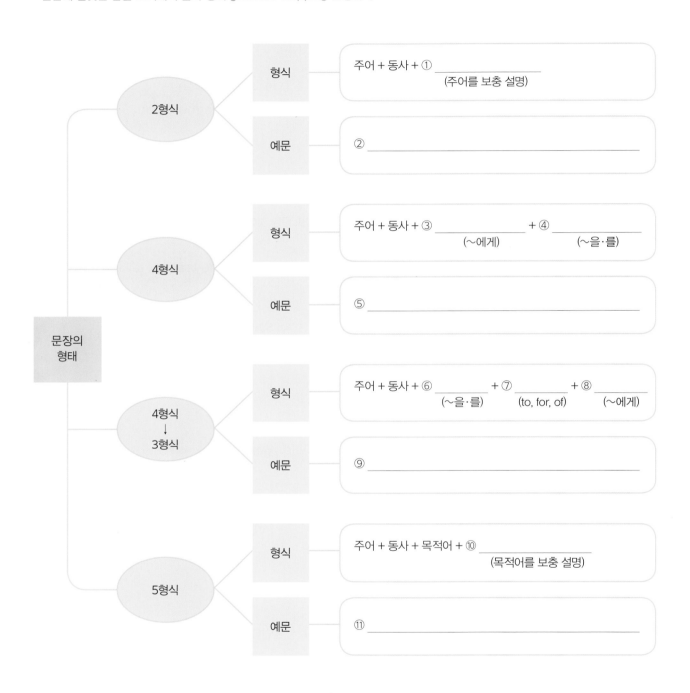

문장의 형태

2형식
- 형식: 주어 + 동사 + ① _____ (주어를 보충 설명)
- 예문: ② _____

4형식
- 형식: 주어 + 동사 + ③ _____ (～에게) + ④ _____ (～을·를)
- 예문: ⑤ _____

4형식 → 3형식
- 형식: 주어 + 동사 + ⑥ _____ (～을·를) + ⑦ _____ (to, for, of) + ⑧ _____ (～에게)
- 예문: ⑨ _____

5형식
- 형식: 주어 + 동사 + 목적어 + ⑩ _____ (목적어를 보충 설명)
- 예문: ⑪ _____

*중복 사용 가능

보기
- 직접목적어
- 주격보어
- 간접목적어
- 목적격보어
- 전치사
- He made me a cake.
- They became friends.
- She keeps her room clean.
- He made a cake for me.

시제

GP 06 현재완료

GP 07 과거와 현재완료

GP 08 현재완료 용법

• Grammar & Writing

• Actual Test

• 한눈에 정리하는 Grammar Mapping

현재완료

GP 06

현재완료는 [have / has + 과거분사]의 형태로 나타낸다. 과거에 발생한 일이 현재까지 영향을 미치거나 현재와 관련성을 가질 때 쓴다.

형태	주어	have / has	과거분사(p.p.)	
부정문	주어	have / has	not	과거분사(p.p.)
의문문	의문사 have / has	주어	과거분사(p.p.)	~?

I **have read** the novel.
☆ Oliver **has** never **seen** snow in Sydney.
☆ A: **Have** you ever **heard** of moving stones?   B: Yes, I have. / ☆ No, I haven't.
A: How long **has** she **been** asleep?   B: For eight hours.

과거와 현재완료

GP 07

과거는 현재와의 관련성 없이 지나간 과거의 상황만을 나타내지만 현재완료는 과거와 관련이 있는 현재의 상황을 나타낸다.

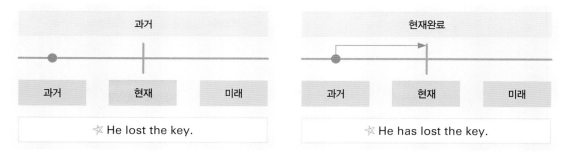

과거	현재완료
☆ He lost the key.	☆ He has lost the key.

❶ 과거
She **lived** in London. (현재는 어디에 살고 있는지 모름)

❷ 현재완료
She **has lived** in London for 12 years. (현재까지 런던에 살고 있음)
[She **started to live** in London 12 years ago. + She still **lives** in London now.]

> **Tip**
> 주로 과거와 함께 쓰는 표현
> yesterday, last night, [~ ago], then, [in + 과거 연도], when…
>
> 주로 현재완료와 함께 쓰는 표현
> just, already, before, twice, since…

GP Practice

A ( ) 안에서 알맞은 것을 고르시오.

1 Dylan (lost, has lost) his bike last Saturday.

2 I have (ate, eaten) Spanish food once.

3 Dr. Morgan (went to, has been to) New York before.

4 The singer was born (in, since) 1998.

5 Where (you have, have you) been today?

B 두 문장이 같은 의미를 갖도록 빈칸을 채우시오.

1 He became a teacher in 2010. He is a teacher now.

→ He _____ a teacher since 2010.

2 Chloe went to Germany. She is still not here.

→ Chloe _____ Germany.

3 Liam forgot my name. He still doesn't remember my name.

→ Liam _____ my name.

C 우리말과 의미가 같도록 ( ) 안의 말을 이용하여 문장을 완성하시오.

1 그 레시피를 이전에 시도해 본 적 있니? (try, recipe)

→ _____ _____ _____ _____ _____ before?

2 우리는 어제 그 마술쇼를 즐겼어. (enjoy, magic show)

→ We _____ _____ _____ _____ yesterday.

3 요즈음 그녀는 충분히 잠을 못 자고 있어. (get enough sleep)

→ She _____ _____ _____ _____ _____ these days.

D 밑줄 친 부분에 대한 설명을 체크하고 틀린 경우엔 바르게 고치시오. (맞으면 'O' 표시)

*p.p.: 과거분사

1	I <u>have met</u> her last week. → ( )	last는 (과거, 현재완료)를 나타내는 부사 (과거, 현재완료)시제와 함께 쓰임
2	He <u>have met</u> the girl before. → ( )	현재완료 형태 3인칭 단수주어 + (has, have) + p.p.
3	They <u>not have come</u> home yet. → ( )	현재완료 부정문 어순 (not + have + p.p., have + not + p.p.)
4	<u>Have you finished</u> college? → ( )	현재완료 의문문 어순 (Did + 주어 + have, Have + 주어) + p.p. ~?

현재완료 용법

현재완료는 의미에 따라 보통 4가지 방법으로 해석한다.

완료	have / has	과거분사(p.p.)	+	just, already, yet

☆ My sister has just come back home. (과거에 시작해서 지금 막) ~했다

경험	have / has	과거분사(p.p.)	+	ever, never, before, ~ times

☆ Have you ever traveled by ship? (과거부터 지금까지) ~한 적이 있다

계속	have / has	과거분사(p.p.)	+	for, since, how long

☆ He has lived in Paris for two years. (과거부터 지금까지) 계속 ~해 오고 있다

결과	have / has	과거분사(p.p.)		lose, go, leave, close

☆ She has lost interest in music. (과거에) ~해서 (그 결과로 지금) ~하다

❶ 완료

Peter **has** just **arrived** at the station.
The ice in my drink **has** already **melted**.

❷ 경험

I **have** never **lived** alone.
☆ She **has watched** the movie ten times.

❸ 계속

He **has had** a cold for three days.
☆ You **have grown** a lot since I last saw you.

❹ 결과

Lucas **has bought** a USB online.
He **has gone** to America.

```
○━ Tip ━○
① [주어 + 완료시제] + [since + 과거시점]
    ~해 오고 있다      ~시점부터 계속

② [주어 + 완료시제] + [for + 기간]
    ~해 오고 있다      ~ 동안 계속
```

• Upgrade •

[have been to] vs. **[have gone to]**
[have been to + 장소 명사]: ~에 갔다 왔다 (경험)
[have gone to + 장소 명사]: ~에 가고 (여기) 없다 (결과)
☆ She **has been to** London. She is here now.
☆ She **has gone to** London. She isn't here now.

GP Practice

A ( ) 안에서 알맞은 것을 고르시오.

1 I (saw, have seen) this beautiful beach before.

2 The puppy hasn't touched its food (for, since) last night.

3 Spring hasn't come (yet, already). It is still cold.

4 Have you (been, gone) to the new theme park in Incheon?

B ( ) 안에 주어진 단어를 알맞게 고쳐 빈칸을 채우시오.

1 I _____ kickboxing for two years. (learn)

2 My dad _____ for the bank for 15 years. (work)

3 How long _____ you _____ together? (live)

4 Sandra _____ never _____ a prize. (win)

C 우리말과 의미가 같도록 ( ) 안의 말을 이용하여 문장을 완성하시오.

1 그녀는 지난주부터 내내 바빴다. (busy, last week)

→ She _____ _____ _____ _____ _____ .

2 우리는 막(방금) 저녁식사를 끝냈어. (just, finish)

→ We _____ _____ _____ _____ .

3 저 화산은 여러 번 폭발해 왔다. (erupt, times)

→ The volcano _____ _____ _____ _____ .

4 Sue는 아직 충분한 돈을 모으지 못했어. (save, enough)

→ Sue _____ _____ _____ _____ yet.

D 밑줄 친 부분에 대한 설명을 체크하고 틀린 경우엔 바르게 고치시오. (맞으면 'O' 표시)

*p.p.: 과거분사

1	She has just finished her report. → (_____)	(끝낸 적 있다, 방금 막 끝냈다) (has + just + p.p., just + 과거동사)
2	I worked on the wall painting since 2015. → (_____)	~부터 계속 (~해 왔다, ~했다) 주어 + (과거, 완료)시제 + since
3	He has been to Italy. So he is not here. → (_____)	(~에 가 본 적 있다, ~로 가버렸다) has + (gone, been) + to 장소
4	He has taught English since 10 years. → (_____)	(~ 동안 계속, ~부터 계속) (since, for) + (기간, 시점)

A   우리말과 의미가 같도록 ( ) 안의 말을 배열하시오.

1 우리 오빠는 내 애완용 뱀을 만져 본 적이 없다. (never, has, touched, my, snake, pet)

→ My brother _____ .

2 그는 이 증상을 2개월째 갖고 있다. (had, has, the symptom, two, for, months)

→ He _____ .

3 우리는 2015년 이후로 네 번 이사했다. (since, moved, four times, 2015, have)

→ We _____ .

4 그녀는 얼마나 오래 그림을 공부해 온 거니? (has, she, how long, studied)

→ _____ painting?

5 반 고흐는 '별이 빛나는 밤' 그림을 1889년에 그렸다. (*The Starry Night*, painted, in)

→ Van Gogh _____ 1889.

6 나는 도쿄에 가 본 적이 없다. (have, been, to, never, Tokyo)

→ I _____ .

B   우리말과 의미가 같도록 ( ) 안의 말을 이용하여 문장을 완성하시오.

1 그들은 지난달부터 그 사자를 추적해 왔다. (track, since, the lion)

→ They _____ _____ _____ _____ _____ last

month.

2 그는 그의 생일선물들을 아직 안 열어 봤다. (open, his birthday gifts)

→ He _____ _____ _____ _____ _____ yet.

3 그녀는 직장을 가진 이후로 가난한 아이들을 후원해 왔다. (sponsor, since)

→ She _____ _____ _____ _____ she started working.

4 그녀는 그녀의 아기를 위해 오늘 기저귀 아홉 번을 갈아 주었어. (change, times, diapers)

→ She _____ _____ _____ _____ _____

_____ _____ _____ today.

5 Sophia는 어제 그녀의 약속을 깼다. (break, promise)

→ Sophia _____ _____ _____ _____ .

6 왜 사람들은 그 섬을 떠나버렸니? (leave, have)

→ _____ _____ _____ _____ the island?

C 주어진 단어를 알맞은 시제로 고쳐 문장을 완성하시오.

1 play   Ella _____ the cello on stage last year.

Ella _____ the cello since last year.

2 arrive   The ship _____ one hour ago.

The ship _____ not _____ yet.

3 live   He _____ in Seoul in 2016.

He _____ in Seoul since 2016.

4 run   She _____ a cafeteria two years ago, and she still runs it.

She _____ a cafeteria for two years now.

D 출장을 자주 다니는 영선이 아버지의 여권을 보고 다음 질문에 답하시오.

1 A: Where did he visit in 2013?

     B: He _____ in 2013.

2 A: Has he visited China?

     B: No, _____.

3 A: How many countries has he visited?

     B: He _____ four countries.

4 A: How many times has he been to Mexico?

     B: He _____ Mexico _____.

(1–5) 빈칸에 들어갈 알맞은 말을 고르시오.

1

> The leaves _____ off the trees.
> No leaves are left on the trees now.

① is falling ② has fallen
③ felled ④ are falling
⑤ have fallen

2

> The plane _____ Seoul 30 minutes ago.

① is leaving ② leaves
③ left ④ has left
⑤ has leaving

3

> _____ you sent the mail to Linda?

① Did ② Do
③ Have ④ Has
⑤ Are

4

> Mr. Kelly _____ to Dubai 12 times.

① was ② went
③ has go ④ has gone
⑤ has been

5

> The movie director has made seven films _____ 2002.

① in ② for
③ during ④ since
⑤ before

6 다음 중 어법상 옳은 것을 고르시오.

① I have learned many things this year.
② He has arrived home yet.
③ We have live in Bundang for 12 years.
④ Has you ever played the game called Simon Says?
⑤ When have you bought the car?

7 다음 두 문장을 한 문장으로 올바르게 연결한 것을 고르시오.

> · I began to use this ID five years ago.
> · And I still use it now.

① I began this ID for five years.
② I have use this ID for five years.
③ I have used this ID since five years.
④ I have begun this ID five years ago.
⑤ I have used this ID for five years.

8 빈칸에 들어가야 할 것끼리 알맞게 짝지어진 것을 고르시오.

> · He painted this picture _____ 2015.
> · He has painted many pictures _____ 2015.

① in - in ② in - ago
③ in - for ④ for - since
⑤ in - since

9 다음 밑줄 친 것 중 어법상 어색한 부분을 고르시오.

> A: How long have you knew him?
>   ⓐ   ⓑ
> B: I have known him since I was six.
>   ⓒ   ⓓ   ⓔ

① ⓐ   ② ⓑ

③ ⓒ   ④ ⓓ

⑤ ⓔ

(10–11) 다음 밑줄 친 부분이 어법상 어색한 것을 고르시오.

10 ① I haven't heard from her lately.

② He has never swum in the sea.

③ Jessy took a walk in the morning.

④ She has already eaten dinner.

⑤ Have she finished college?

11 ① I have gone to the Internet café.

② He bought a new car last week.

③ Have you ever cleaned your room?

④ The couple got married yesterday.

⑤ I have used this bag since 2012.

(12–13) 빈칸에 들어갈 수 없는 말을 고르시오.

12

> He _____ last night.

① took pictures

② called him

③ didn't study math

④ had a headache

⑤ has been busy

13

> I have been a member of the soccer club since _____.

① two months   ② three days ago

③ last week   ④ this May

⑤ yesterday

(14–15) 두 문장을 한 문장으로 고칠 때 빈칸에 알맞은 말을 쓰시오.

14 Only my sister ate the cookies in the jar. The jar is empty now.

⇨ My sister _____ all the cookies.

15 Emma went to the meeting. She is still not here.

⇨ Emma _____ _____ the meeting.

(16-17) 보기의 밑줄 친 부분과 쓰임이 같은 것을 고르시오.

16

She has never worn high heels.

① Sally has not washed the dishes yet.
② My brother has just arrived home.
③ We have stayed at the resort once.
④ I haven't seen her since yesterday.
⑤ The kids have gone to the park.

17

My brother has been in the army for 13 months.

① He has cooked for me many times.
② I have known her since we were 12.
③ I have never raised any pets.
④ We have been to the bakery once.
⑤ She has just finished her work.

18 다음 중 어법상 올바른 것을 모두 고르시오.

ⓐ Bella have broken her arm.
ⓑ I have been to visit Hollywood.
ⓒ He has worked as a chef for 10 years.
ⓓ Have you answered his call?
ⓔ We were at school since 9 a.m.

① ⓐ, ⓑ   ② ⓐ, ⓑ, ⓒ
③ ⓑ, ⓒ, ⓔ   ④ ⓒ, ⓓ
⑤ ⓒ, ⓓ, ⓔ

19 ( ) 안의 단어를 빈칸에 공통으로 들어갈 형태로 고치시오.

Tom has _____ in the library all day.
He has _____ to Boston only once.

(be) ⇨ _____

20 주어진 문장을 ( ) 안의 말을 이용하여 부정문으로 바꿔 쓰시오.

우리는 이 새끼 고양이 이름을 지었어.
We have named this kitten. (yet)

⇨ We _____
_____ this kitten _____ .

(21-22) 다음 글을 읽고 물음에 답하시오.

My mother began to play the piano in 1988. She (① play) almost every day then. Now, (② 그녀는 약 30년 동안 피아노를 연주해 오셨다.)

21 ①의 play를 알맞게 고쳐 쓰시오.

⇨ _____

22 ②의 영작을 완성하시오.

⇨ She _____
_____
about 30 years.

(23–24) 우리말과 의미가 같도록 ( ) 안의 말을 배열하시오.

23 나는 그 파일들을 실수로 삭제해버렸어.
(deleted, the, files, have, by mistake)

⇨ I _____
_____ .

24 당신은 열기구를 타 본 적 있나요?
(you, ever, have, ridden, in)

⇨ _____
_____ a hot-air balloon?

25 다음 대화에 알맞은 대답을 완성하시오.

A: Have you finished your meal?
B: No, I _____ . Can I have
some more soup?

⇨ _____

(26–27) 우리말과 의미가 같도록 ( ) 안의 말을 이용하여 문장을 완성하시오.

26 그녀는 피규어들을 3년째 모아 오고 있어.
(collect, figurines, for)

⇨ She _____
_____ .

27 그 아이들은 동물원에 여러 번 가 본 적 있어.
(been, to)

⇨ The children _____
_____ .

(28–29) 틀린 것이 있으면 고치고 그 이유를 설명하시오.

28 Dinosaurs have died out a long time
ago.

고치기: _____ ⇨ _____

이유: ago는 (과거, 과거부터 현재)를 의미하는
부사여서 (과거, 현재완료)시제와 사용

29 The musical not has started yet.

고치기: _____ ⇨ _____

이유: 현재완료 부정문의 어순은 (not + has + p.p.,
has + not + p.p.)이고, 의미는 (이미 ～했다,
아직 ～ 안 했다)

30 다음 조건을 이용하여 알맞게 영작하시오.

이 회사는 지난해 이후로 17채의 건물을 지어 왔다.
조건 1: build, since
조건 2: 9단어, 현재완료시제

⇨ _____
_____ .

한눈에 정리하는 Grammar Mapping

빈칸에 알맞은 답을 보기에서 골라 넣어 grammar mapping 완성하기

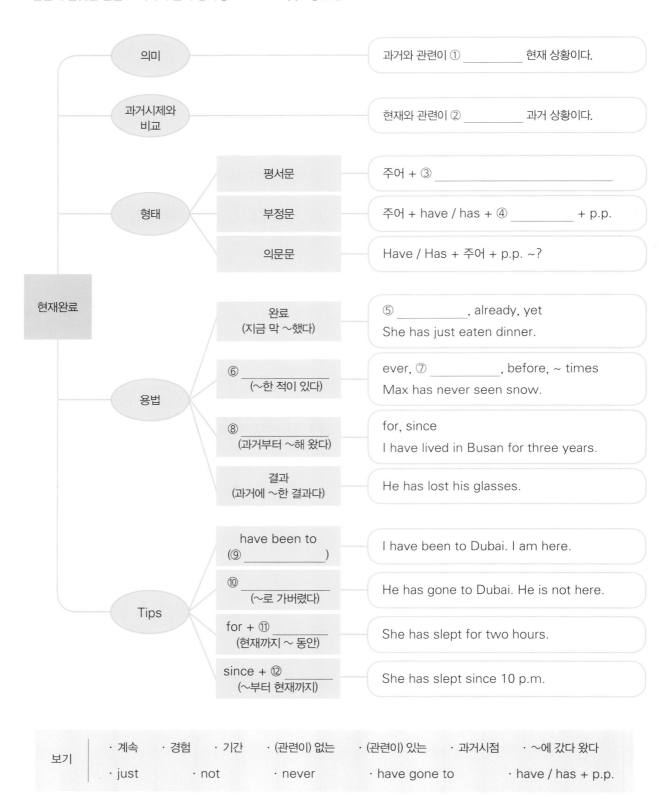

현재완료			
	의미		과거와 관련이 ① _____ 현재 상황이다.
	과거시제와 비교		현재와 관련이 ② _____ 과거 상황이다.
	형태	평서문	주어 + ③ _____
		부정문	주어 + have / has + ④ _____ + p.p.
		의문문	Have / Has + 주어 + p.p. ~?
	용법	완료 (지금 막 ~했다)	⑤ _____, already, yet She has just eaten dinner.
		⑥ _____ (~한 적이 있다)	ever, ⑦ _____, before, ~ times Max has never seen snow.
		⑧ _____ (과거부터 ~해 왔다)	for, since I have lived in Busan for three years.
		결과 (과거에 ~한 결과다)	He has lost his glasses.
	Tips	have been to (⑨ _____)	I have been to Dubai. I am here.
		⑩ _____ (~로 가버렸다)	He has gone to Dubai. He is not here.
		for + ⑪ _____ (현재까지 ~ 동안)	She has slept for two hours.
		since + ⑫ _____ (~부터 현재까지)	She has slept since 10 p.m.

보기	· 계속 · 경험 · 기간 · (관련이) 없는 · (관련이) 있는 · 과거시점 · ~에 갔다 왔다
	· just · not · never · have gone to · have / has + p.p.

38

조동사

GP 09 can, may, will

GP 10 must, have to, should

GP 11 had better, used to, would like to

• Grammar & Writing

• Actual Test

• 한눈에 정리하는 Grammar Mapping

can, may, will

❶ can / could

	can	
능력, 가능	~할 수 있다 (be able to)	☀ She can read people's minds. = She is able to read people's minds.
허락	~해도 된다	You can take a break.
요청, 부탁	~해 주시겠어요?	Can (Could) you deliver the pizza here?

	could	
can의 과거	~할 수 있었다	I could not answer your call yesterday.
요청, 부탁	~해 주시겠어요?	Could (Can) you deliver the pizza here?

• Upgrade •

can(~할 수 있다)의 과거와 미래 표현
❶ 과거: could, was (were) able to   He was able to find the answer.
❷ 미래: will be able to   ☀ He will be able to find the answer.

❷ may / might

	may	
허락	~해도 된다 ~해도 될까요?	You may use my eraser. May (Can) I see your student ID card?
불확실한 추측	~일지도 모른다	☀ The bird may look ugly, but it is very clever.

	might	
may의 과거	~해도 된다	She said her son might eat some ice cream.
불확실한 추측	~일지도 모른다	The bird might look ugly, but it is very clever.

❸ will / would

	will	
예정	~일 것이다 (be going to)	We will be 17 years old next year. = We are going to be 17 years old next year.
의지	~하겠다	☀ I will keep my promise.
요청, 부탁	~해 주시겠어요?	Will you wait a minute, please?

	would	
will의 과거	~일 것이다	He thought she would buy shoes for him.
요청, 부탁	~해 주시겠어요?	Would you wait a minute, please?

GP Practice

A ( ) 안에서 알맞은 것을 고르시오.

1 (May, Will) I please try on this jacket?

2 (Would, May) you lower your voice a bit?

3 Mike is not here. You (can, will) leave a message for him.

4 My grandmother will (turns, turn) 70 years old next year.

5 He didn't say a word to me. He (will, might) be angry with me.

B 두 문장이 같은 의미를 갖도록 빈칸을 채우시오.

1 It is possible that Julia knows our secret.

→ Julia _____ know our secret.

2 The little girl was able to climb up the tall tree.

→ The little girl _____ climb up the tall tree.

3 Are you going to pick me up at the station?

→ _____ you pick me up at the station?

C 우리말과 의미가 같도록 ( ) 안의 말을 이용하여 문장을 완성하시오.

1 은행이 지금은 문을 닫았을지도 몰라. (may, be)

→ Banks _____ _____ closed at this time.

2 일부 물개들은 두 시간 동안 잠수를 할 수 있어. (be able to, dive)

→ Some seals _____ _____ _____ _____ for two hours.

3 이 유리잔에 금이 갔네요. 다른 컵을 주시겠어요? (can, bring)

→ This cup has a crack in it. _____ _____ _____ me another one?

D 밑줄 친 부분에 대한 설명을 체크하고 틀린 경우엔 바르게 고치시오. (맞으면 'O' 표시)

1	Will I use your computer? → ( )	(허락, 추측)을 의미하는 조동사 (Will, May)
2	The robot can works 24 hours a day. → ( )	조동사 뒤에 오는 동사는 (동사원형, 현재형 동사)
3	She said that she will help me then. → ( )	조동사 will은 시제 변화가 (불가능, 가능)하며 과거형은 (will, would)
4	They will can arrive here in time. → ( )	[조동사 + 조동사]는 (가능, 불가능)하므로 can은 (be going to, be able to)로 대체

must, have to, should

❶ must

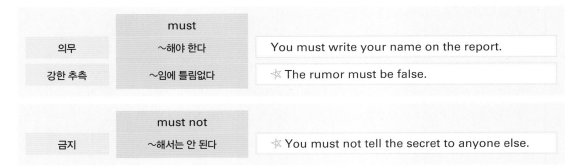

	must	
의무	~해야 한다	You must write your name on the report.
강한 추측	~임에 틀림없다	☆ The rumor must be false.

	must not	
금지	~해서는 안 된다	☆ You must not tell the secret to anyone else.

We **must** slow down at the crosswalk. (= have to)

She didn't have breakfast. She **must** be hungry now.

You **must not** wake the baby.

❷ have to

	have to	
의무	~해야 한다	He has to read the book before class.

	don't have to	
불필요	~할 필요가 없다	We don't have to climb the stairs.

She **has to** feed her dog. (= must)

Robert **had to** take out the garbage.

☆ You **will have to** hurry.

☆ She **doesn't have to** get up early on Sundays.

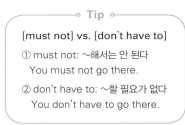

Tip

[must not] vs. [don't have to]

① must not: ~해서는 안 된다
You must not go there.

② don't have to: ~할 필요가 없다
You don't have to go there.

❸ should

	should	
충고, 조언 (긍정)	(도덕적) ~해야 한다	You should get a haircut.

	should not	
충고, 조언 (부정)	~해서는 안 된다	We should not use bad words.

The model is too skinny. She **should** eat more.

You **shouldn't** play the guitar at this hour.

GP Practice

A ( ) 안에서 알맞은 것을 고르시오.

1 He (must, had to) blow up 20 balloons yesterday.

2 I wasn't sick. So I (must not, didn't have to) go to the hospital.

3 You (has to, should) be polite to older people.

4 John never does his homework. His teacher (must, have to) be upset.

B 보기에서 알맞은 것을 골라 빈칸을 채우시오. (한 번씩만 사용)

| 보기 | must | must not | had to | didn't have to |

1 The baby monkey has lost its mom. It _____ be very sad.

2 We _____ prepare dinner. We ordered some Chinese food.

3 You _____ talk to strangers.

4 Anna missed the last train. So she _____ take a taxi.

C 우리말과 의미가 같도록 ( ) 안의 말을 이용하여 문장을 완성하시오.

1 내가 엄마에게 죄송하다고 먼저 말해야 할까? (should, say)

→ _____ _____ _____ _____ to mom first?

2 밤 9시 이후에 풀장에서 수영하면 안 됩니다. (must, swim)

→ _____ _____ _____ _____ in the pool after 9 p.m.

3 이것은 네 잘못이 아니야. 미안해 할 필요 없어. (have to, feel)

→ It's not your fault. You _____ _____ _____ _____ sorry.

4 여러분 중 상당수는 가족 중에 외동일 것입니다. (must, the only child)

→ Many of you _____ _____ _____ _____ in your family.

D 밑줄 친 부분에 대한 설명을 체크하고 틀린 경우엔 바르게 고치시오. (맞으면 'O' 표시)

1	You <u>don't should</u> say bad words. → ( )	조동사의 부정형은 (don't + 조동사, 조동사 + not)
2	Kelly will <u>must</u> see a doctor soon. → ( )	[조동사 + 조동사]는 (가능, 불가능)하므로 must를 (그대로, have to로) 사용
3	I <u>not have to</u> bring my lunch today. → ( )	(~하면 안 된다, ~할 필요 없다)란 의미로 (don't, not) + have to
4	Carl <u>must busy</u> with his homework. → ( )	조동사 뒤엔 (형용사, 동사원형)이므로 조동사 + (형용사, be + 형용사) 어순

had better, used to, would like to

❶ had better

	had better	
강한 충고 (긍정)	~하는 것이 낫겠다	☆ You had better turn off your cell phone.

	had better not	
강한 충고 (부정)	~하지 않는 게 낫겠다	☆ Jack had better not eat junk food.

We **had better** wait and see.
You **had better not** waste your time.

❷ used to

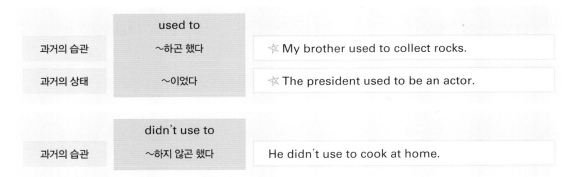

	used to	
과거의 습관	~하곤 했다	☆ My brother used to collect rocks.
과거의 상태	~이었다	☆ The president used to be an actor.

	didn't use to	
과거의 습관	~하지 않곤 했다	He didn't use to cook at home.

(1) 과거의 습관: ~하곤 했다 (= would)

We **used to** play hide-and-seek together.
We **would** play hide-and-seek together.
She **didn't use to** like living here.

> ○ Tip ○
> 조동사 would는 과거의 습관을 나타내어 used to를 대신할 수 있으나 과거의 상태에는 사용하지 않는다.

(2) 과거의 상태: ~이었다

There **used to** be a bridge over there.
There ~~would~~ be a bridge over there. (X)

❸ would like to

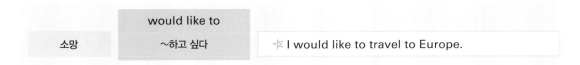

	would like to	
소망	~하고 싶다	☆ I would like to travel to Europe.

Would you like to leave a message?

GP Practice

A ( ) 안에서 알맞은 것을 고르시오.

1 You (have better, had better) bring your pet to an animal doctor.

2 I would like (join, to join) the drama club.

3 My aunt (used to, uses to) run a Thai restaurant.

4 You (don't have better, had better not) go out on this rainy day.

B 보기에서 알맞은 것을 골라 빈칸을 채우시오. (한 번씩만 사용)

보기	had better	used to	would like to	would

1 The play starts soon. You _____ find your seat now.

2 The country _____ be quiet and peaceful.

3 She _____ visit her grandmother every month when she was young.

4 Excuse me? I _____ ask some questions.

C 우리말과 의미가 같도록 ( ) 안의 말과 조동사를 이용하여 문장을 완성하시오.

1 일부 물고기는 오랜 옛날에는 육지에 살았었다. (live, on land)

→ Some fish _____ _____ _____ _____ a long time ago.

2 여드름을 짜지 않는 것이 낫겠어. 흉터를 남길 거야. (pop)

→ You _____ _____ _____ _____ that pimple. It will leave a scar.

3 언제 방문하고 싶으세요? (visit)

→ When _____ you _____ _____ _____ ?

4 나는 이 버릇을 깨는 것이 낫겠어. (break)

→ I _____ _____ _____ this habit.

D 밑줄 친 부분에 대한 설명을 체크하고 틀린 경우엔 바르게 고치시오. (맞으면 'O' 표시)

1	Jane used to <u>visits</u> the museum. → ( )	과거의 (상태, 습관) 의미는 used to + (일반동사, 동사원형)
2	She <u>has</u> better wear sunscreen. → ( )	(충고, 허락)의 의미는 (has, had) better + 동사원형
3	I <u>not had better</u> open the window. → ( )	had better의 부정형은 바로 (앞, 뒤)에 (don't, not)
4	I would like <u>order</u> now. → ( )	'~하고 싶다'의 의미는 would like + (동사원형, to + 동사원형)

A 우리말과 의미가 같도록 ( ) 안의 말을 배열하시오.

1 믿든 안 믿든, 네 삼촌은 정말 귀여웠단다. (cute, very, used to, your, uncle, be)

→ Believe it or not, _____ .

2 우리는 케이크를 더 먹지 않는 것이 낫겠다. (better, not, had, eat)

→ We _____ any more cake.

3 너는 새치기를 하면 안 돼. (cut, in, line, must, not)

→ You _____ .

4 우리는 미래에는 로봇과 경쟁을 해야 할 거야. (have, will, to, compete, we)

→ _____ against robots in the future.

5 저것은 개가 아닐지도 몰라. 여우처럼 생겼잖아. (may, that, be, not, a, dog)

→ _____ . It looks like a fox.

6 그녀가 나에게 고마워할 필요는 없어. (have, to, doesn't, thank)

→ She _____ me.

B 우리말과 의미가 같도록 ( ) 안의 말을 이용하여 문장을 완성하시오.

1 저 나무 좀 봐. 분명히 100미터가 넘겠는걸. (be, 100 meters, tall, over)

→ Look at the tree. It _____ _____ _____ _____ _____ _____ .

2 오늘 비가 올지도 몰라, 그러니 빨래를 걷자. (rain)

→ _____ _____ _____ _____ , so let's bring in the laundry.

3 그녀는 내년에 엄마가 될 거야. (become)

→ She _____ _____ _____ _____ _____ _____ .

4 너는 반 친구들을 놀려서는 안 돼. (make fun of, should)

→ _____ _____ _____ _____ _____ _____ your classmates.

5 그는 혼자서 수영장을 채울 수 없어. (fill)

→ He _____ _____ the swimming pool by himself.

6 그는 혼자서 그 테이블을 옮길 수 있었어. (able, move, the table)

→ He _____ _____ _____ _____ _____ _____ by himself.

7 피곤해 보이네. 너 좀 쉬는 것이 낫겠어. (better, some rest, get)

→ You look tired. You _____ _____ _____ _____ _____ .

C 두 문장의 의미가 같도록 보기에서 골라 문장을 완성하시오. (한 번씩만 사용)

> 보기 | must   can   had better   used to   has to

1 She must wear a uniform at school.

  → She _____ wear a uniform at school.

2 Tom lived in Paris before. But he doesn't live there anymore.

  → Tom _____ live in Paris.

3 Are you able to lift this heavy box?

  → _____ you lift this heavy box?

4 You should watch out for that dog.

  → You _____ watch out for that dog.

5 I am sure that Daniel is at the library now.

  → Daniel _____ be at the library now.

D 보기의 표현과 had better, had better not을 사용하여, Sandra에게 그림과 같은 충고를 하시오.

> 보기 | add some salt to it   buy the ticket online   wear the cap

1 This soup needs a bit more salt. _____.

2 You _____. It is 33% off on this website.

3 _____. It doesn't go well with your dress.

(1–5) 빈칸에 들어갈 알맞은 말을 고르시오.

1

> 그는 분명 왼손잡이일 거야.
> → He _____ be left-handed.

① must ② will
③ used to ④ had better
⑤ would like to

2

> 그 수다스러운 코미디언이 예전엔 조용한 소년이었어.
> → The talkative comedian _____
>   be a shy boy.

① can ② would
③ must ④ used to
⑤ had to

3

> 그 아기는 곧 설 수 있을 거야.
> → The baby will _____ stand up
>   soon.

① can ② is able to
③ should ④ may
⑤ be able to

4

> 너는 지금 네 강아지를 산책시키는 것이 낫겠다.
> → You _____ walk your puppy
>   now.

① can ② will
③ may ④ had better
⑤ would like to

5

> 창가 쪽 좌석으로 옮기고 싶으신가요?
> → _____ you like to move to a
>   window seat?

① Can ② Would
③ May ④ Should
⑤ Must

6 다음 우리말을 영어로 잘못 옮긴 것은?

① 그 계곡은 예전에는 물에 잠겼었지.
   The valley used to be under water a
   long time ago.
② 너는 당근을 더 먹는 것이 좋겠어.
   You had better eat more carrots.
③ 주소가 틀린 것이 분명해.
   The address must be wrong.
④ 이 주스를 마셔보시겠어요?
   Would you like to try this juice?
⑤ 그는 전혀 움직일 필요가 없어.
   He must not move at all.

7 다음 중 어법상 어색한 것을 고르시오.

① We would like cancel our travel
   plans.
② She could open the bottle herself.
③ Tom would take a walk along the
   river.
④ You should dry your hair carefully.
⑤ She will have to explain the reason.

(8–9) 밑줄 친 부분과 바꿔 쓸 수 있는 것은?

8

> My family <u>will</u> have a garage sale this weekend.

① used to   ② are able to

③ must   ④ had to

⑤ is going to

9

> She <u>must</u> prepare some firewood for a campfire.

① will   ② may

③ would   ④ can

⑤ has to

(10–11) 다음 상황을 고려하여 빈칸에 알맞은 것을 고르시오.

10

> A: Would you like to go out for dinner?
> B: I would love to.
>   But I am afraid I _____.

① would   ② can

③ must   ④ can't

⑤ used to

11

> A: Sally is in a good mood.
>   You _____ talk to her now.
> B: Thank you for the advice.

① will   ② used to

③ might   ④ had better

⑤ would like to

12 밑줄 친 부분의 쓰임이 보기와 같은 것을 고르시오.

> He is not Jane's type. She <u>must</u> dislike him.

① My mom <u>must</u> be angry at me.

② I <u>must</u> finish this report today.

③ <u>Must</u> I do the dishes right now?

④ You <u>must</u> not make any noise.

⑤ He <u>must</u> stop complaining.

(13–15) 빈칸에 공통으로 들어갈 단어를 쓰시오.

13

> · Cars _____ stop at red lights.
> · The movie _____ be about his childhood.

⇨ _____

14

> · We _____ like to order now.
> · I _____ go running every morning.

⇨ _____

15

> · Look at the no-pets sign.
>   You _____ bring in your pets.
> · I _____ give you a fish.
>   But I can teach you how to fish.

⇨ _____

16 다음 중 밑줄 친 부분의 의미가 나머지와 다른 것을 고르시오.

① It <u>may</u> not be true.

② Only buses <u>may</u> use this lane.

③ She <u>may</u> not know you.

④ He <u>may</u> be late today.

⑤ Tim <u>may</u> not be happy with the news.

17 다음 우리말과 의미가 다른 것은?

여기서 사진을 찍으면 안 됩니다.

① You must not take pictures here.

② Don't take pictures here.

③ You cannot take pictures here.

④ You don't have to take pictures here.

⑤ You should not take pictures here.

(18–19) 다음 빈칸에 들어갈 수 없는 말은?

18 _____ you tell me the address again?

① Can   ② Could

③ Will   ④ Would

⑤ May

19 We will make an English-only zone. There, you _____ speak English only.

① should   ② can

③ must   ④ used to

⑤ have to

(20–21) 두 문장이 같은 의미를 갖도록 빈칸을 채우시오.

20 He could not write poems well.

⇨ He _____

_____

poems well.

21 The city will hold a spring flower festival.

⇨ The city _____

_____ a spring flower

festival.

(22–23) 우리말과 의미가 같도록 ( ) 안의 말을 배열하시오.

22 너는 더 큰 사이즈로 입어 볼 필요 없어.
(have, don't, try, to, you, on, bigger, size, a)

⇨ _____

_____.

23 나는 이 선물상자를 재활용하는 것이 낫겠어.
(I, recycle, had, this, better, gift, box)

⇨ _____

_____.

24 어법상 <u>틀린</u> 것으로 짝지어진 것은?

> ⓐ Will you stay at home today?
> ⓑ You have better get enough sleep.
> ⓒ We should careful at the lake.
> ⓓ She was used to live alone.
> ⓔ You must not talk to strangers.

① ⓐ, ⓑ
② ⓐ, ⓑ, ⓒ
③ ⓑ, ⓒ, ⓓ
④ ⓒ, ⓓ, ⓔ
⑤ ⓓ, ⓔ

(25–27) 우리말과 의미가 같도록 빈칸에 알맞은 말을 쓰시오.

25 이 귀여운 손글씨는 분명 Matilda의 것일 거야.

⇨ This cute handwriting _____
be Matilda's.

26 나는 이 가방을 반품하고 싶습니다.

⇨ I _____ _____
_____ return this bag.

27 사람들은 이전에 지구가 평평하다고 믿었었지.

⇨ People _____ _____
believe that the Earth was flat.

(28–30) 틀린 것이 있으면 고치고 이유를 설명하시오.

28 This song will popular soon.

고치기: _____ ⇨ _____
이유: 조동사 뒤에는 동사원형이 오므로
조동사 + (형용사, be + 형용사) 어순

29 We will can see new baby pandas
next month.

고치기: _____ ⇨ _____
이유: [조동사 + 조동사]는 (가능, 불가능)하므로
will + (can, be able to)를 사용

30 You don't had better play the piano
late at night.

고치기: _____ ⇨ _____
이유: had better의 부정형은 바로 (앞, 뒤)에
(don't, not)을 붙임

31 다음 문장을 미래시제로 고쳐 쓰시오.

You must enter the correct password.
조건: 8단어

⇨ _____

_____ .

한눈에 정리하는 Grammar Mapping

빈칸에 알맞은 답을 보기에서 골라 넣어 grammar mapping 완성하기

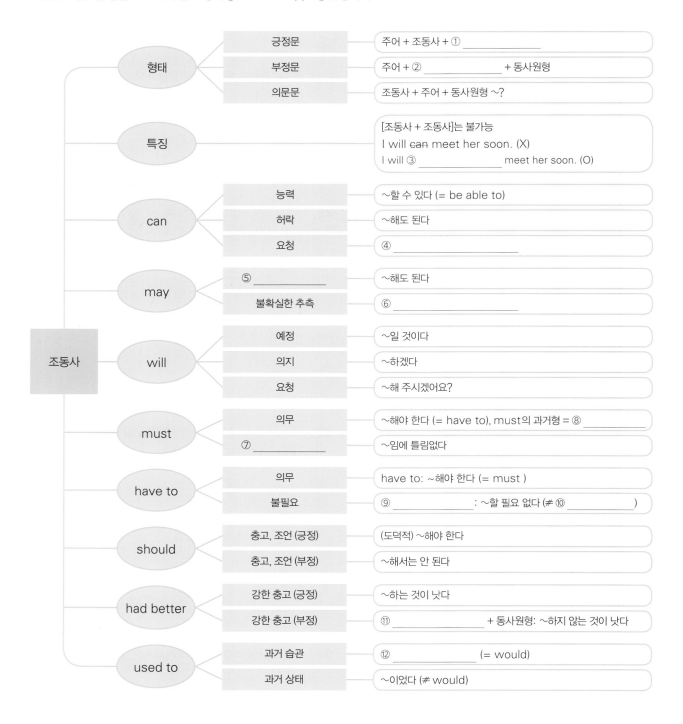

	긍정문	주어 + 조동사 + ① _____
형태	부정문	주어 + ② _____ + 동사원형
	의문문	조동사 + 주어 + 동사원형 ~?

특징
[조동사 + 조동사]는 불가능
I will c̶a̶n̶ meet her soon. (X)
I will ③ _____ meet her soon. (O)

	능력	~할 수 있다 (= be able to)
can	허락	~해도 된다
	요청	④ _____

	⑤ _____	~해도 된다
may	불확실한 추측	⑥ _____

	예정	~일 것이다
will	의지	~하겠다
	요청	~해 주시겠어요?

	의무	~해야 한다 (= have to), must의 과거형 = ⑧ _____
must	⑦ _____	~임에 틀림없다

	의무	have to: ~해야 한다 (= must)
have to	불필요	⑨ _____ : ~할 필요 없다 (≠ ⑩ _____)

	충고, 조언 (긍정)	(도덕적) ~해야 한다
should	충고, 조언 (부정)	~해서는 안 된다

	강한 충고 (긍정)	~하는 것이 낫다
had better	강한 충고 (부정)	⑪ _____ + 동사원형: ~하지 않는 것이 낫다

	과거 습관	⑫ _____ (= would)
used to	과거 상태	~이었다 (≠ would)

조동사

보기 | · 허락   · 강한 추측   · 동사원형   · ~하곤 했다   · ~해 주시겠어요?   · ~일지도 모른다
· don't have to   · 조동사 + not   · had better not   · be able to   · must not   · had to

수동태

GP 12 능동태와 수동태

GP 13 수동태의 시제

GP 14 수동태의 여러 형태

GP 15 동사구 수동태

GP 16 by 이외의 전치사를 쓰는 수동태

• Grammar & Writing

• Actual Test

• 한눈에 정리하는 Grammar Mapping

능동태와 수동태

능동태는 주어가 동작을 직접 행하는 것으로 '(주어가) ~하다'란 의미이다. 수동태는 주어가 동작의 영향을 받거나 당하는 형태로 '(주어가) ~당하다 / ~되다'란 의미이다.

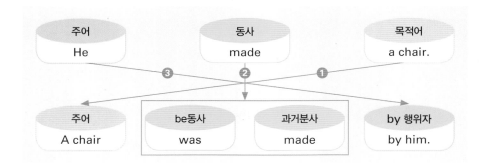

수동태를 만드는 방법

❶ 능동태의 목적어를 수동태의 주어로 쓴다.

❷ 능동태의 동사를 [be동사 + 과거분사] 형태로 바꾼다.

❸ 능동태의 주어를 [by + 행위자(목적격)] 형태로 바꾼다.

He **broke** the window. (능동태)

→ The window **was broken by** him. (수동태)

A lot of girls **love** the singer. (능동태)

→ ⚹ The singer **is loved by** a lot of girls. (수동태)

• Upgrade •

수동태로 쓸 수 없는 동사

❶ **목적어를 갖지 않는 자동사**

arrive(도착하다), rise(오르다), happen(발생하다), appear(나타나다), look(~해 보이다)...

We arrived at the airport in time.

→ The airport ~~was arrived by~~ us in time. (×)

❷ **상태나 소유를 나타내는 타동사**

have(가지다), meet(만나다), resemble(닮다), belong to(속하다)...

We have a nice garden.

→ A nice garden ~~is had by~~ us. (×)

GP Practice

A ( ) 안에서 알맞은 것을 고르시오.

1 The baker (bakes, is baked) bread every morning.

2 English (speaks, is spoken) all over the world.

3 Alex (threw, was thrown) a dart.

4 The bright sun (appeared, was appeared) over the horizon.

5 The first paper money (made, was made) in China.

B 다음 문장을 수동태로 바꿀 때 빈칸에 알맞은 말을 쓰시오.

1 People grow rice in many countries.

→ Rice _____ people.

2 Leonardo da Vinci painted the *Mona Lisa*.

→ The *Mona Lisa* _____ Leonardo da Vinci.

3 I wrote my report last night.

→ My report _____ last night.

C 우리말과 의미가 같도록 ( ) 안의 말을 이용하여 문장을 완성하시오.

1 많은 집들이 폭풍에 의해 파괴되었다. (destroy)

→ Many houses _____ _____ _____ the storm.

2 스마트폰은 다양한 방식으로 사용된다. (use)

→ A smartphone _____ _____ in various ways.

3 Alex가 파란 꽃병을 어제 깼어. (break)

→ The blue vase _____ _____ _____ Alex yesterday.

D 밑줄 친 부분에 대한 설명을 체크하고 틀린 경우엔 바르게 고치시오. (맞으면 'O' 표시)

*p.p.: 과거분사

1	The mystery was <u>solve</u> by him. → ( )	미스터리가 (푸는, 풀리는) 것이므로 (be동사 + 동사원형, be동사 + p.p.)
2	The car <u>loves</u> by ladies. → ( )	그 차가 (사랑하는, 사랑받는) 것이므로 (동사, be동사 + p.p.)
3	The train <u>was arrived</u> late. → ( )	기차가 (도착하다, 도착 당하다)이므로 수동태로 사용 (가능, 불가능)
4	These dolls <u>was</u> made in Paris. → ( )	복수형 주어의 수동태는 (are / were, is / was) + p.p.

수동태의 시제

GP 13

수동태의 시제는 be동사의 현재·과거·미래·진행시제 형태로 나타낸다.

현재시제	am / are / is	과거분사	The soup is cooked by him.
과거시제	was / were	과거분사	The soup was cooked by him.
미래시제	will be	과거분사	The soup will be cooked by him.
진행시제	be동사 + being	과거분사	The soup is being cooked by him.

The Olympic Games **are held** every four years.　　　(~되다)
All her fans **were invited** by the actress.　　　(~되었다)
This program **will be used** by college students.　　　(~될 것이다)
My car **is being washed** by Sam.　　　(~되는 중이다)
Dinner **was being prepared** in the kitchen by my dad.　(~되는 중이었다)

수동태의 여러 형태

GP 14

부정문		주어	be동사	not	과거분사		The ring was not found.
의문문		Be동사	주어		과거분사	~?	Was the ring found?
	의문사	be동사	주어		과거분사	~?	When was the ring found?
조동사		주어	조동사	be	과거분사		The ring must be found.

❶ 부정문

He didn't write the book.
→ The book **was not written** by him.

❷ 의문문

Did Fred design the building?
→ **Was** the building **designed** by Fred?
When did King Sejong create Hangeul?
→ **When was** Hangeul **created** by King Sejong?

❸ 조동사 수동태

The rules **should be followed** by people.

> **Tip**
>
> 의문사가 주어인 문장의 수동태
> [By whom + be동사 + 주어 + 과거분사 ~?]
> · Who wrote the book?
>   → By whom was the book written?

GP Practice

A ( ) 안에서 알맞은 것을 고르시오.

1 The e-mail (wasn't, doesn't) sent to me.

2 How (do, are) cans and bottles recycled?

3 The video clip will (post, be posted) on Facebook.

4 Bananas (are eating, are being eaten) by the monkeys now.

B 다음 문장을 수동태로 바꿀 때 빈칸에 알맞은 말을 쓰시오.

1 We cannot copy the files.

→ The files _____ by us.

2 Did Dave return the book yesterday?

→ _____ the book _____ by Dave yesterday?

3 His mom is watching the newborn baby.

→ The newborn baby _____ by his mom.

C 우리말과 의미가 같도록 ( ) 안의 말을 이용하여 문장을 완성하시오.

1 그것은 언제 주문되었니? (order)

→ _____ _____ it _____ ?

2 나는 그 사진들을 찍지 않았다. (take)

→ The pictures _____ _____ _____ _____ me.

3 그는 경찰관에 의해 붙잡힐 것이다. (catch)

→ He _____ _____ _____ _____ the police.

D 밑줄 친 부분에 대한 설명을 체크하고 틀린 경우엔 바르게 고치시오. (맞으면 'O' 표시)

*p.p.: 과거분사

1	<u>Did</u> this tree planted by you? → ( )	수동태 의문문은 (Did + 주어 + 동사, Was + 주어 + p.p.)?
2	The elevator is <u>be</u> repaired now. → ( )	현재진행 수동태는 (is + being, is + be) + p.p.
3	The shop will <u>is</u> closed soon. → ( )	조동사 수동태는 조동사 + (be + p.p., is + p.p.)
4	I <u>not was</u> invited to the party. → ( )	수동태 부정문은 (not + be동사, be동사 + not) + p.p.

동사구 수동태

GP 15

두 개 이상의 단어로 이루어진 동사구는 하나의 단어 개념으로 생각하고 수동태로 바꾼다.

run over	(차로) 치다	turn on / off	켜다 / 끄다	bring up	기르다
laugh at	비웃다	put off	연기하다	carry out	실행하다
look after	돌보다	take care of	돌보다	make use of	사용하다

He **turned on** the music app.
→ ※ The music app **was turned on** by him.
The mother eagle **took care of** the egg.
→ ※ The egg **was taken care of** by the mother eagle.

by 이외의 전치사를 쓰는 수동태

GP 16

수동태에서 행위자를 나타내는 전치사 by 대신 다른 전치사가 쓰일 수도 있다.

| 주어 | be동사 | 과거분사 | by | Cheese is made by him. |
| | | | 기타 전치사 | Cheese is made from milk. |

be interested in	~에 관심이 있다	be worried about	~에 걱정하다
be covered with	~로 덮여 있다	be filled with	~로 가득 차 있다
be satisfied with	~에 만족하다	be pleased with	~에 기뻐하다
be surprised at	~에 놀라다	be made of / from	~로 만들어지다
be known to	~에게 알려져 있다	be known for	~로 유명하다

Chris **is interested in** space research.
※ We **are satisfied with** the English class.
※ K-pop **is known to** most teenagers in Asia.

• Upgrade •

[by + 행위자]의 생략: 행위자가 일반인이거나 불분명하고 중요하지 않을 때는 생략한다.
The dollar is used all over the world (by people).
My laptop computer was stolen (by someone).

GP Practice

A ( ) 안에서 알맞은 것을 고르시오.

1 Judy's piano was covered (with, on) dust.

2 I am worried (for, about) my school report.

3 The artist is interested (at, in) sand painting.

4 The theory is known (to, as) all scientists.

B 다음 문장을 수동태로 바꿀 때 빈칸에 알맞은 말을 쓰시오.

1 Wolves looked after the boy in a forest.

→ The boy _____ by wolves in a forest.

2 The soldiers will carry out the mission.

→ The mission _____ by the soldiers.

3 The couple brought up five children.

→ Five children _____ by the couple.

C 우리말과 의미가 같도록 ( ) 안의 말을 이용하여 문장을 완성하시오.

1 런던은 안개로 유명하다. (know)

→ London _____ _____ _____ its fog.

2 그녀는 생일 선물에 기뻐했다. (please)

→ She _____ _____ _____ her birthday gift.

3 가로등은 자동으로 켜진다. (turn on)

→ Street lamps _____ _____ _____ automatically.

D 밑줄 친 부분에 대한 설명을 체크하고 틀린 경우엔 바르게 고치시오. (맞으면 'O' 표시)

1	I was satisfied <u>of</u> the bubble bath. → ( )	'~에 만족하다'는 be동사 + satisfied + (of, with)
2	He was surprised <u>for</u> my IQ. → ( )	'~에 놀라다'는 be동사 + surprised + (at, for)
3	The game <u>was put</u> because of snow. → ( )	동사구 put off(미루다)의 수동태는 be동사 + (put, put off)
4	Wine is made <u>for</u> grapes. → ( )	'~로 만들어지다'는 be동사 + made + (for, from) + 재료

A 우리말과 의미가 같도록 ( ) 안의 말을 배열하시오.

1 내 생활 방식은 이 책에 의해 바뀌었다. (by, changed, book, was, this)

→ My lifestyle _____ .

2 콘서트홀에서 첼로가 연주되고 있었다. (was, cello, played, being, the)

→ _____ in the concert hall.

3 너는 새로운 컴퓨터에 매우 만족할 거야. (satisfied, be, will, with, you)

→ _____ the new computer.

4 그 학습 자료는 언제 업로드 되니? (uploaded, is, the learning material)

→ When _____ ?

5 그의 연기는 모두에게서 비웃음을 당했다. (at, by, was, everyone, laughed)

→ His acting _____ .

6 나는 똑같은 학교 점심 메뉴에 싫증이 난다. (of, am, the same, tired, lunch menu)

→ I _____ at school.

B 우리말과 의미가 같도록 ( ) 안의 말을 이용하여 문장을 완성하시오.

1 오늘 아침에 우유가 배달되지 않았다. (deliver)

→ Milk _____ _____ _____ this morning.

2 아홉 번째 행성은 언제 발견되었나요? (discover, the ninth planet)

→ When _____ _____ _____ _____ _____ ?

3 공공도서관이 우리 동네에 지어지고 있다. (build)

→ A public library _____ _____ _____ in our town.

4 거짓 정보가 인터넷에서 수집될 수 있다. (can, collect)

→ False information _____ _____ _____ on the Internet.

5 대부분의 사용자들이 그 앱에 만족한다. (satisfy)

→ Most of the users _____ _____ _____ the app.

6 그 연구는 캐나다의 연구원들에 의해 실행되었다. (carry out, researchers)

→ The study _____ _____ _____ _____ in Canada.

C 주어진 ( ) 안의 단어를 이용하여 질문에 대한 대답을 완성하시오.

1

Q: Who made the big mistake?

A: The big mistake _____. (Andrew)

2

Q: What causes many accidents?

A: Many accidents _____. (speeding)

3

Q: Who is reading the magazine?

A: The magazine _____. (young women)

4

Q: Who didn't see the rainbow?

A: The rainbow _____. (they)

D 주어진 말을 이용하여 그림에 맞게 문장을 완성하시오. (현재시제 사용)

cover   teach   disappoint   look after

1 The roof _____ snow.

2 My English class _____ Mrs. Ryan.

3 The girl _____ her hairstyle.

4 My puppy _____ my little sister.

(1–5) 빈칸에 들어갈 알맞은 말을 고르시오.

1

> The copy machine _____ by Chester Carlson in 1938.

① invents　　　② invented

③ was inventing　　④ is invented

⑤ was invented

2

> The bookstore can _____ easily.

① find　　　② is found

③ be found　　④ is finding

⑤ be finding

3

> Many people are interested _____ a healthy diet.

① in　　　② of

③ to　　　④ for

⑤ with

4

> This poem _____ by Jack.

① doesn't write

② doesn't be written

③ not written

④ was not written

⑤ not be written

5

> The baby panda is _____ by its mom.

① looked　　　② look after

③ looked after　　④ looking after

⑤ be looked after

(6–7) 다음 문장을 수동태로 바르게 고친 것을 고르시오.

6

> Did she bake the cookies?

① Did the cookies bake by her?

② Did the cookies baked by her?

③ Were the cookies bake by her?

④ Were the cookies baked by her?

⑤ Was the cookies baked by her?

7

> Justin trains his new puppy.

① His new puppy is trained by Justin.

② His new puppies is trained Justin.

③ His new puppy trains Justin.

④ Justin trains by his new puppy.

⑤ Justin is trained by his new puppy.

(8-9) 문장의 밑줄 친 부분이 <u>어색한</u> 것을 고르시오.

8 ① The ball <u>was kicked</u> into the air.
② The photo <u>was taking</u> by her.
③ The car will <u>be washed</u> by him.
④ Many girls <u>are standing</u> by the gate.
⑤ Her speech <u>is being recorded</u>.

9 ① A photo <u>was sent</u> to her cell phone.
② Things <u>are kept</u> in place.
③ My pencil <u>was disappeared</u>.
④ Toy cars <u>are bought</u> by many kids.
⑤ The radio <u>was fixed</u> yesterday.

10 다음 문장을 능동태로 바르게 고친 것을 고르시오.

> The show is being watched by the girls.

① The show is watching the girls.
② The show is being watched the girls.
③ The girls are being watching the show.
④ The girls are being watched the show.
⑤ The girls are watching the show.

(11-12) 다음 문장을 수동태 문장으로 고쳐 쓰시오.

11 People laughed at the great idea at first.

⇨ The great idea _____ _____ _____ _____ people at first.

12 The huge waves surprised me.

⇨ I _____ _____ _____ the huge waves.

(13-14) 빈칸에 들어갈 말을 바르게 짝지은 것을 고르시오.

13
· We can _____ the starving children in Africa.
· They can _____ by our love.

① save - are saved
② save - be saved
③ be saved - saves
④ be saving - are saving
⑤ be saved - saved

14
· We were satisfied _____ the results of the project.
· _____ all the tickets sold out?

① with - Are ② with - Do
③ for - Are ④ for - Do
⑤ by - Do

15 다음 우리말을 영어로 바르게 옮긴 것을 고르시오.

> 이 컴퓨터는 누가 사용했었니?

① Who be used this computer?
② Who was used this computer by?
③ By whom used this computer?
④ By whom this computer was used?
⑤ By whom was this computer used?

(16-18) 우리말과 의미가 같도록 ( ) 안의 말을 이용하여 문장을 완성하시오.

16 질문에 대답하기 전에 너는 주의깊게 읽어 보아야 한다. (answer)

⇨ Before questions _____
_____, you have to read them carefully.

17 오늘 아침에 구름 때문에 일출이 안 보였어. (see)

⇨ The sunrise _____
_____ this morning because of the clouds.

18 내 아기 여동생은 할머니께서 돌봐주셨다.
(take care of)

⇨ My baby sister _____
_____ by my grandmother.

(19-20) 다음 중 어법상 어색한 문장을 고르시오.

19 ① The box is made of paper.
② Free lunches were offered to the homeless.
③ A secret should be kept forever.
④ The skater is pleased with the silver medal.
⑤ The novel was readed by her in one day.

20 ① Who will be invited to the party?
② A new apartment is being built.
③ The window is not locked.
④ When does Disneyland created?
⑤ Your chicken will be delivered soon.

21 다음 중 밑줄 친 부분을 생략할 수 있는 문장을 고르시오.

① French is spoken in Canada <u>by people</u>.
② He was helped <u>by his sister</u>.
③ Police dogs were first used in Scotland <u>by the police</u>.
④ This tree was planted <u>by my grandfather</u>.
⑤ Was this picture taken <u>by you</u>?

(22–23) 다음 대화의 빈칸에 주어진 단어를 이용하여 문장을 완성하시오.

22　A: Who made this great movie?

　　B: This movie _____ _____ _____ John Favreau. (make)

23　A: Mom, I don't want to go to the dentist.

　　B: Sorry. Your tooth must _____ _____ right away. (pull)

24　어법상 맞는 것끼리 짝지어진 것은?

> ⓐ The pyramids was built in Egypt.
> ⓑ Was the fish caught by Jill?
> ⓒ The car will be covered with snow.
> ⓓ A car is be chased by the police.
> ⓔ You were looked after a babysitter.

① ⓐ, ⓑ　　　　② ⓐ, ⓓ

③ ⓑ, ⓒ　　　　④ ⓑ, ⓓ

⑤ ⓓ, ⓔ

25　빈칸에 동사 write를 알맞은 형태로 바꿔 쓰시오.

> A: Who ___ⓐ___ *Harry Potter*?
> B: Henry Lewes wrote it.
> C: No. It was ___ⓑ___ by J.K. Rowling.

ⓐ _____

ⓑ _____

(26–27) 틀린 것이 있으면 고치고 이유를 설명하시오.

26　This box must opened by Catherine.

고치기: _____ ⇨ _____

이유: 상자가 (열다, 열리다)이므로

　　조동사 + (p.p., be + p.p.)

27　My mom was disappointed for the size of the kitchen.

고치기: _____ ⇨ _____

이유: 엄마가 실망을 (시키다, 느끼다)이므로

　　be 동사 + disappointed + (for, with)

28　우리말과 의미가 같도록 (　) 안의 말을 배열하시오.

> 제주도는 아름다운 풍경으로 세계에 알려져 있다.
> (beautiful, known, scenery, is, for, its)

⇨ Jeju Island _____

_____ around the world.

(29–30) 다음 밑줄 친 단어를 알맞게 고쳐 쓰시오.

> The Eiffel Tower in Paris (29) build in 1889. The French people hated it. Some said that it looked like a big chimney. But it is still (30) visit by many tourists.

29　build ⇨ _____

30　visit ⇨ _____

한눈에 정리하는 Grammar Mapping

빈칸에 알맞은 답을 보기에서 골라 넣어 grammar mapping 완성하기

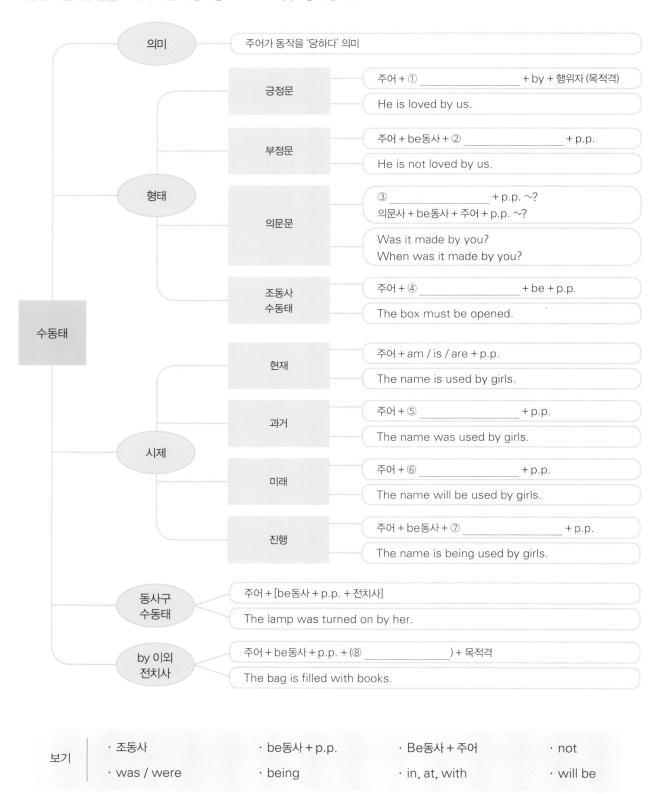

수동태

- **의미** — 주어가 동작을 '당하다' 의미

- **형태**
  - **긍정문**
    - 주어 + ① _____ + by + 행위자 (목적격)
    - He is loved by us.
  - **부정문**
    - 주어 + be동사 + ② _____ + p.p.
    - He is not loved by us.
  - **의문문**
    - ③ _____ + p.p. ~?
      의문사 + be동사 + 주어 + p.p. ~?
    - Was it made by you?
      When was it made by you?
  - **조동사 수동태**
    - 주어 + ④ _____ + be + p.p.
    - The box must be opened.

- **시제**
  - **현재**
    - 주어 + am / is / are + p.p.
    - The name is used by girls.
  - **과거**
    - 주어 + ⑤ _____ + p.p.
    - The name was used by girls.
  - **미래**
    - 주어 + ⑥ _____ + p.p.
    - The name will be used by girls.
  - **진행**
    - 주어 + be동사 + ⑦ _____ + p.p.
    - The name is being used by girls.

- **동사구 수동태**
  - 주어 + [be동사 + p.p. + 전치사]
  - The lamp was turned on by her.

- **by 이외 전치사**
  - 주어 + be동사 + p.p. + (⑧ _____) + 목적격
  - The bag is filled with books.

보기
- · 조동사
- · was / were
- · be동사 + p.p.
- · being
- · Be동사 + 주어
- · in, at, with
- · not
- · will be

to부정사

GP 17　to부정사의 명사적 쓰임

GP 18　to부정사의 형용사적 쓰임

GP 19　to부정사의 부사적 쓰임

GP 20　to부정사의 의미상 주어

GP 21　to부정사를 이용한 구문

• Grammar & Writing

• Actual Test

• 한눈에 정리하는 Grammar Mapping

to부정사의 명사적 쓰임

GP 17

'~하는 것'의 의미를 가지며 문장에서 명사처럼 주어, 목적어, 보어 역할을 한다.

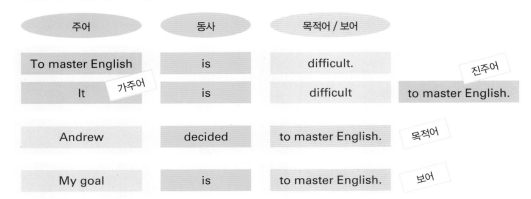

① **주어 역할**: ~하는 것은

To invent a flying car is my dream.

= ☆ It is my dream **to invent** a flying car.

② **목적어 역할**: ~하는 것을

They wanted **to stay** together.

☆ My friends promised **to keep** my secret.

③ **보어 역할**: ~하는 것이다

My plan is **to draw** cartoons.

His job is **to help** the homeless.

> **Tip**
>
> to부정사 주어가 길면 문장 앞에 가주어 it을 쓰고 뒤에 진주어 to부정사를 쓴다.

• Upgrade •

to부정사의 부정은 to부정사 앞에 not이나 never를 쓴다.

He promised **not to be** late again.

④ **의문사 + to부정사**: to부정사가 의문사와 같이 쓰여 주어, 목적어, 보어 역할을 한다.

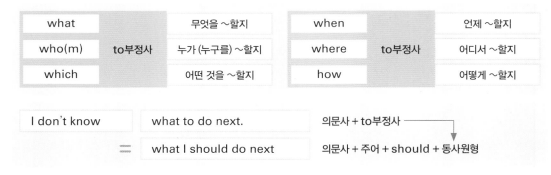

The child didn't know **how to open** the bottle.

☆ Please don't tell me **when to study**.

Let's talk about **where to go** for our vacation.

(= **where we should go** for our vacation)

A 보기의 말을 알맞은 형태로 바꿔 빈칸을 채우시오. (한 번씩만 사용)

보기 | hear   invite   have   keep

1 It was my mom's plan _____ three children.

2 He wanted _____ you to his concert.

3 The question is how _____ a promise.

4 It was wonderful _____ your voice again.

B 두 문장이 같은 의미를 갖도록 빈칸을 채우시오.

1 Do you know where you should get off?

→ Do you know _____?

2 The model knows how she should pose.

→ The model knows _____.

3 To spend our vacation on the moon sounds amazing.

→ _____ sounds amazing _____.

C 우리말과 의미가 같도록 ( ) 안의 말을 이용하여 문장을 완성하시오.

1 그의 직업은 영화 촬영에 적합한 장소를 찾는 것이다. (find)

→ His job _____ _____ _____ the right places for movie shootings.

2 네 글씨체는 읽기가 어려워. (read)

→ _____ is hard _____ _____ your handwriting.

3 우리는 이번 주 금요일 밤에 파자마 파티를 열기로 동의했어. (agree, hold)

→ We _____ _____ _____ a pajama party this Friday night.

D 밑줄 친 부분에 대한 설명을 체크하고 틀린 경우엔 바르게 고치시오. (맞으면 'O' 표시)

1	<u>That</u> is fun to talk with Sam. → ( )	to부정사 주어가 길면 문장 앞에 (가주어, 진주어)인 (That, It) 사용
2	They planned <u>have</u> a small wedding. → ( )	주어 + plan + 목적어 (to부정사, 동사원형)
3	She decided <u>don't</u> to waste time. → ( )	to부정사를 부정할 땐 (don't, not)을 to부정사 (앞, 뒤)에 사용
4	He knows <u>what</u> to take his medicine. → ( )	'(무엇을, 언제) 복용할지를'이므로 의문사 (what, when) + to부정사

to부정사의 형용사적 쓰임

'~하는, ~할'의 의미를 가지며 형용사처럼 명사를 수식한다. 이때 to부정사는 명사 뒤에 위치한다.

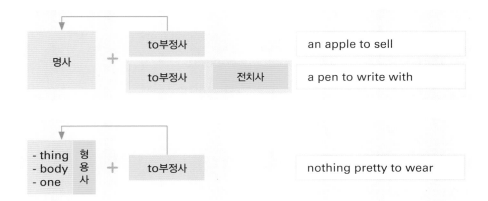

❶ 명사 + [to부정사]

I bought *a book* **to read**. (← read a book)

I have *a lot of homework* **to do**. (← do a lot of homework)

❷ 명사 + [to부정사 + 전치사]

I need *a chair* **to sit on**. (← sit on a chair)

★ She bought *a house* **to live in**. (← live in a house)

❸ [-thing / -body / -one + 형용사] + [to부정사]

I need *something delicious* **to eat**.

★ Do you have *anything cold* **to drink**?

> ○ Tip ○
>
> **[명사 + to부정사 + 전치사]**
> 수식하는 명사가 to부정사에 이어지는 전치사의 목적어인 경우 전치사가 필요하다.
> · paper to write on
> · a pencil to write with
> · a friend to play with
> · something to talk about

• Upgrade •

[be동사 + to부정사] 용법

be동사 뒤에 to부정사가 와서 주어의 상태에 대해서 보충 설명하는 형용사 역할을 한다. 이때 to부정사는 예정, 가능, 의무, 운명, 의도 등의 의미를 가진다.

❶ 예정(~할 예정이다)　　The movie **is to start** soon.

❷ 가능(~할 수 있다)　　No stars **were to be seen** in the night sky.

❸ 의무(~해야 한다)　　You **are to bring** your own food.

❹ 운명(~할 운명이다)　　The soldier **was never to return** again.

❺ 의도(~하고자 하다)　　If you **are to help** me, please be quiet.

A 보기의 말을 알맞은 형태로 바꿔 빈칸을 채우시오.

보기 |　　　　eat　　　　　feed　　　　　explain　　　　　succeed

1 There is nothing _____ in the refrigerator.

2 Can you give me a chance _____ ?

3 It was time _____ my dog.

4 If you are _____ , you must work hard.

B 보기에서 알맞은 전치사를 골라 문장을 완성하시오.

보기 |　　　　in　　　　　on　　　　　with　　　　　about

1 The water is warm enough to swim _____ .

2 Do you have time? I have something to talk _____ .

3 He is looking for paper to write _____ .

4 She made new friends to play _____ .

C 우리말과 의미가 같도록 ( ) 안의 말을 이용하여 문장을 완성하시오.

1 그는 도서관에 반납할 책이 두 권 있다. (books, return)

→ He has _____ _____ _____ _____ to the library.

2 오늘은 텔레비전에 볼 만한 흥미로운 것이 없네. (interesting, nothing, watch)

→ There is _____ _____ _____ _____ on TV today.

3 스트레스를 푸는 가장 좋은 방법이 무엇일까? (way, release)

→ What is _____ _____ _____ _____ _____ stress?

D 밑줄 친 부분에 대한 설명을 체크하고 틀린 경우엔 바르게 고치시오. (맞으면 'O' 표시)

1	Write down a bad habit <u>to broke</u>. → ( )	형용사처럼 명사 (앞, 뒤)에서 수식하는 to + (동사원형, 과거동사)
2	We found a house <u>to buy</u>. → ( )	'구입할 집'을 의미하며 (명사 + to부정사, to부정사 + 명사)
3	We found a house <u>to live</u>. → ( )	(live a house, live in a house)이므로 명사 + to부정사 + 전치사 (in, 없음)
4	He had <u>special nothing</u> to say. → ( )	-thing으로 끝나는 명사의 수식은 (명사 + 형용사, 형용사 + 명사) + to부정사

to부정사의 부사적 쓰임

GP 19

'~하기 위해, ~해서, ~하기에, ~하다니' 등의 의미를 가지며 문장에서 부사처럼 동사, 형용사, 문장을 수식한다.

목적	주어 + 동사 ~		to부정사	He ran to catch the bus.
감정의 원인	주어 + 동사	(감정) 형용사	to부정사	I am happy to see you again.
형용사 수식	주어 + 동사	형용사	to부정사	The house is easy to build.
판단의 근거	주어 + (판단) 동사 ~		to부정사	Jane must be kind to help me.
결과	주어 + (무의지) 동사 ~		to부정사	She lived to be 85 years old.

❶ **목적: ~하기 위해 (~하다)**

Cathy *got up* early **to go** to school on time.

☀ I *work out* every day **to stay** healthy.

❷ **감정의 원인: ~해서 (~한 감정이 들다)**

☀ He was *surprised* **to hear** the news.

Julie felt *scared* **to walk** into the dark woods.

❸ **형용사 수식: ~하기에 (~한 상태이다)**

The dance was *easy* **to learn**.

❹ **판단의 근거: ~하는 것을 보아 (~이겠다)**

☀ You *must* be popular **to have** so many fans.

❺ **결과: ~해서, (결국) ~하게 되다**

James *grew up* **to be** a world-famous photographer.

The army fought hard *only* **to lose** the battle.

- **Upgrade** •

결과를 나타내는 대표적 표현 (무의지 동사)

❶ grow up + to부정사: 자라서 ~가 되다

❷ live + to부정사: 살아서 ~가 되다

❸ wake up + to부정사: 깨어나서 ~하게 되다

> ○ **Tip** ○
>
> **감정을 나타내는 형용사**
> happy, glad, sad, pleased, bored, scared, disappointed, surprised, shocked…

GP Practice

A 밑줄 친 부분을 해석하고 보기에서 해당 쓰임을 골라 번호를 쓰시오.

보기	① 목적	② 감정의 원인	③ 형용사 수식	④ 판단의 근거	⑤ 결과

1 The dog was excited to see snow.   쓰임 _____   해석 _____

2 This potato is too hot to eat.   쓰임 _____   해석 _____

3 She grew up to be a singer.   쓰임 _____   해석 _____

4 I practiced a lot to win the game.   쓰임 _____   해석 _____

5 He must be rich to buy the airplane.   쓰임 _____   해석 _____

B 주어진 표현과 어울리는 표현을 찾아 연결하시오.

1 He was **excited** •   • Ⓐ to buy a new bag.

2 Pizza is not **easy** •   • Ⓑ to drive a car for the first time.

3 You **must be honest** •   • Ⓒ to make.

4 Lucy **went shopping** •   • Ⓓ to tell me the truth.

5 The girl **grew up** •   • Ⓔ to be the queen of the country.

C 우리말과 의미가 같도록 ( ) 안의 말을 이용하여 문장을 완성하시오.

1 Tom은 그의 여자친구와 헤어지게 되어 슬펐다. (sad, break up with)

→ Tom _____ _____ _____ _____ _____ _____ his girlfriend.

2 그녀는 결국 120살까지 살았다. (live, be)

→ She _____ _____ _____ 120 years old.

3 너의 질문은 대답하기에 어렵구나. (difficult, answer)

→ Your question _____ _____ _____ _____.

D 밑줄 친 부분에 대한 설명을 체크하고 틀린 경우엔 바르게 고치시오. (맞으면 'O' 표시)

1	I was <u>happily</u> to see you again. → ( )	행복한 (부사, 감정형용사)	+	보게 되어서 [to부정사]
2	His painting is <u>easily</u> to understand. → ( )	쉬운 (부사, 형용사)	+	이해하기에 [to부정사]
3	He saved money <u>buy</u> an airplane. → ( )	저축하다	+	사기 위해 (to부정사, 동사원형)
4	He must be smart <u>solve</u> the quiz. → ( )	똑똑한 것이 분명해 [(판단)동사]	+	푸는 것을 보니 (to부정사, 동사원형)

to부정사의 의미상 주어

GP 20

to부정사의 행위자를 의미상 주어라고 한다. 의미상 주어는 to부정사 앞에 [for + 목적격] 또는 [성품을 나타내는 형용사 + of + 목적격]의 형태로 쓴다.

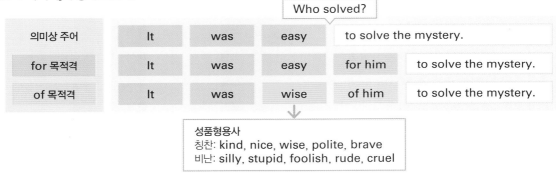

☆ It is hard **for me** *to study* all night.
The dog is not easy **for you** *to train*.

☆ It was brave **of the firefighter** *to save* the boy.
It was nice **of her** *to take care of* the lost cat.

to부정사를 이용한 구문

GP 21

to부정사를 이용한 구문에는 [형용사 / 부사 + enough + to부정사]와 [too + 형용사 / 부사 + to부정사] 등이 있다.

❶ enough to

☆ He is **strong enough to lift** the wooden box.
→ ☆ He is **so strong that he can lift** the wooden box.

❷ too ~ to

☆ Cathy was **too tired to wake up** at six.
→ Cathy was **so tired that she could not wake up** at six.

A ( ) 안에서 알맞은 것을 고르시오.

1 It is very kind (of, for) you to say that.

2 This game app is easy (of, for) me to download.

3 He is (too, enough) honest to tell a lie.

4 This elephant was (enough strong, strong enough) to crush the car.

5 It was brave of (she, her) to catch the robber.

B 두 문장이 같은 의미를 갖도록 문장을 완성하시오.

1 He was so strong that he could lift a car.

→ He was _____ a car.

2 The kid is so short that he can't reach the shelf.

→ The kid is _____ the shelf.

3 She ran fast enough to come in first place.

→ She ran _____ fast _____ she _____ come in first place.

C 우리말과 의미가 같도록 ( ) 안의 말을 이용하여 문장을 완성하시오.

1 그가 그녀의 충고를 받은 것은 현명했어. (take, wise)

→ It was _____ _____ _____ _____ _____ her advice.

2 나의 영어 선생님은 중국어 말하는 것을 어려워하셔. (speak)

→ It is hard _____ _____ _____ _____ _____ _____
Chinese.

3 포장도로가 계란을 익힐 만큼 충분히 뜨거웠어. (fry, hot)

→ The pavement _____ _____ _____ _____ _____ an egg on.

D 밑줄 친 부분에 대한 설명을 체크하고 틀린 경우엔 바르게 고치시오. (맞으면 'O' 표시)

1	It was fun <u>of him</u> to make a doll. → ( )	성품형용사가 (있으면, 없으면) 의미상 주어는 (of, for) + 목적격
2	It was kind <u>for her</u> to help us. → ( )	성품형용사가 (있으면, 없으면) 의미상 주어는 (of, for) + 목적격
3	Tom is <u>enough old</u> to drive a car. → ( )	(~하기에 충분한, ~하기엔 너무 ~한)의 의미 (enough + 형용사, 형용사 + enough) + to부정사
4	I was <u>too busy</u> to do my homework. → ( )	(~하기에 충분한, ~하기엔 너무 ~한)의 의미 (too + 형용사, 형용사 + too) + to부정사

A 우리말과 의미가 같도록 ( ) 안의 말을 배열하시오.

1 당신은 언제 화가가 되기로 결심했나요? (become, decide, to, artist, an)

→ When did you _____ ?

2 나는 같이 일할 파트너를 찾고 있습니다. (to, work, a, partner, with)

→ I am looking for _____ .

3 이 텐트는 우리가 들어가서 잠자기에 너무 작아. (small, too, to, sleep, us, in, for)

→ This tent is _____ .

4 그녀는 프리즈비(원반) 던지는 방법을 잘 알아. (frisbee, a, to, how, throw)

→ She knows _____ well.

5 그 새로운 놀이공원은 다음 달에 오픈할 예정이야. (to, is, next month, open)

→ The new amusement park _____ .

6 새로운 출발을 할 시간이야. (make, to, time)

→ It is _____ a fresh start.

B 우리말과 의미가 같도록 ( ) 안의 말을 이용하여 문장을 완성하시오.

1 그의 계획은 이번 달에 최소한 3권의 책을 읽는 것이었어. (plan, be, read)

→ _____ _____ _____ _____ at least 3 books this month.

2 용돈을 다 웹툰에 사용하다니 너는 어리석구나. (silly, spend)

→ It was _____ _____ _____ _____ all your pocket money on webtoons.

3 당신은 빈칸을 채우셔야 합니다. (be, fill out)

→ You _____ _____ _____ _____ the blanks.

4 그 요리사는 언제 오븐을 꺼야 하는지 잊어버렸어. (turn off)

→ The cook forgot _____ _____ _____ _____ the oven.

5 관광객들은 다음에 어디를 가야 할지 알고 있었어. (go)

→ The tourists knew _____ _____ _____ next.

6 그는 그의 가족과 식사하는 것이 매우 큰 즐거움이었어. (have)

→ It was a great pleasure _____ _____ _____ _____ dinner with his family.

7 그녀는 아주 어려서 그 전쟁을 기억할 수 없었어. (so, remember, that)

→ She was _____ _____ _____ _____ _____ the war.

C to부정사를 이용하여 두 문장을 한 문장으로 쓰시오.

1 Jake arrived too late. So he couldn't watch the concert.

→ Jake arrived _____ _____ _____ _____ the concert.

2 They were brave. They saved a child from the fire.

→ It was brave _____ _____ _____ _____ a child from the fire.

3 The birds are making a nest. They will live in the nest.

→ The birds are making a nest _____ _____ _____.

4 Can you teach me? How should I wrap this gift?

→ Can you teach me _____ _____ _____ this gift?

5 I met my Korean fans again. So I was excited.

→ I was excited _____ _____ _____ _____ _____ again.

D 주어진 단어를 이용하여 그림 속 **Fred**의 상황에 알맞은 문장을 쓰시오. (한 번씩만 사용)

보기   1   2   3

This bag	difficult	listen to
Bumper cars	**heavy**	**carry**
His speech	fun	solve
The math question	boring	ride

보기	This bag is heavy for Fred to carry.

1 His speech is _____ for Fred _____ _____ _____.

2 The math question is _____ for Fred _____ _____.

3 Bumper cars are _____ for Fred _____ _____.

(1–5) 빈칸에 들어갈 알맞은 말을 고르시오.

1

It was fun _____ to appear on TV.

① she   ② her

③ for she   ④ of her

⑤ for her

2

I can't find the bus stop. Can you tell me where _____ ?

① go   ② went

③ to went   ④ to goes

⑤ to go

3

It is important _____ realistic goals.

① set   ② sets

③ to set   ④ to setting

⑤ to sets

4

You are _____ to think about your future.

① older   ② old so

③ enough old   ④ old too

⑤ old enough

5

He is a great roommate _____ .

① to live   ② to living

③ live   ④ to live in

⑤ to live with

(6–7) 우리말을 영어로 바르게 옮긴 것을 고르시오.

6

나는 너무 늦게 도착해서 기차를 못 탔어.

① I arrived so late to catch the train.

② I arrived late enough to catch the train.

③ I arrived enough late to catch the train.

④ I arrived too late to catch the train.

⑤ I arrived too late to caught the train.

7

나는 특별히 할 말이 없었어.

① I had nothing special to say.

② I had to say nothing special.

③ I had special nothing to say.

④ I didn't have nothing special to say.

⑤ I didn't have special nothing to say.

8 보기의 밑줄 친 부분과 쓰임이 같은 것을 고르시오.

We will get you some paper to write on.

① I hope to grow taller.

② To make model airplanes takes time.

③ It was time to say goodbye.

④ We wanted to watch the movie.

⑤ The rules were easy to remember.

9 빈칸에 들어갈 수 <u>없는</u> 말을 고르시오.

> We will tell you _____ to cook.

① where ② why
③ when ④ how
⑤ what

10 밑줄 친 부분이 나머지와 쓰임이 <u>다른</u> 것은?

① My dad lost weight <u>to be</u> healthy.
② He called me <u>to ask</u> about you.
③ She came to Seoul <u>to visit</u> you.
④ Don't forget <u>to bring</u> your glasses.
⑤ We arrived early <u>to get</u> better seats.

(11-12) 주어진 단어를 알맞게 고쳐 빈칸을 채우시오.

11 It was fun _____ to ride the roller coaster. (me)

⇨ _____

12 It was difficult _____ the Russian actor's name. (remember)

⇨ _____

(13-14) 다음 중 어법상 <u>어색한</u> 것을 고르시오.

13 ① He lost the chance to say sorry.
② We tried not to make the same mistake.
③ It was necessary of her to tell the truth.
④ He was never to see his mom again.
⑤ You must be busy to take a taxi.

14 ① Did you decide whom to invite?
② You are old enough to know better.
③ We have something fun to do today.
④ This was fantastic to sing with my favorite singer.
⑤ Brian needed a fork to eat with.

15 빈칸에 들어갈 말이 나머지와 <u>다른</u> 것을 고르시오.

① It was nice _____ her to forgive you.
② The promise was easy _____ me to keep.
③ The musical is boring _____ us to watch.
④ The book was fun _____ him to read.
⑤ It was exciting _____ me to ride a horse.

16 다음 중 명사적 쓰임의 to부정사로 짝지어진 것을 고르시오.

> ⓐ She bought a hat to put on.
> ⓑ Do you want to order now?
> ⓒ I hurried not to be late for school.
> ⓓ It was his first time to babysit.
> ⓔ It was fun to talk with Jack.

① ⓐ, ⓑ   ② ⓐ, ⓔ

③ ⓑ, ⓔ   ④ ⓒ, ⓓ

⑤ ⓒ, ⓔ

(17–18) 우리말과 의미가 같도록 빈칸을 채우시오.

17 너는 이 책을 먼저 읽어야 해.

⇨ You are _____ _____ this book first.

18 우리는 일출을 볼 수 있도록 충분히 일찍 일어났어.

⇨ We got up early _____ _____ _____ the sunrise.

19 빈칸에 들어갈 말로 알맞은 것은?

> 너는 오렌지 껍질을 쉽게 벗기는 방법을 아니?
> Do you know _____ to peel an orange easily?

① what   ② when

③ how   ④ where

⑤ why

(20–21) 우리말과 의미가 같도록 ( ) 안의 말을 배열하시오.

20 나는 그에게 말해 줄 무언가 중요한 것이 있어.
(important, tell, something, to)

⇨ I have _____

_____ him.

21 Lucas는 그 어려운 책을 이해하는 것을 보니 영리한 것이 분명해.
(must, brilliant, be, understand, to)

⇨ Lucas _____

_____ the difficult book.

22 친구의 어법 실수를 잘못 설명해 준 학생은?

① To made new friends is not easy.
채빈: to부정사의 형태는 [to + 동사원형]이지.

② He agreed to not make any noise.
유리: to부정사를 부정할 땐 not을 to부정사 바로 앞에 써야 해.

③ I am enough young to live alone.
승아: '~하기엔 너무 ~한'은 [too + 형용사 + to부정사]이지.

④ This was dangerous to travel alone.
범희: 가주어는 항상 it을 써야 해.

⑤ He brought me a chair to sit.
보민: '~위에 앉을 의자'는 to sit at을 써.

(23–24) 우리말과 의미가 같도록 ( ) 안의 말을 이용하여 문장을 완성하시오.

23 우리는 아기를 깨우지 않기 위해 조용히 걸었어.
(wake, not)

⇨ We walked quietly _____ _____

_____ _____ _____ .

24 그 영화는 네가 혼자 보기에 무섭다.
(you, watch)

⇨ The movie is scary _____

_____ _____ _____ alone.

(25–26) 두 문장이 같은 의미를 갖도록 빈칸을 채우시오.

25 Do you know what you should buy on the way home?

⇨ Do you know _____ _____

_____ on the way home?

26 The panda was so lazy that it didn't move a lot.

⇨ The panda was _____ _____

_____ _____ a lot.

(27–29) 틀린 것이 있으면 고치고 이유를 설명하시오.

27 The two countries agreed end the war.

고치기: _____ ⇨ _____

이유: agree는 (주어, 목적어)로
(동사원형, to부정사)를 가짐

28 Evan was enough kind to lend his book to me.

고치기: _____ ⇨ _____

이유: (~하기에 충분한, 너무 ~해서)의 어순은
(enough + 형, 형 + enough) + to부정사

*형: 형용사

29 It was very kind for you to share your food with me.

고치기: _____ ⇨ _____

이유: 성품형용사가 (있으면, 없으면)
의미상 주어는 (of, for) + 목적격

30 다음 조건을 이용하여 알맞게 영작하시오.

10분은 휴식을 취하기엔 너무 짧은 시간이야.
조건 1: short, take a break, is
조건 2: 9단어, too ~ to

⇨ _____

_____ .

한눈에 정리하는 Grammar Mapping

빈칸에 알맞은 답을 보기에서 골라 넣어 grammar mapping 완성하기

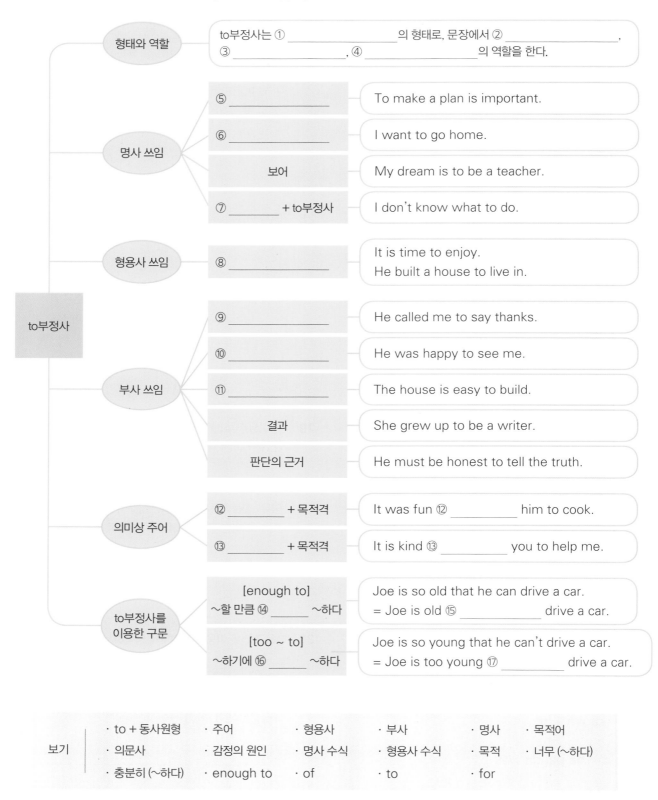

to부정사

형태와 역할
to부정사는 ① _____의 형태로, 문장에서 ② _____, ③ _____, ④ _____의 역할을 한다.

명사 쓰임
- ⑤ _____ — To make a plan is important.
- ⑥ _____ — I want to go home.
- 보어 — My dream is to be a teacher.
- ⑦ _____ + to부정사 — I don't know what to do.

형용사 쓰임
- ⑧ _____ — It is time to enjoy. / He built a house to live in.

부사 쓰임
- ⑨ _____ — He called me to say thanks.
- ⑩ _____ — He was happy to see me.
- ⑪ _____ — The house is easy to build.
- 결과 — She grew up to be a writer.
- 판단의 근거 — He must be honest to tell the truth.

의미상 주어
- ⑫ _____ + 목적격 — It was fun ⑫ _____ him to cook.
- ⑬ _____ + 목적격 — It is kind ⑬ _____ you to help me.

to부정사를 이용한 구문
- [enough to] ~할 만큼 ⑭ _____ ~하다 — Joe is so old that he can drive a car. = Joe is old ⑮ _____ drive a car.
- [too ~ to] ~하기에 ⑯ _____ ~하다 — Joe is so young that he can't drive a car. = Joe is too young ⑰ _____ drive a car.

보기
- to + 동사원형
- 주어
- 형용사
- 부사
- 명사
- 목적어
- 의문사
- 감정의 원인
- 명사 수식
- 형용사 수식
- 목적
- 너무 (~하다)
- 충분히 (~하다)
- enough to
- of
- to
- for

동명사

GP 22 동명사의 명사적 쓰임

GP 23 동명사의 관용적 쓰임

GP 24 동명사와 to부정사

• Grammar & Writing

• Actual Test

• 한눈에 정리하는 Grammar Mapping

동명사의 명사적 쓰임

[동사원형 + -ing] 형태로 '~하는 것'의 의미이다. 문장에서 명사처럼 주어, 목적어, 보어 역할을 한다.

주어	동사	목적어 / 보어	
☆ Watching musicals	is	fun.	
☆ She	enjoys	singing loudly.	동사의 목적어
☆ I	am interested in	making robots.	전치사의 목적어
☆ His hobby	is	taking pictures.	보어

❶ 주어 역할: ~하는 것은

☆ Using chopsticks is good for the brain.
= To use chopsticks is good for the brain.

❷ 목적어 역할: ~하는 것을

She *finished* **packing** her bag for the trip.　(동사의 목적어)
I was excited *about* **seeing** a whale in the ocean.　(전치사의 목적어)

❸ 보어 역할: ~하는 것이다

The best part of camping is **meeting** new people.

• Upgrade •

동명사의 부정은 동명사 앞에 not이나 never를 쓴다.
We are sorry for **not answering** your questions.

> ○ Tip ○
> 동명사 주어는 to부정사로 바꿔 쓸 수 있고, 항상 단수취급을 한다.

동명사의 관용적 쓰임

go -ing	~하러 가다	be busy -ing	~하느라 바쁘다
how / what about -ing	~하는 것이 어때?	spend 시간 / 돈 (in) -ing	~하는 데 ~을 소비하다
look forward to -ing	~을 고대하다	have difficulty (in) -ing	~하는 데 어려움이 있다

He **is busy** study**ing** for the final exam.
How about go**ing** to a seafood buffet for dinner?

A ( ) 안에서 알맞은 것을 고르시오.

1 Do you mind (designs, designing) shoes for me?

2 (Cooking, Cook) Japanese food is easy for her.

3 Don't be afraid of (to make, making) mistakes.

4 Kevin enjoys (playing, to play) virtual games.

5 Don't spend too much time (to watch, watching) TV.

B 두 문장이 같은 의미를 갖도록 빈칸을 채우시오.

1 He took a shower. He finished it.

→ He finished ＿＿＿＿＿＿ ＿＿＿＿＿＿ ＿＿＿＿＿＿.

2 She builds ships. It is her job.

→ Her job is ＿＿＿＿＿＿ ＿＿＿＿＿＿.

3 We made noise. We are sorry about that.

→ We are sorry about ＿＿＿＿＿＿ ＿＿＿＿＿＿.

C 우리말과 의미가 같도록 ( ) 안의 말을 이용하여 문장을 완성하시오.

1 그 꿀벌은 꿀을 모으느라 바쁘다. (busy, collect)

→ The honeybee ＿＿＿＿＿＿ ＿＿＿＿＿＿ ＿＿＿＿＿＿ nectar.

2 세 명의 아들을 키우는 것은 쉽지 않아. (raise)

→ ＿＿＿＿＿＿ ＿＿＿＿＿＿ ＿＿＿＿＿＿ is not easy.

3 매일 밤 달은 형태를 계속 바꾼다. (keep, change)

→ The moon ＿＿＿＿＿＿ ＿＿＿＿＿＿ its shape every night.

D 밑줄 친 부분에 대한 설명을 체크하고 틀린 경우엔 바르게 고치시오. (맞으면 'O' 표시)

1	Sleep enough is important. → ( )	'충분히 자는 것'은 (주어, 목적어) 역할의 (동사, 동명사)
2	He enjoyed to sing the same song. → ( )	주어 + enjoy + 목적어 (동명사, to부정사)
3	Thank you for don't making noise. → ( )	동명사를 부정할 때는 (don't, not)을 동명사 (앞, 뒤)에 위치
4	Beavers are good at build dams. → ( )	주어 + 동사 + 전치사 + 목적어 (동사, 동명사)

동명사와 to부정사

주어	동사	목적어	
동명사를 목적어로 취하는 동사	S — enjoy, finish, mind, keep, give up, avoid, practice, stop, quit	동명사	
to부정사를 목적어로 취하는 동사	S — want, hope, agree, plan, expect, decide, learn, promise	to부정사	
동명사와 to부정사를 모두 목적어로 취하는 동사 (의미 차이 없는 경우)	S — like, love, hate, begin, start, continue	동명사 / to부정사	
동명사와 to부정사를 모두 목적어로 취하는 동사 (의미 차이 있는 경우)	S — remember, forget	동명사 / to부정사	~했던 것을 ~하다 / ~할 것을 ~하다
	S — try	동명사 / to부정사	시험 삼아 ~해 보다 / ~하려고 노력하다

❶ 동명사를 목적어로 취하는 동사

Don't *give up* **climbing** to the top of the mountain.

James *avoided* **looking** into her eyes.

❷ to부정사를 목적어로 취하는 동사

Daniel *is planning* **to build** his own house.

❸ 동명사와 부정사를 모두 목적어로 갖고 의미 변화가 없는 동사

Jane *began* **dancing** on the stage. = Jane *began* **to dance** on the stage.

❹ 동명사와 부정사를 모두 목적어로 갖지만 의미 차이가 있는 동사

I *remember* **visiting** the museum before. (이미 방문했던 것을)

Remember **to hand in** your report tomorrow. (앞으로 제출할 것을)

She *forgot* **meeting** you last year. (이미 만났던 것을)

Don't *forget* **to bring** your lunch today. (앞으로 가져올 것을)

We *tried* **solving** the puzzle for fun. (시험 삼아 풀어 보았다)

We *tried* **to solve** the puzzle to win a prize. (풀려고 노력했다)

• Upgrade •

❶ stop + 동명사: ~하는 것을 멈추다 (동명사가 stop의 목적어)

He *stopped* **drinking** water.

❷ stop + to부정사: ~하기 위해 멈추다 (to부정사의 부사적 쓰임)

He *stopped* **to drink** water.

GP Practice

A ( ) 안에서 알맞은 것을 고르시오. (복수 정답 가능)

1 Please don't forget (calling, to call) me tomorrow.

2 She likes (to ride, riding) her bike in the morning.

3 He hoped (to study, studying) in America.

4 When do you practice (to play, playing) the violin?

B ( ) 안에 주어진 단어를 동명사 또는 to부정사로 바꿔 문장을 완성하시오.

1 He hopes _____ snow on Christmas. (see)

2 Do you mind _____ in the lobby for a minute? (wait)

3 Don't forget _____ a helmet for your safety. (wear)

4 I promised _____ my cousin to the museum. (take)

C 우리말과 의미가 같도록 ( ) 안의 말을 이용하여 문장을 완성하시오.

1 그들은 새 집으로 이사 가는 것을 포기했다. (move)

→ They _____ _____ _____ to a new house.

2 너를 여기서 만날 줄은 예상치 못했어. (see)

→ I did not _____ _____ _____ you here.

3 Tom은 영화를 보는 도중에 코를 골기 시작했다. (start, snore)

→ Tom _____ _____ _____ during the movie.

4 내가 일할 때는 귀찮게 하는 것을 그만해. (bother)

→ Please _____ _____ me when I am working.

D 밑줄 친 부분에 대한 설명을 체크하고 틀린 경우엔 바르게 고치시오. (맞으면 'O' 표시)

*가능한 답은 모두 체크

1	Tom began <u>to keep</u> a diary. → ( )	~하는 것을 시작하다 begin + (to부정사, 동명사)
2	The police will try <u>finding</u> evidence. → ( )	(~하려고 노력하다, 시험 삼아 ~해 보다) try + (to부정사, 동명사)
3	Stop <u>to worry</u> about me. I am okay. → ( )	(~하는 것을, ~하기 위해) 멈추다 stop + (to부정사, 동명사)
4	I remember <u>visiting</u> the island before. → ( )	(~했던 것을, ~할 것을) 기억하다 remember + (to부정사, 동명사)

A 우리말과 의미가 같도록 ( ) 안의 말을 배열하시오.

1 왜 계속 시계를 보는 거니? (looking, keep, the, at, clock)

→ Why do you _____?

2 그 개가 갑자기 나를 보며 짖는 것을 멈췄어. (barking, stopped, me, at)

→ The dog suddenly _____.

3 그 배우는 영화를 위해 말 타는 것을 배웠어. (a, horse, learned, ride, to)

→ The actor _____ for the movie.

4 그는 사람들의 이름 외우는 것을 어려워한다. (has, remembering, difficulty)

→ He _____ people's names.

5 발을 조금만 움직여 주시겠어요? (moving, foot, mind, your)

→ Would you _____ a little?

6 William은 숙제를 하는 데 3시간이 걸렸어. (spent, doing, his, hours, homework, three)

→ William _____.

B 우리말과 의미가 같도록 ( ) 안의 말을 이용하여 문장을 완성하시오.

1 그녀는 고아원에서 자원봉사 활동하기를 원했어. (do, volunteer work)

→ She _____ _____ _____ _____ _____ at an orphanage.

2 Bill은 파충류 키우는 것을 좋아해. (be fond of, raise, reptiles)

→ Bill _____ _____ _____ _____ _____.

3 나는 왜 사람들이 투우 보는 것을 즐기는지 이해가 안 가. (watch, bullfighting)

→ I don't understand why people _____ _____ _____.

4 Jessica는 지난주 나한테 1달러 빌렸던 것을 잊어버렸어. (borrow)

→ Jessica _____ _____ _____ _____ from me last week.

5 불이 났을 때, 그는 비상구를 찾으려고 노력했다. (find an exit)

→ When the fire started, he _____ _____ _____ _____.

6 NASA는 이 프로젝트로 태양에 대해 더 많이 알아낼 것을 기대한다. (expect, find out)

→ NASA _____ _____ _____ _____ _____ about the sun

with this project.

C 두 문장을 의미가 같은 한 문장으로 고칠 때 빈칸에 알맞은 말을 쓰시오.

1 You call me at night. Stop it.

→ Stop _____ me at night.

2 You eat food late at night. It is bad for your health.

→ _____ food late at night is bad for your health.

3 Brian paints with oil paints. He is good at it.

→ Brian is good at _____ with oil paints.

4 My cousin stayed at home all weekend. He enjoyed it.

→ My cousin enjoyed _____ at home all weekend.

5 She will invite me to her concert. She promised me.

→ She promised _____ _____ me to her concert.

6 Brian bought the T-shirt himself. Then, he forgot it.

→ Brian forgot _____ the T-shirt himself.

D Carmella가 해변에서 보낸 하루이다. 주어진 표현을 이용하여 그림에 알맞는 문장을 완성하시오.

take a sand bath

build a sandcastle

run along the beach

1 _____ _____ _____ _____ was very fun.

2 Carmella enjoyed _____ _____ _____ .

3 Her favorite activity was _____ _____ _____ _____ .

(1–5) 빈칸에 들어갈 알맞은 말을 고르시오.

1

_____ breakfast is a healthy habit.

① Eat   ② To eats

③ Eats   ④ Eating

⑤ To eating

2

She didn't expect _____ so much.

① succeed   ② to succeed

③ succeeding   ④ to succeeds

⑤ to succeeding

3

We are sorry for _____ the rules.

① breaking   ② to breaks

③ breaks   ④ break

⑤ to breaking

4

Do you remember _____ the aquarium with me before?

① visit   ② to visits

③ visits   ④ visiting

⑤ to visiting

5

Jane stopped _____ on the phone to answer the door.

① talk   ② talking

③ talks   ④ to talks

⑤ to talking

6 밑줄 친 부분이 나머지 문장들과 쓰임이 다른 것은?

① He finished repairing the broken door.

② She enjoyed watching the musical.

③ Are you interested in saving the Earth?

④ Her job is writing stories for kids.

⑤ I don't mind eating alone.

(7–8) 다음 중 어법상 어색한 것을 고르시오.

7

① She wanted to take a walk.

② I practiced to play the cello a lot.

③ Do you agree to take the train?

④ She was busy moving the boxes.

⑤ We learned to paint with sand.

8

① He quit working for the company.

② Do you mind passing me the bread?

③ My brother loved learning German.

④ I enjoyed to go down the water slides.

⑤ What about eating Mexican food?

9 어법상 어색한 것으로만 짝지어진 것은?

ⓐ He never gave up trying.
ⓑ Drink coffee is not good for you.
ⓒ The baby bird began flying.
ⓓ She avoids to drive at night.
ⓔ Let's go surfing tomorrow.

① ⓐ, ⓑ, ⓒ   ② ⓑ, ⓒ
③ ⓑ, ⓓ   ④ ⓓ, ⓔ
⑤ ⓔ

(10–11) 빈칸에 들어갈 말을 바르게 짝지은 것을 고르시오.

10
· Remember _____ this plant soon.
· Don't forget _____ your hands.

① water - wash
② to water - washing
③ watering - to wash
④ to water - to wash
⑤ watering - washing

11
· The soldiers kept _____ in the rain.
· They hoped _____ the battle.

① walk - win
② to walk - winning
③ walking - to win
④ to walk - to win
⑤ walking - winning

12 빈칸에 공통으로 들어갈 say의 형태는?

I hated _____ sorry to my brother.
But I finally decided _____ it to him.

⇨ _____

(13–14) 빈칸에 들어갈 수 없는 말은?

13 My cousin _____ cleaning her room.

① began   ② hates
③ stopped   ④ enjoys
⑤ plans

14 He _____ to get a job at the TV company.

① minds   ② wants
③ expects   ④ agrees
⑤ decides

15 다음 두 문장의 의미가 같도록 빈칸에 알맞은 말을 고르시오.

To wash dishes is my daddy's job.
= _____ dishes is my daddy's job.

① Wash   ② Washes
③ Washing   ④ Washed
⑤ To washing

(16–18) 두 문장을 한 문장으로 바꿀 때 빈칸에 알맞은 말을 쓰시오.

16 Tom made fun of his sister.
He doesn't do that any more.

⇨ Tom stopped _____ fun
of his sister.

17 I saw a rainbow when I was 12.
I still remember it.

⇨ I remember _____
a rainbow when I was 12.

18 We walked in the forest.
We enjoyed it a lot.

⇨ We enjoyed _____ in the
forest.

19 짝지어진 두 문장의 의미가 서로 다른 것은?

① He began to play the guitar.
= He began playing the guitar.

② It was fun to read the comics.
= Reading the comics was fun.

③ We forgot to lock the door.
= We forgot locking the door.

④ Jane hated wearing a raincoat.
= Jane hated to wear a raincoat.

⑤ To see is to believe.
= Seeing is believing.

(20–21) 두 문장의 의미가 같도록 빈칸에 알맞은 말을 쓰시오.

20 Miranda tried not to eat unhealthy
food.

⇨ Miranda avoided _____
unhealthy food.

21 The young girl couldn't draw a circle
well.

⇨ The young girl was not good at
_____ a circle.

22 친구의 어법 실수를 잘못 설명해 준 학생을 고르시오.

① He left without <u>say</u> goodbye.
② I expect <u>getting</u> better grades.
③ She imagined <u>don't living</u> in Korea.
④ Don't forget <u>bringing</u> a raincoat.
⑤ Reading many books <u>are</u> important.

① 지민: 전치사 without 뒤에는 동명사를 써.

② 찬호: expect의 목적어는 to부정사야.

③ 채빈: 동명사의 부정은 바로 앞에 not이 와야 해.

④ 수현: '~해야 할 것을 잊다'를 의미할 때는
forget이 to부정사를 목적어로 갖지.

⑤ 재민: books가 복수니까 are가 맞아.

23 다음 우리말을 영어로 바르게 옮긴 것을 고르시오.

> 그는 두려움을 안 보이려고 노력했어.

① He tried not show his fear.
② He tried not showing his fear.
③ He didn't try showing his fear.
④ He didn't try to show his fear.
⑤ He tried not to show his fear.

(24-25) 우리말과 의미가 같도록 ( ) 안의 말을 배열하시오.

24 Emily는 그의 전화를 받는 것을 피했다.
(his, call, answering, avoided)

⇨ Emily _____

_____ .

25 나는 더운 날씨 때문에 머리를 기르는 것을 포기했어.
(gave, growing, hair, my, up)

⇨ I _____

because of the hot weather.

(26-27) 우리말과 의미가 같도록 ( ) 안의 말을 이용하여 문장을 완성하시오.

26 그는 어렸을 때 밤하늘의 별을 세었던 것을 잊고 있었어. (forget, count)

⇨ He _____ the stars
in the night sky when he was young.

27 나는 그의 기분을 상하게 할까 봐 두려웠다.
(be afraid of, hurt)

⇨ I _____

his feelings.

(28-29) 틀린 것이 있으면 고치고 이유를 설명하시오.

28 Remember speaking nicely to others starting today.

고치기: _____ ⇨ _____
이유: (말할 것을, 말했던 것을) 기억하다
remember + (to부정사, 동명사)

29 Bees never stop to move their wings when they fly.

고치기: _____ ⇨ _____
이유: (~하기 위해, ~하던 것을) 멈추다
stop + (to부정사, 동명사)

30 다음 조건을 이용하여 알맞게 영작하시오.

> 우리는 다음 달에 너를 만나는 것을 고대하고 있어.
> 조건1: look forward to, meet
> 조건2: 9단어, 현재진행시제

⇨ _____

_____ .

한눈에 정리하는 Grammar Mapping

빈칸에 알맞은 답을 보기에서 골라 넣어 grammar mapping 완성하기

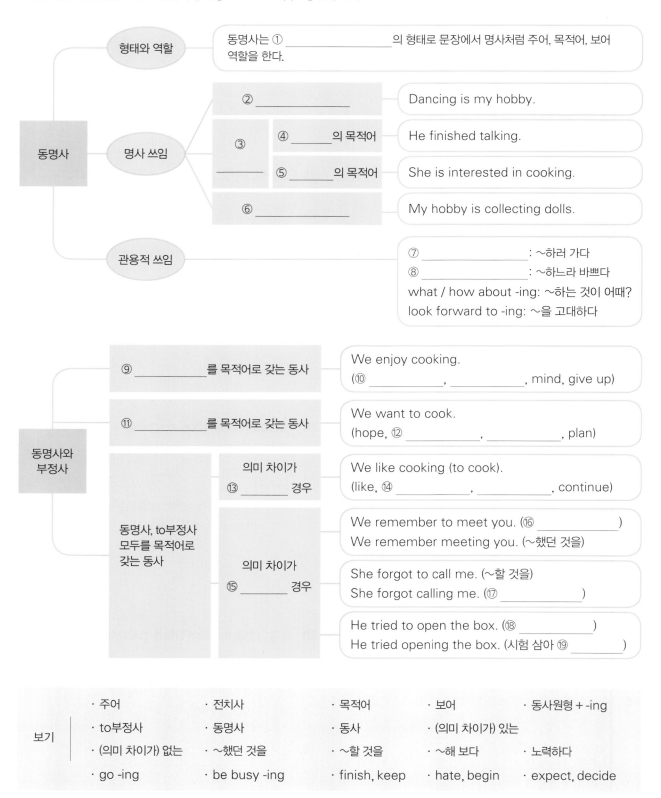

동명사

형태와 역할
동명사는 ① _____의 형태로 문장에서 명사처럼 주어, 목적어, 보어 역할을 한다.

명사 쓰임
② _____ Dancing is my hobby.
③ _____ ④ _____의 목적어 He finished talking.
_____ ⑤ _____의 목적어 She is interested in cooking.
⑥ _____ My hobby is collecting dolls.

관용적 쓰임
⑦ _____ : ~하러 가다
⑧ _____ : ~하느라 바쁘다
what / how about -ing: ~하는 것이 어때?
look forward to -ing: ~을 고대하다

동명사와 부정사

⑨ _____를 목적어로 갖는 동사
We enjoy cooking.
(⑩ _____, _____, mind, give up)

⑪ _____를 목적어로 갖는 동사
We want to cook.
(hope, ⑫ _____, _____, plan)

동명사, to부정사 모두를 목적어로 갖는 동사

의미 차이가 ⑬ _____ 경우
We like cooking (to cook).
(like, ⑭ _____, _____, continue)

의미 차이가 ⑮ _____ 경우
We remember to meet you. (⑯ _____)
We remember meeting you. (~했던 것을)

She forgot to call me. (~할 것을)
She forgot calling me. (⑰ _____)

He tried to open the box. (⑱ _____)
He tried opening the box. (시험 삼아 ⑲ _____)

보기

· 주어	· 전치사	· 목적어	· 보어	· 동사원형 + -ing
· to부정사	· 동명사	· 동사	· (의미 차이가) 있는	
· (의미 차이가) 없는	· ~했던 것을	· ~할 것을	· ~해 보다	· 노력하다
· go -ing	· be busy -ing	· finish, keep	· hate, begin	· expect, decide

분사

GP 25 현재분사와 과거분사

GP 26 분사의 형용사적 쓰임

GP 27 감정을 나타내는 분사

GP 28 현재분사와 동명사

GP 29 분사구문

● Grammar & Writing

● Actual Test

● 한눈에 정리하는 Grammar Mapping

현재분사와 과거분사

GP 25

[동사원형 + -ing] 형태의 현재분사는 진행, 능동의 의미를 갖고, [동사원형 + -ed] 형태의 과거분사는 완료, 수동의 의미를 갖는다.

종류	형태	의미	
현재분사	동사원형 + -ing	진행: ~하고 있는	boiling water
		능동: ~하는, ~하게 하는	shocking news
과거분사	동사원형 + -ed	완료: ~된	boiled eggs
		수동: ~되는, ~당하는	shocked people

• Upgrade •

분사는 be동사나 have와 결합하여 진행형, 완료형, 수동태를 만든다.

He **is writing** a letter. (진행형)

He **has written** a letter. (완료형)

The letter **was written** by him. (수동태)

분사의 형용사적 쓰임

GP 26

❶ **명사 수식**: 명사 앞이나 뒤에서 명사를 수식한다.

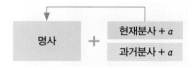

☆ a **moving** robot
☆ a **used** bike

☆ a robot **moving** underwater
a bike **used** for 7 years

❷ **보어 역할**: 주어나 목적어의 상태를 보충 설명한다.

주어	동사	주격보어	
The plan	was	amazing.	현재분사
She	looked	amazed.	과거분사

주어	동사	목적어	목적격보어	
We	saw	Henry	cleaning ~.	현재분사
He	kept	the rooms	cleaned.	과거분사

She sat **listening** to music.   (들으면서: 현재분사)

He designed a dress **made** out of chocolate.   (만들어진: 과거분사)

GP Practice

A ( ) 안에서 알맞은 것을 고르시오.

1 He bought a (using, used) car.

2 Look at the (singing, sing) dog.

3 How many (boiling, boiled) eggs did you eat today?

4 The cat (playing, played) on the sofa is cute.

B ( ) 안에 주어진 단어를 알맞게 고쳐 빈칸을 채우시오.

1 The tourists saw a white lion _____ on a rock. (sleep)

2 AlphaGo is a program _____ by Google. (make)

3 The robber _____ away is very fast. (run)

4 They saved a _____ soldier. (wound)

C 우리말과 의미가 같도록 ( ) 안의 말을 이용하여 문장을 완성하시오.

1 그녀는 마침내 그녀의 잃어버린 목걸이를 찾았다. (lose, necklace)

→ She finally found _____ _____ _____.

2 선글라스를 쓰고 있는 저 남자가 우리 삼촌이야. (wear, sunglasses)

→ The man _____ _____ is my uncle.

3 구르는 돌은 이끼가 끼지 않아. (roll, stone)

→ A _____ _____ gathers no moss.

4 그 소녀는 장난감으로 가득 찬 상자를 열었다. (fill, with)

→ The girl opened a box _____ _____ toys.

D 밑줄 친 부분에 대한 설명을 체크하고 틀린 경우엔 바르게 고치시오. (맞으면 'O' 표시)

1	Look at the <u>danced</u> boy. → ( )	'춤추고 있는'은 (진행, 완료) 의미이므로 (현재, 과거)분사
2	I love any food <u>cooking</u> by my dad. → ( )	'요리된'은 (수동, 능동) 의미이므로 (현재, 과거)분사
3	He put a <u>fallen</u> leaf inside a book. → ( )	'떨어진 잎(낙엽)'은 (진행, 완료) 의미이므로 (현재, 과거)분사
4	I have a <u>made in Italy</u> scarf. → ( )	[분사+α]가 명사를 수식할 때, [분사+α]는 명사 (앞, 뒤)에 위치

감정을 나타내는 분사

GP 27

현재분사는 '～한 감정을 느끼게 하는', 과거분사는 '～한 감정을 느끼는'을 의미한다.

동사 (～한 감정이 들게 하다)	현재분사 (～한 감정을 느끼게 하는)	과거분사 (～한 감정을 느끼는)
excite / shock	exciting / shocking	excited / shocked
interest (흥미롭게 하다)	interesting (흥미로운)	interested (흥미를 가진)
surprise (놀라게 하다)	surprising (놀라운)	surprised (놀란)
satisfy (만족하게 하다)	satisfying (만족스러운)	satisfied (만족한)
bore (지루하게 하다)	boring (지루한)	bored (지루해 하는)

☆ The book *bores* him.
☆ The book *is* **boring** to him.
☆ He *is* **bored** with the book.

○ Tip ○

감정을 유발하는 주어는 보통 사물이고 감정을 느끼는 주어는 일반적으로 사람이다.

현재분사와 동명사

GP 28

[동사원형 + -ing]가 현재분사로 쓰이면 형용사 역할이고, 동명사로 쓰이면 명사 역할이다.

	be동사	동사원형 + -ing	동사원형 + -ing	명사
현재분사	She	is	playing the piano.	☆ a sleeping lion
		≠	～하고 있는 중	～하고 있는
동명사	My hobby	is	playing the piano.	☆ a sleeping bag
		=	～하는 것	～하는 용도의

Jack *is* **wrapping** birthday gifts.　　　(포장하고 있는 중: 현재분사)
My role *is* **wrapping** birthday gifts.　　(포장하는 것: 동명사)

• Upgrade •
용도나 목적을 나타내는 동명사는 [for + 동사원형 + -ing] 형태로 바꿀 수 있다.
a sleeping bag = a bag *for* **sleeping**
running shoes = shoes *for* **running**

GP Practice

A ( ) 안에서 알맞은 것을 고르시오.

1 He was (satisfying, satisfied) with a silver medal.

2 The report on UFOs sounds very (surprising, surprised).

3 Jane was (exciting, excited) about her vacation plans.

4 The news was (shocking, shocked) to me.

B 밑줄 친 부분의 해석을 쓰고, 현재분사인지 동명사인지를 고르시오.

보기 ㅣ The old lady needs a <u>walking</u> stick.	해석	지팡이	현재분사, 동명사
1 He bought a new <u>washing</u> machine.			현재분사, 동명사
2 This book is about a <u>sleeping</u> beauty.			현재분사, 동명사
3 <u>Swimming</u> is my hobby.			현재분사, 동명사
4 This book is very <u>boring</u>.			현재분사, 동명사

C 우리말과 의미가 같도록 ( ) 안의 말을 이용하여 문장을 완성하시오.

1 그들은 대기실에 들어갔어. (wait)

→ They entered the _____ _____.

2 우리 엄마는 어제 운전면허 시험을 통과하셨어. (drive)

→ My mom passed the _____ _____ yesterday.

3 우리 아빠는 내 성적표에 충격을 받지 않으셨어. (shock)

→ My dad _____ _____ _____ at my school report.

4 너의 아이디어는 나에게 흥미롭게 들리는걸. (sound, interest)

→ Your idea _____ _____ to me.

D 밑줄 친 부분에 대한 설명을 체크하고 틀린 경우엔 바르게 고치시오. (맞으면 'O' 표시)

1	Her English class is never <u>bored</u>. → ( )	수업이 지루함을 (느끼게 하는, 느낀)이므로 (현재, 과거)분사
2	We were <u>surprising</u> at the noise. → ( )	우리가 놀람을 (느끼게 하는, 느낀)이므로 (현재, 과거)분사
3	The mosquito was <u>annoying</u>. → ( )	모기가 짜증을 (느끼게 하는, 느낀)이므로 (현재, 과거)분사
4	I need new <u>run</u> shoes. → ( )	(달리는 중, 달리는 용도)의 신발이므로 (동명사, 현재분사)

분사구문

분사구문은 [접속사 + 주어 + 동사]로 이루어진 부사절을 [동사원형 + -ing]의 부사구로 줄여 쓴 것을 말하고, 문맥에 따라 시간, 이유, 양보, 조건 등의 의미를 가진다.

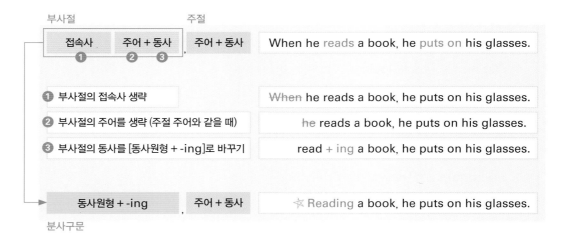

①시간: when, as(~할 때), while(~하는 동안), before, after(~하기 전에, 후에)

When butterflies taste food, they use their feet.

→ **Tasting** food, butterflies use their feet.

②이유: because, as, since(~ 때문에, ~이므로)

Because I didn't hear the alarm, I kept sleeping.

→ ☆ **Not hearing** the alarm, I kept sleeping.

③양보: although, though(~일지라도)

Although Emily has a driver's license, she never drives.

→ ☆ **Although having** a driver's license, Emily never drives.

> **Tip**
> 양보, 조건을 나타내는 접속사는 뜻을 분명하게 하기 위해 생략되지 않을 수도 있다.

④조건: if(만약 ~한다면)

If you read this book, you will find the answer.

→ ☆ **Reading** this book, you will find the answer.

⑤동시동작: while, as(~하면서)

While he was listening to music, he searched the Internet.

→ ☆ **(Being) Listening** to music, he searched the Internet.

> **Tip**
> being으로 시작하는 분사구문에서 being은 생략 가능하다.

• Upgrade •

분사구문의 부정은 분사구문 앞에 not이나 never를 쓴다.

Not feeling good, he didn't say a word.

GP Practice

A   ( ) 안에서 알맞은 것을 고르시오.

1 (Waited, Waiting) for me, she read a magazine.

2 (Buy, Buying) this computer today, you will get a mouse for free.

3 (Hearing, Heard) the good news, Justin began to cry.

4 (Don't wanting, Not wanting) to hurt her feelings, I said nothing.

B   분사구문을 이용하여 두 문장의 의미가 같도록 문장을 완성하시오.

1 If you wear these glasses, you can see better.

→ _____ _____ _____, you can see better.

2 When a starfish loses an arm, it can grow another.

→ _____ _____ _____, a starfish can grow another.

3 Because he was tired, he slept until noon.

→ _____ _____, he slept until noon.

C   주어진 접속사를 사용하여 분사구문을 부사절(접속사 + 주어 + 동사)로 고치시오.

1 Taking off their shoes, the boys jumped into the pool. (after)

→ _____ _____ _____ _____ _____ their shoes, they jumped into the pool.

2 Leaving the stage, he gave me a wink. (when)

→ _____ _____ _____ _____ _____, he gave me a wink.

3 Loving Eric, she decided to marry him. (because)

→ _____ _____ _____ _____, she decided to marry him.

D   밑줄 친 부분에 대한 설명을 체크하고 틀린 경우엔 바르게 고치시오. (맞으면 'O' 표시)

1	He <u>loving</u> animals, he has three dogs. → ( )	주절과 같은 부사절의 (주어, 목적어)는 삭제 (함, 안 함)
2	<u>Hear</u> the news, she got excited. → ( )	(부사절, 주절)의 동사는 (동사원형, 동사원형 + -ing) 형태로 씀
3	<u>Knowing not</u> the area, I got lost. → ( )	분사의 부정은 (don't, not)을 분사 바로 (앞, 뒤)에 씀
4	<u>Although</u> being short, I am good at basketball. → ( )	명확한 의미를 위해 (접속사, 주어)는 생략하지 않을 수도 있음

A 우리말과 의미가 같도록 ( ) 안의 말을 배열하시오.

1 잠자리를 보자, 그 강아지는 그것을 따라가기 시작했어. (dragonfly, a, seeing)

→ _____ , the puppy began to chase it.

2 킬트는 스코틀랜드 남자들이 입는 치마야. (worn, a skirt, Scottish, men, by)

→ A kilt is _____ .

3 그녀는 거울에 비친 자신의 모습을 보고 놀랐어. (surprised, she, was)

→ _____ to see herself in the mirror.

4 유리에 열을 가한 후에, 그 유리 공예가는 이것을 풍선처럼 불었어. (heating, after, glass)

→ _____ , the glass artist blew it up like a balloon.

5 우리 선생님이 내게 엄청나게 많은 과제를 주셨어. 벌써 지친 느낌이야. (exhausted, feel)

→ My teacher gave me tons of homework. I already _____ .

6 물속에서는 매우 빠르지만, 펭귄들은 땅 위에서는 느려. (being, although, fast, water, in)

→ _____ , penguins are slow on land.

B 우리말과 의미가 같도록 ( ) 안의 말을 이용하여 문장을 완성하시오.

1 이봐요, 잠자는 공주님! 일어나라고! (sleep, beauty)

→ Hey, _____ _____ ! Wake up!

2 랩뮤직을 좋아해서, 그는 항상 이것을 차에서 틀어. (love, rap music)

→ _____ _____ _____ , he always plays it in his car.

3 조카는 내 그림에 실망했어. (disappoint, drawing)

→ My nephew _____ _____ _____ _____

_____ .

4 운전하는 동안, 삼촌은 절대 휴대폰을 사용하지 않으셔. (while, drive)

→ _____ _____ , my uncle never uses his cell phone.

5 그 의사에 관한 이야기는 매우 감동적이야. (very, touch)

→ The story about the doctor _____ _____ _____ .

6 너 오늘 왜 걱정스럽게 보이니? (look, worry)

→ Why do you _____ _____ today?

C 분사구문을 만드는 방법을 정리한 노트이다. 보기에서 알맞은 말을 골라 ( )의 설명을 완성하시오. (중복 사용 가능)

보기	주어	동사원형	접속사	부사절

	1 (_____)을 분사구문으로 만들기	주절
부사절은 2 ( ) + 주어 + 동사	<u>When she reads</u> a book,	she listens to music.
3 ( ) 생략	~~When~~ she reads a book,	she listens to music.
4 주절과 같은 부사절의 ( ) 생략	~~she~~ reads a book,	she listens to music.
분사구문은 5 ( ) + -ing	<u>Reading</u> a book,	she listens to music.

D 주어진 ( ) 안의 단어를 이용하여 다음 그림과 일치하는 문장을 완성하시오.

1 _____ _____ _____, some dolphins jumped in and out of the water. (follow, our boat)

2 _____ _____ _____, I fell asleep right away. (open, a book)

3 _____ _____ _____, she found some money in the pocket. (wash, her jacket)

(1–5) 빈칸에 들어갈 알맞은 말을 고르시오.

1 Wash strawberries with _____ water.

① run   ② runs

③ runned   ④ to run

⑤ running

2 The woman _____ at me is my aunt.

① wave   ② waves

③ waved   ④ to wave

⑤ waving

3 He gave me a toy horse _____ of wood.

① make   ② makes

③ made   ④ to make

⑤ making

4 His soccer skills were _____.

① amaze   ② amazes

③ amazed   ④ to amaze

⑤ amazing

5 _____ a shower, he sang a song loudly.

① Takes   ② Took

③ Taken   ④ Taking

⑤ To take

(6–7) 밑줄 친 부분이 어법상 어색한 것은?

6 ① Look at the star shining in the sky.

② The dragon drawn by Tom looks cute.

③ The rising sun is very beautiful.

④ Who is the smiled man?

⑤ He is a well-known reporter.

7 ① Your plan sounds interested.

② Are you pleased with the present?

③ He had a boring vacation.

④ My baby was surprised by the noise.

⑤ The music sounds depressing.

8 빈칸에 들어갈 수 없는 말을 고르시오.

The cake _____ by my dad was very delicious.

① cutting   ② made

③ bought   ④ chosen

⑤ decorated

(9~10) 밑줄 친 부분을 분사구문으로 고칠 때 가장 알맞은 것은?

9

> After she peeled the apple, she cut it into eight pieces.

① She peeled the apple

② She peeling the apple

③ Peeled the apple

④ Peeling the apple

⑤ Peels the apple

10

> Because I didn't have an umbrella, I ran in the rain.

① I didn't having an umbrella

② Didn't have an umbrella

③ Didn't having an umbrella

④ Having not an umbrella

⑤ Not having an umbrella

11 밑줄 친 부분이 '~하기 때문에'라고 해석되는 것은?

① Wearing his seatbelt, he was not hurt.

② Feeling sick, he went to school.

③ Turning left, you will find the ATM.

④ Seeing her for the first time, I fell in love.

⑤ Arriving at home, I ran into my room.

12 밑줄 친 부분을 [접속사 + 주어 + 동사]로 바꿀 때 알맞은 것은?

> Staying in Korea, she worked as a reporter.

① If she stayed in Korea

② Although she stayed in Korea

③ While she was staying in Korea

④ Unless she stayed in Korea

⑤ If she didn't stay in Korea

13 주어진 단어를 다음 빈칸에 공통으로 들어갈 형태로 고치시오.

· Alex and I went to a _____ room once.

· There, we saw my sister _____ loudly in the next room.

sing ⇨ _____

(14~15) ( ) 안의 말을 알맞게 고쳐 빈칸을 채우시오.

14 The end of the story was _____. (shock)

⇨ _____

15 _____ a cookbook, he cooked rice noodles. (read)

⇨ _____

(16–17) 밑줄 친 부분의 쓰임이 나머지와 다른 것은?

16 ① Try on the skirt in the fitting room.

② When did your driving lesson start?

③ The singer is waiting for his turn.

④ He bought a sleeping bag.

⑤ Where is a washing machine?

17 ① Being tired from work, he went to bed.

② Being shy, he never talks to people.

③ Being late, she had to hurry.

④ Being a teacher, he speaks very well.

⑤ Being a pilot is his dream.

18 어법상 올바른 것으로만 짝지어진 것은?

ⓐ Working hard, you will succeed.

ⓑ The pants buying online are nice.

ⓒ Don't having time, he had to hurry.

ⓓ Be careful of the boiling water.

ⓔ Eat salty soup, he became thirsty.

① ⓐ, ⓑ   ② ⓐ, ⓓ

③ ⓑ, ⓒ   ④ ⓑ, ⓓ

⑤ ⓓ, ⓔ

19 다음 밑줄 친 부분을 [접속사 + 주어 + 동사]로 고칠 때 알맞은 접속사는?

Hitting the target, you will get a doll as a prize.

① If   ② But

③ Because   ④ Although

⑤ And

(20–21) 우리말과 의미가 같도록 ( ) 안의 말을 고쳐서 빈칸을 채우시오.

20 그녀는 어떻게 유리로 만들어진 신발을 신을 수 있었지? (make)

⇨ How could she wear shoes _____ out of glass?

21 엄마는 이번 낚시여행에 매우 만족해하셨어. (satisfy)

⇨ Mom was very _____ with the fishing trip this time.

22 밑줄 친 부분을 틀리게 설명하는 학생은?

① He is interesting in cooking.

아리: 감정을 '느낀' 것이니까 interested야.

② I feeling hot, I opened the window.

성은: 주절과 같은 분사구문의 주어는 생략해야 해.

③ The news was disappointed.

승현: '실망한' 감정을 느낀 거니까 맞네.

④ Finding not his mom, the boy cried.

찬호: 분사의 부정은 not을 분사 바로 앞에 써야 해.

⑤ The bird drawn by Tim looks real.

소미: '~그려진'이란 수동의 의미니까 과거분사네.

(23-24) 밑줄 친 부사절을 알맞게 고쳐 분사구문으로 만드시오.

23 <u>Although he is young</u>, he acts like my dad.

⇨ _____ _____, he acts like my dad.

24 <u>When she finished her meal</u>, she ordered dessert.

⇨ _____ _____ _____, she ordered dessert.

(25-26) 우리말과 의미가 같도록 ( ) 안의 말을 배열하시오.

25 이 지름길을 택하면, 너는 학교에 지각하지 않을 거야.
(this, taking, shortcut)

⇨ _____,
you won't be late for school.

26 첫째 줄에 앉아 있는 저 소녀는 내 사촌이야.
(sitting, the, in, first row)

⇨ The girl _____
_____ is my cousin.

(27-28) 우리말과 의미가 같도록 ( ) 안의 말을 이용하여 문장을 완성하시오.

27 그는 그 작가에 의해 쓰여진 모든 소설을 좋아했어.
(write, by, the writer)

⇨ He liked all of the novels _____
_____ _____ _____.

28 카멜레온은 두려움을 느낄 때 몸 색깔을 바꾼다.
(feel, frightened)

⇨ _____ _____, the chameleon changed colors.

(29-30) 틀린 것이 있으면 고치고 이유를 설명하시오.

29 He felt sorry for the animals keeping in the zoo.

고치기: _____ ⇨ _____
이유: 동물원에 '갇힌'은 (수동, 능동)의 의미이므로 (과거, 현재)분사

30 She taking a picture with her cell phone, she sent it to me.

고치기: _____ ⇨ _____
이유: 분사구문에서, 주절과 같은 부사절의 (주어, 목적어)는 생략

한눈에 정리하는 Grammar Mapping

빈칸에 알맞은 답을 보기에서 골라 넣어 grammar mapping 완성하기

분사의 종류와 의미

현재분사의 형태
① _____

② _____ ~하게 하는
③ 감정을 _____

falling leaves
shocking news

과거분사의 형태
④ _____

~하게 된
⑤ _____
⑥ 감정을 _____

fallen leaves
shocked people

분사의 쓰임

⑦ _____

⑧ _____ + 명사
명사 + ⑨ _____

a singing bird
a bird singing in the tree

보어

⑩ _____를 보충설명

This game was exciting.

⑪ _____를 보충설명

We found the game exciting.

현재분사 VS. 동명사

현재분사

~하고 있는

a sleeping baby

동명사

⑫ _____
~하는 것

a sleeping bag

분사구문 만들기

⑬ _____을 분사구문으로 만들기

– 부사절의 ⑭ _____ 생략
– 주절과 같은 ⑮ _____ 생략
– ⑯ _____ 로 바꾸기

As he saw me, he smiled.
As he saw me, he smiled.
he saw me, he smiled.
⇨ Seeing me, he smiled

*중복 사용 가능

보기 | · 동사원형 + -ing · 동사원형 + -ed · 명사 수식 · 부사절 · 분사 + 수식어구
· 분사 · 주어 · 목적어 · 접속사 · ~당하는
· ~하고 있는 · ~하는 용도의 · (감정을) 느낀 · (감정을) 갖게 하는

대명사

GP 30 재귀대명사

GP 31 부정대명사 one, another, other

GP 32 one, another, other(s)의 표현

GP 33 부정대명사 all, both

GP 34 부정대명사 each, every

• Grammar & Writing

• Actual Test

• 한눈에 정리하는 Grammar Mapping

재귀대명사

GP 30

재귀대명사는 인칭대명사의 소유격이나 목적격에 -self(단수)나 -selves(복수)를 붙인 형태로 '~자신, ~자체'의 의미이다.

	1인칭	2인칭	3인칭
단수	myself	yourself	himself / herself / itself
복수	ourselves	yourselves	themselves

❶ **재귀용법**: 동사와 전치사의 목적어로 사용하고, 생략할 수 없다.

	주어	동사	목적어
동사의 목적어	He	loved	himself.
전치사의 목적어	She	talked to	herself.

The teacher introduced **herself** to the class.
☆ *You* must be proud of **yourself**.

❷ **강조용법**: 주어나 목적어를 강조하기 위해 사용하고, 생략할 수 있다.

주어 강조	I *myself*	built	the house.
주어 강조	I	built	the house *myself.*
목적어 강조	I	built	the house *itself.*

Allen **himself** fixed the broken car.
☆ *Allen* fixed the broken car **himself**.
I want to meet *the doctor* **himself**.

❸ **관용적 표현**

by oneself	혼자서(alone)	in itself	본래, 그 자체로
for oneself	혼자 힘으로	beside oneself	제정신이 아닌
of itself	저절로	between ourselves	우리끼리 얘기지만
enjoy oneself	즐거운 시간을 갖다	help oneself to	~을 마음껏 먹다
talk to oneself	혼잣말하다	make oneself at home	편하게 있다

☆ *Young children* should not swim **by themselves**.
☆ *He* always enjoys learning new things **for himself**.

GP Practice

A ( ) 안에서 알맞은 것을 고르시오.

1 There is a saying, "Know (you, yourself)."

2 We should protect (ourselves, us) from the tornado.

3 My sister found the answer (her, herself).

4 Did they enjoy (themself, themselves) at the party?

B 밑줄 친 부분의 문장 내 역할과 생략 가능 여부를 고르시오.

1 He often talks to <u>himself</u>.   (목적어, 강조) 역할   생략 (가능, 불가)

2 I <u>myself</u> got a call from Jane.   (목적어, 강조) 역할   생략 (가능, 불가)

3 You should trust <u>yourself</u>.   (목적어, 강조) 역할   생략 (가능, 불가)

4 The singer wrote the song <u>himself</u>.   (목적어, 강조) 역할   생략 (가능, 불가)

C 우리말과 의미가 같도록 ( ) 안의 말을 이용하여 문장을 완성하시오.

1 너는 몸조심 하렴. (take care of)

→ You _____ _____ _____ _____.

2 그 아이들은 진흙 축제에서 즐거운 시간을 가졌다. (enjoy)

→ The children _____ _____ at the mud festival.

3 신선한 과일을 마음껏 드세요. (help, to)

→ _____ _____ _____ some fresh fruit.

4 그녀가 직접 이 감사편지를 썼어. (thank-you letter)

→ She _____ _____ _____ _____.

D 밑줄 친 부분에 대한 설명을 체크하고 틀린 경우엔 바르게 고치시오. (맞으면 'O' 표시)

1	We protected <u>ourself</u> from wild animals. → ( )	주어와 목적어가 (같음, 다름) (인칭대명사, 재귀대명사) 사용
2	They looked at <u>myself</u>. → ( )	주어와 목적어가 (같음, 다름) (인칭대명사, 재귀대명사) 사용
3	She cleaned the house <u>herself</u>. → ( )	(주어, 목적어)를 강조하는 재귀대명사 (그녀를, 그녀가 직접)(으)로 해석
4	He traveled to India by <u>oneself</u>. → ( )	He가 (혼자서, 저절로) 행한 의미 by + (oneself, himself)

부정대명사 one, another, other

GP 31

부정대명사는 특정하게 정해지지 않은 사람, 사물, 수량 등을 나타내는 대명사이다.

one	앞에 언급한 명사와 같은 종류의 불특정한 사람이나 사물을 나타낸다.	
	He broke his watch, so he bought a new one.	
another	또 다른 하나 (같은 종류의 다른 하나)	another (+ 단수명사)
	Can I have another piece of pizza?	
other	(그 밖의) 다른	other + 복수명사
	Is there life on other planets?	

☆ This *bag* is too big. I need a smaller **one**.

☆ I don't like this *ring*. Could you show me **another**?

This *song* is more famous than **other** songs.

• Upgrade •

❶ **부정대명사 one**: 앞에 언급한 불특정한 명사를 대신하는 대명사

I lost my cell phone, so I have to buy a new one. (one = a cell phone)

❷ **인칭대명사 it**: 앞에 나온 특정한 명사를 대신하는 대명사

I lost my cell phone, but I found it. (it = my cell phone)

one, another, other(s)의 표현

GP 32

one ~, the other ~	(둘 중) 하나는 ~, 나머지 하나는 ~
	Here are *two* dogs. One is mine, and the other is hers.
one ~, another ~, the other ~	(셋 중) 하나는 ~, 다른 하나는 ~, 나머지 하나는 ~
	☆ I bought *three* pens. One is black, another is red, and the other is blue.
one ~, the others ~	(제한된 범위의 다수) 하나는 ~, 나머지 전부는 ~
	I have *five* students. One is a boy, and the others are girls.
some ~, the others ~	(여러 개 중) 몇몇은 ~, 나머지 전부는 ~
	Some of my guests arrived on time, and the others arrived late.
some ~, others ~	(불특정 다수) 몇몇은 ~, 다른 몇몇은 ~
	☆ Some like going out, and others like staying at home.

GP Practice

A ( ) 안에서 알맞은 것을 고르시오.

1 I need your math book. Can you lend (one, it, ones) to me?

2 I am still thirsty. Can you give me (another, other) cup of water?

3 Her pants are too short now. I will buy her some new (one, it, ones).

B 보기에서 알맞은 것을 골라 빈칸을 채우시오.

| 보기 | the other | another | the others | others |

1 I have two pets. One is a parrot, and _____ is a dog.

2 This skirt is too small for me. Please show me _____ one.

3 The movie has a sad ending. Some like the sad ending, but _____ don't.

4 He has three kids. One is left-handed, and _____ are right-handed.

C 우리말과 의미가 같도록 부정대명사를 이용하여 문장을 완성하시오.

1 나는 펜이 없어. 펜 하나 빌려줄래?

→ I don't have a pen. Could you lend me _____ ?

2 그는 취미가 두 개야. 하나는 스키타기이고, 다른 하나는 노래하기야.

→ He has two hobbies. _____ is skiing, and _____ is singing.

3 나는 형제가 셋 있는데, 한 명은 10살, 또 한 명은 7살, 나머지 한 명은 2살이야.

→ I have three brothers. One is ten, _____ is seven, and _____ is two years old.

4 어떤 사람들은 외식하는 것을 좋아하지만, 다른 사람들은 그렇지 않다.

→ _____ like eating out, but _____ don't.

D 밑줄 친 부분에 대한 설명을 체크하고 틀린 경우엔 바르게 고치시오. (맞으면 'O' 표시)

1	He dropped a fork. I picked <u>one</u> up for him. → ( )	앞에서 언급한 '포크'와 (같은, 다른) '포크'는 (one, it)
2	I lost my hat, so I bought a new <u>one</u>. → ( )	앞에서 언급한 '모자'와 (같은, 다른) '모자'는 (one, it)
3	My left arm is hurt, but <u>another</u> is not. → ( )	두 개 중 하나는 one, 나머지 하나는 (other, the other)
4	Some like sunny days, and <u>other</u> don't. → ( )	불특정 다수 중 몇몇은 some, 다른 몇몇은 (others, the others)

부정대명사 all, both

all은 '모든, 모두'의 의미로 셋 이상의 사람이나 사물을 나타내고 뒤에 오는 명사에 따라 단수나 복수 취급한다.
both는 '둘 다(의)'의 의미로 항상 복수 취급한다.

| all | 모든 모두 | all (of) + 복수명사 | 복수동사 | All (of) my students are diligent. |
| | | all (of) + 셀 수 없는 명사 | 단수동사 | All (of) the money was stolen. |

| both | 둘 다(의) | both + (of) 복수명사 | 복수동사 | Both (of) my parents have jobs. |

* **All (of) the children** *need* care and love.
* **All the advice** *was* very helpful.
* **Both of them** *are* high school students.
  Both teams *were* ready to win the game.

부정대명사 each, every

each는 둘 이상에서 '각각의' 의미로 단수 취급하고 every는 셋 이상에서 '(개개인에 중점을 둔) 모든'의 의미로 단수 취급한다.

| each | 각각(의) | each + 단수명사 | 단수동사 | Each player has seven cards. |
| | | each of + 복수명사 | 단수동사 | Each of us is special. |

| every | 모든 | every + 단수명사 | 단수동사 | Every dog has its day. |

* **Each person** *is* important for our team's victory.
  Each of my friends *has* a cell phone.
* **Every student** *wants* to get a good grade.

> ○ **Tip** ○
> [every + 단수명사]: ~마다
> · I go swimming every Sunday.

• Upgrade •

부정대명사 either / neither

either은 '둘 중 하나'의 의미이고 neither은 '둘 중 어느 것도 아닌'의 의미이다.
[not + either]을 neither로 나타낼 수 있다.

I wrote two letters. **Neither** of them was sent to her.
I don't want **either** of those caps. (= I want **neither** of those caps.)

GP Practice

A   ( ) 안에서 알맞은 것을 고르시오.

1 She has two cousins. (All, Both) of them are pilots.

2 (All, Every) the seats are already taken.

3 Look at the beautiful flowers. (Each, Every) has its own color.

4 (All, Every) boy jumped into the swimming pool.

B   ( ) 안에 주어진 단어를 알맞게 고쳐 빈칸을 채우시오. (현재시제 사용)

1 Every child _____ the right to be happy. (have)

2 All the milk _____ spilled all over the floor. (be)

3 Each of the answers _____ worth five points. (be)

4 Both of his cars _____ parked in front of his house. (be)

C   우리말과 의미가 같도록 ( ) 안의 말을 이용하여 문장을 완성하시오.

1 세 학생이 지각했다. 각각 다른 이유가 있었다. (have)

→ Three students were late. _____ _____ a different reason.

2 모든 질문들이 Judy에게는 매우 쉬웠다. (the questions)

→ _____ _____ _____ were very easy for Judy.

3 모든 여정은 한 걸음부터 시작한다. (journey)

→ _____ _____ begins with a step.

4 그들은 한국인이지만, 그들 둘 다 런던에 산다. (them)

→ They are Koreans, but _____ _____ _____
in London.

D   밑줄 친 부분에 대한 설명을 체크하고 틀린 경우엔 바르게 고치시오. (맞으면 'O' 표시)

1	All his money <u>are</u> saved in the bank. → ( )	all + 단수명사 + (단수, 복수)동사
2	Every <u>cat</u> looks the same to me. → ( )	every + (단수, 복수)명사
3	<u>Both</u> three boys are cute. → ( )	셋 이상의 '모두'는 (all, both)
4	Each boy <u>have</u> a dream. → ( )	each + (단수, 복수)명사 + (단수, 복수)동사

A 우리말과 의미가 같도록 ( ) 안의 말을 배열하시오.

1 언니는 이 모든 음식을 혼자서 요리했어. (herself, dishes, the, all)

→ My sister cooked _____.

2 각각의 여자아이들이 독특한 헤어밴드를 하고 있다. (the, girls, of, is, each)

→ _____ wearing a unique hairband.

3 나는 자전거를 잃어버려서 새것을 주문했다. (a, ordered, one, new)

→ I lost my bike and _____.

4 그의 가족은 6명인데, 몇몇은 K-pop을 좋아하고, 나머지는 좋아하지 않는다.
(don't, some, the, like, others, K-pop)

→ There are six people in his family. _____,

and _____.

5 그는 그 두 권의 책 모두 읽지 않았어. (did not, either, read, of)

→ He _____ the books.

6 그녀는 내가 아니라 그녀 자신에게 화가 났어. (was, with, angry, herself)

→ She _____, not with me.

B 우리말과 의미가 같도록 ( ) 안의 말을 이용하여 문장을 완성하시오.

1 여름에 어떤 사람들은 해변에 가고 어떤 사람들은 산에 간다. (visit, go)

→ In summer, _____ _____ beaches, and _____ _____ to
the mountains.

2 그녀는 그 두 대의 차 모두 사지 않았어. (of)

→ She bought _____ _____ _____ _____.

3 Mike는 자신에 관한 모든 것들에 만족한다. (everything)

→ Mike is satisfied with _____ _____ _____.

4 우리 둘은 그 계획에 관해 다른 생각을 가지고 있다. (both, us)

→ _____ _____ _____ _____ different thoughts about the plan.

5 나는 클래식 음악을 듣고 싶어요. 몇 곡 연주해 주시겠어요? (could, play)

→ I want to listen to classical music. _____ _____ _____ _____?

6 왜 신발 한 쪽만 신고 있니? 나머지는 어디 있니? (be)

→ Why are you wearing only one shoe? Where _____ _____ _____ one?

C 보기에서 알맞은 말을 골라 그림의 상황에 맞도록 빈칸을 채우시오. (중복 사용 가능)

보기 | others   another   the other   some

1

There are three dogs in the garden. One is lying under the tree, _____ is
playing with the ball, and _____ is barking at the children.

2

This castle has two gates. One is closed, and _____ is open.

3

There are many people on the street. _____ are running in the
marathon, and _____ are cheering for the runners.

D 보기에서 알맞은 말을 골라 이야기를 완성하시오. (한 번씩만 사용)

보기 | all   each   herself   themselves   some   the others

There are twenty-five students in the park. _____ are riding bicycles. _____
_____ are drawing flowers. Their teacher _____ is preparing twenty-
five sandwiches, potato salad, and some fruit for her students. _____ of the
students is waiting to eat. Fortunately, _____ of the food tastes great, and
the students enjoy _____.

(1–4) 빈칸에 들어갈 알맞은 말을 고르시오.

1
I am good at making paper flowers.
I will make _____ for you.

① another   ② the other
③ other   ④ it
⑤ one

2
Some people like winter, but _____ like summer.

① another   ② others
③ other   ④ the other
⑤ the others

3
Between _____, our soccer team did not play well in the game.

① ourselves   ② themselves
③ yourself   ④ herself
⑤ yourselves

4
I can speak three languages. One is English, another is Chinese, and _____ is Korean.

① another   ② other
③ the other   ④ others
⑤ the others

(5–6) 빈칸에 공통으로 들어갈 알맞은 말을 고르시오.
(대문자와 소문자 적용)

5
· _____ student is wearing a name tag.
· He goes to the gym _____ Sunday.

① Some, some   ② All, all
③ Any, any   ④ Every, every
⑤ Each, each

6
· I don't like this skirt. Can you show me _____?
· I'd like _____ glass of juice.

① some   ② other
③ others   ④ another
⑤ any

7 빈칸에 들어갈 수 <u>없는</u> 것을 고르시오.

Teachers will test _____ of the students this week.

① all   ② both
③ some   ④ each
⑤ every

(8–9) 우리말을 영어로 바르게 옮긴 것을 고르시오.

8
아빠는 아빠의 차를 직접 수리하셨다.

① My dad repaired his car with him.
② Himself my dad repaired his car.
③ My dad him repaired his car.
④ My dad himself repaired his car.
⑤ My dad repaired his car him.

9 나는 기뻐서 제정신이 아니었어.

① I was for myself with joy.

② I was beside myself with joy.

③ I was by myself with joy.

④ I was in myself with joy.

⑤ I was of myself with joy.

10 밑줄 친 부분이 바르게 쓰인 것은?

① My cat cannot be with <u>other</u> cats.

② I need a pencil. Do you have <u>it</u>?

③ I'd like to have <u>other</u> piece of pizza.

④ Some like summer, and <u>the others</u> like winter.

⑤ There were four windows in my room. I closed <u>both of them</u>.

11 밑줄 친 부분이 어법상 어색한 것은?

① We must love <u>ourselves</u>.

② The boy put on his seatbelt <u>himself</u>.

③ He <u>himself</u> washed his car.

④ We decorated the classroom <u>ourselves</u>.

⑤ Becky and I introduced <u>herself</u> to each other.

(12-13) 빈칸에 들어갈 말이 차례대로 짝지어진 것은?

12 · She can't move this box _____.
· _____ three boys can speak English.

① herself - Both　　② her - All

③ sheself - Both　　④ herself - All

⑤ her - Both

13 · One of the twin girls has curly hair. _____ has straight hair.
· Let's paint our room _____.

① The other - yourselves

② Other - ourselves

③ The other - ourselves

④ Another - yourselves

⑤ Another - yourselves

(14-15) 빈칸에 공통으로 들어갈 말을 쓰시오.
(대문자와 소문자 적용)

14 · _____ of us has different talents.
· There are tall trees on _____ side of the road.

⇨ _____, _____

15 · The students _____ will find the answers.
· After winning the game, they felt proud of _____.

⇨ _____

(16–18) 우리말과 의미가 같도록 빈칸에 알맞은 말을 쓰시오.

16 두 개의 영화관 모두가 오늘 예약이 꽉 차 있다.

⇨ _____ of the theaters are fully booked today.

17 저기 있는 뷔페를 마음껏 드세요.

⇨ Please _____ yourself to the buffet over there.

18 모든 문장은 적어도 하나의 동사를 가지고 있다.

⇨ _____ sentence has at least one verb.

19 두 문장의 의미가 같도록 알맞은 전치사를 쓰시오.

Mark lived in the big house alone.
= Mark lived in the big house _____ himself.

⇨ _____

20 다음 문장의 밑줄 친 부분과 같은 쓰임을 모두 고르시오.

> Did you enjoy yourself at the amusement park?

① She grew the vegetables herself.
② The kid hid himself under the desk.
③ He designed his house himself.
④ I myself decided to take the job.
⑤ He taught himself how to swim.

21 밑줄 친 부분 중 생략할 수 있는 것을 고르시오.

① He drew a picture of himself.
② I looked at myself in the mirror.
③ My cousin planted this tree herself.
④ Your behavior in itself is a big problem.
⑤ They should protect themselves first.

22 빈칸에 들어갈 말이 다른 것은?

① A: Did you read my message?
   B: Yes, I read _____.
② If you don't like your cap, give _____ to me.
③ A: Where is the closest bank?
   B: _____ is across from the grocery store.
④ I lost my eraser, so I have to buy _____.
⑤ Where is my key? Have you seen _____?

(23-24) 우리말과 의미가 같도록 ( ) 안의 말을 배열하시오.

23 나는 세 명의 외국인 친구들이 있는데, 그들 각각은 국적이 다르다.

(of, is, them, each)

⇨ I have three foreign friends.

_____

from a different country.

24 Jenny는 긴장할 때 보통 혼잣말을 한다.
(to, talks, usually, herself)

⇨ Jenny _____

when she feels nervous.

(25-27) 보기에서 적절한 대명사를 골라 빈칸을 완성하시오.

보기	each	all	the other
	the others	one	another

I keep three dogs.

white	white	black
2 years old	3 years old	5 years old
female	female	male
Korea	Korea	Korea

25 One is two years old, _____ is three years old, and the other is five years old.

26 One of them is a black dog.

_____ are white.

27 _____ of them is from Korea.

(28-29) 틀린 것이 있으면 고치고 이유를 설명하시오.

28 Look at the four koalas in the tree. Three are eating leaves, and other is sleeping.

고치기: _____ ⇨ _____

이유: 네 마리의 코알라 중 셋을 제외한 나머지는
(other, the other)

29 She always looks at her in the mirror before leaving home.

고치기: _____ ⇨ _____

이유: 주어와 목적어가 (같음, 다름)
(인칭대명사, 재귀대명사) 사용

30 다음 조건을 이용하여 알맞게 영작하시오.

캠프에 참가한 10명의 소년이 있다. 몇몇은 한국인이고, 나머지는 캐나다인이다.

조건 1: Koreans, Canadians, and
조건 2: 8단어

⇨ There are ten boys joining the camp.

_____

_____.

한눈에 정리하는 Grammar Mapping

빈칸에 알맞은 답을 보기에서 골라 넣어 grammar mapping 완성하기

	1인칭	2인칭	3인칭
단수	myself	yourself	① _____ / herself / itself
복수	② _____	③ _____	④ _____

재귀대명사

종류

용법
- ⑤ _____
  동사, 전치사의 ⑥ _____ (생략 ⑦ _____)
  She introduced herself to us.
- **강조용법**
  주어나 목적어를 ⑧ _____ (생략 ⑨ _____)
  I fixed it myself.

관용 표현
by oneself (⑩ _____), for oneself (⑪ _____)
enjoy oneself (즐기다), talk to oneself (혼잣말하다)

부정대명사

제한된 범위

- one(s)
  앞에 언급된 명사와 같은 종류의 것
  cf) it: 앞에 나온 특정한 명사

- ⑫ _____
  (같은 종류의) 또 다른 하나 (+ 단수명사)

- ⑬ _____
  (그 밖의) 다른 + 복수명사

- one ~
  ⑭ _____ ~
  (둘 중) 하나는 ~, 나머지 하나는 ~

- one ~
  another ~
  the other ~
  (셋 중) 하나는 ~, ⑮ _____ ~, 나머지 하나는 ~

- some ~
  the others ~
  (여러 개 중) 몇몇은 ~, 나머지 전부는 ~

불특정 대상
- some ~
  ⑯ _____ ~
  몇몇은 ~, 다른 몇몇은 ~

보기
- another
- other
- yourselves
- others
- ourselves
- himself
- the other
- themselves
- 재귀용법
- 목적어
- 강조
- 가능
- 불가
- 스스로
- 홀로
- 다른 하나는

Chapter

09

비교표현

GP 35   원급, 비교급, 최상급

GP 36   원급을 이용한 표현

GP 37   비교급을 이용한 표현

GP 38   최상급을 이용한 표현

• Grammar & Writing

• Actual Test

• 한눈에 정리하는 Grammar Mapping

원급, 비교급, 최상급

GP 35

❶ 원급

| A | as | 원급 | as | B | A가 B만큼 ~한(하게) |

☆ His speech is **as powerful as** his rival's.
☆ Today is not **as hot as** yesterday.

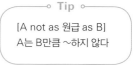

Tip
[A not as 원급 as B]
A는 B만큼 ~하지 않다

❷ 비교급

| A | 비교급 | than | B | A가 B보다 ~한(하게) |

☆ Hot air is **lighter than** cold air.
☆ Your idea is **more creative than** mine.

❸ 최상급

| A | the | 최상급 | in / of | B | A가 B에서 가장 ~한(하게) |

☆ The thumb is **the shortest** *of all five fingers*.
☆ Vatican City is **the smallest** nation *in the world*.

Tip
최상급 + in / of
① in + 단수명사 (장소)
② of + 복수명사 (사람, 사물)

❹ 비교급과 최상급 만들기

			원급	비교급	최상급
규칙 변화	기본 변화	+ -er / -est	long	long**er**	long**est**
	-e로 끝나는 경우	+ -r / -st	close	close**r**	close**st**
	[단모음 + 단자음] 경우	끝자음 하나 더 + -er / -est	big	big**ger**	big**gest**
	[자음 + y]로 끝나는 경우	y → i + -er / -est	busy	bus**ier**	bus**iest**
	3음절 이상, -ous, -ful	more / most + 원급	famous	**more** famous	**most** famous
	-ly로 끝나는 부사	more / most + 원급	slowly	**more** slowly	**most** slowly
불규칙 변화			good / well	**better**	**best**
			bad / ill	**worse**	**worst**
			many / much	**more**	**most**
			little	**less**	**least**

A ( ) 안에서 알맞은 것을 고르시오.

1 His eyesight is (worse, worst) than mine.

2 The snail moves the (slowliest, most slowly) of all animals.

3 The water was as (smooth, smoother) as glass.

4 His second album is (popularer, more popular) than his first one.

B ( ) 안에 주어진 단어를 알맞게 고쳐 빈칸을 채우시오.

1 New York is _____ than Paris. (small)

2 I think I am the _____ person in the world. (luck)

3 This carpet is not as _____ as the floor. (large)

4 Saving money is as _____ as making money. (important)

C 우리말과 의미가 같도록 ( ) 안의 말을 이용하여 문장을 완성하시오.

1 걷기는 수영하는 것만큼 건강에 좋아. (healthy)

→ Walking is _____ _____ _____ swimming.

2 그 댄서는 새털만큼 가벼웠다. (light, a feather)

→ The dancer was _____ _____ _____ _____ _____.

3 나의 남동생은 언제나 나보다 더 일찍 일어난다. (early, me)

→ My brother always gets up _____ _____ _____.

4 많은 학생들에게 월요일은 일주일 중 최악의 날이다. (bad)

→ To many students, Monday is _____ _____ _____ of the week.

D 밑줄 친 부분에 대한 설명을 체크하고 틀린 경우엔 바르게 고치시오. (맞으면 'O' 표시)

1	Tom walked <u>fast</u> than I. → ( )	(원급 + than, 비교급 + than)
2	He was as <u>poorer</u> as a church mouse. → ( )	(as + 원급 + as, as + 비교급 + as)
3	I play the guitar <u>better</u> than Dylan. → ( )	well((잘)의 비교급은 (weller, better)
4	Russia is <u>biggest</u> country in the world. → ( )	(최상급, the + 최상급) + 명사

원급을 이용한 표현

GP 36

❶

| 배수사 | as | 원급 | as | ···보다 몇 배 ~한(하게) |

☆ The KTX is **three times as fast as** the train.
= The KTX is **three times faster than** the train.

○ Tip ○
[배수사 + as + 원급 + as]
= [배수사 + 비교급 + than]

❷

| as | 원급 | as | possible / 주어 can | 가능한 한 ~한(하게) |

☆ Smile **as often as possible.** = Smile **as often as you can.**

비교급을 이용한 표현

GP 37

❶

| even, much, far, a lot, still | 비교급 | than | 훨씬 더 ~한(하게) |

☆ I feel **much** *healthier* than before.

❷

| 비교급 | and | 비교급 | 점점 더 ~한(하게) |

☆ Cell phones are getting **smarter and smarter.**

❸

| the | 비교급 | (s + v) | , | the | 비교급 | (s + v) | ~할수록 더 ~하다 |

☆ **The more** we share, **the happier** we become.

최상급을 이용한 표현

GP 38

❶

| one | of | the | 최상급 | 복수명사 | 가장 ~한 것들 중 하나 |

☆ The wheel is **one of the greatest inventions** in history.

❷

| the | 최상급 | 명사 | that 주어 + have / has + ever + p.p. | 지금껏 한 것 중 가장 ~한 |

☆ This is **the worst hairstyle (that) I have ever had.**

GP Practice

A ( ) 안에서 알맞은 것을 고르시오.

1 Summer is getting (hot and hot, hotter and hotter).

2 Light travels (very, a lot) faster than sound.

3 (The little, The less) I sleep, the fatter I get.

4 She is one of the most humorous (girl, girls) at my school.

B ( ) 안에 주어진 단어를 이용하여 빈칸을 채우시오.

1 She cleaned her sports car _____ _____ _____ possible. (gently)

2 His battery lasts three times _____ _____ _____ mine. (long)

3 This is _____ _____ joke that I have ever heard. (fun)

4 The warmer it got, _____ _____ the snowman melted. (much)

C 우리말과 의미가 같도록 ( ) 안의 말을 이용하여 문장을 완성하시오.

1 가능한 한 조심스럽게 상자를 옮겨라. (carefully)

→ Carry the box _____ _____ _____ _____.

2 그의 가방은 내 가방보다 두 배 무겁다. (heavy, as)

→ His backpack is _____ _____ _____

_____ mine.

3 빨리 걸으면 걸을수록, 더 빨리 거기에 도착할 것이다. (fast, early)

→ _____ _____ you walk, _____ _____ you will get there.

4 이것은 가장 맛있는 피자 중 하나이다. (delicious)

→ This is one of _____ _____ _____ _____.

D 밑줄 친 부분에 대한 설명을 체크하고 틀린 경우엔 바르게 고치시오. (맞으면 'O' 표시)

1	May is <u>very</u> warmer than March. → ( )	비교급 강조는 (매우, 훨씬) (very, much) + 비교급
2	The older we get, <u>the wiser</u> we become. → ( )	'~할수록 더 ~하다' the + 비교급, (비교급, the + 비교급)
3	He is one of the fastest <u>runner</u> in Korea. → ( )	'가장 ~한 것들 중 하나' one of the 최상급 + (단수, 복수)명사
4	Her report is <u>as twice</u> long as mine. → ( )	'~보다 몇 배 더 ~한' (as + 배수사, 배수사 + as) + 원급 + as

A   우리말과 의미가 같도록 ( ) 안의 말을 배열하시오.

1 그 카페는 그 식당만큼 붐비지 않아요. (as, as, not, crowded)

→ The café is _____ the restaurant.

2 네 가방이 내 가방보다 훨씬 무겁구나. (than, much, mine, heavier)

→ Your bag is _____.

3 감기에 걸리지 않으려면, 가능한 한 자주 손을 씻어라. (often, possible, as, as)

→ Wash your hands _____ to avoid catching a cold.

4 나의 아빠는 우리 가족 중 가장 멋을 낸다. (fashionable, most, the, person)

→ My dad is _____ in my family.

5 Frozen은 내가 봤던 최고의 영화이다. (that, have, I, seen, ever, the, movie, best)

→ *Frozen* is _____.

6 Tom에게 가까이 갈수록, 내 심장은 더 빨리 뛰었다. (faster, the, the, closer)

→ _____ I walked to Tom, _____ my heart beat.

B   우리말과 의미가 같도록 ( ) 안의 말을 이용하여 문장을 완성하시오.

1 우리 사장님은 다른 사람들만큼 열심히 일한다. (hard)

→ My boss works _____ _____ _____ everyone else.

2 일부 개는 고양이보다 더 영리하다. (clever)

→ Some dogs are _____ _____ _____.

3 가능하면 빨리 나에게 다시 전화주세요. (soon)

→ Please call me back _____ _____ _____ _____.

4 날씨가 더우면 더울수록, 아이스크림은 더 많이 팔린다. (hot, much)

→ _____ _____ it becomes, _____ _____ ice cream is sold.

5 이것은 그가 그렸던 것 중 최고의 그림이다. (good, paint)

→ This is _____ _____ _____

_____ _____ _____.

6 판다는 가장 멸종위기에 처한 동물 중 하나이다. (one, endangered)

→ The panda is _____ _____ _____

_____ _____.

C 다음 그림과 일치하도록 ( ) 안의 단어를 이용하여 문장을 완성하시오.

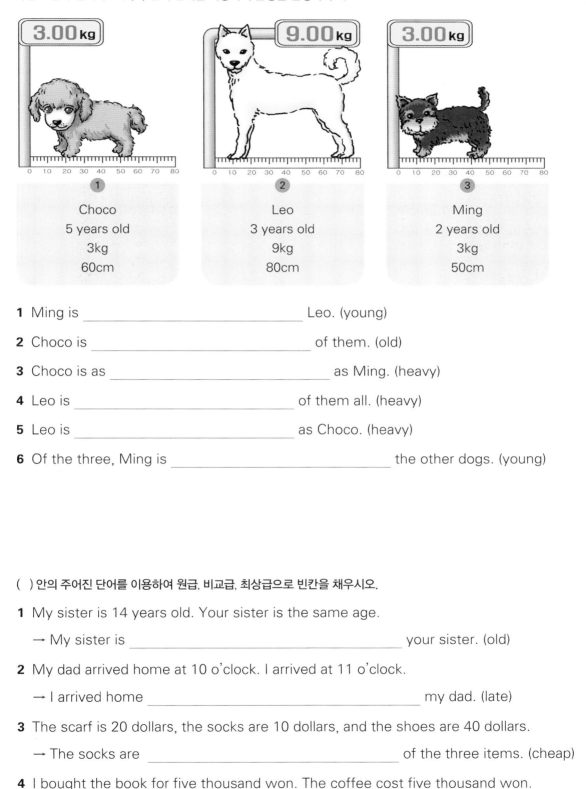

① Choco
5 years old
3kg
60cm

② Leo
3 years old
9kg
80cm

③ Ming
2 years old
3kg
50cm

1 Ming is _____ Leo. (young)

2 Choco is _____ of them. (old)

3 Choco is as _____ as Ming. (heavy)

4 Leo is _____ of them all. (heavy)

5 Leo is _____ as Choco. (heavy)

6 Of the three, Ming is _____ the other dogs. (young)

D ( ) 안의 주어진 단어를 이용하여 원급, 비교급, 최상급으로 빈칸을 채우시오.

1 My sister is 14 years old. Your sister is the same age.

→ My sister is _____ your sister. (old)

2 My dad arrived home at 10 o'clock. I arrived at 11 o'clock.

→ I arrived home _____ my dad. (late)

3 The scarf is 20 dollars, the socks are 10 dollars, and the shoes are 40 dollars.

→ The socks are _____ of the three items. (cheap)

4 I bought the book for five thousand won. The coffee cost five thousand won.

→ The book cost _____ the coffee. (much)

1 원급, 비교급, 최상급이 <u>잘못</u> 짝지어진 것을 고르시오.

① good - better - best
② hot - hotter - hottest
③ easy - easier - easiest
④ little - less - lest
⑤ slowly - more slowly - most slowly

(2–5) 빈칸에 들어갈 알맞은 말을 고르시오.

2 The frog's body is as _____ as your fingernail.

① small   ② smaller
③ smallest   ④ more small
⑤ most small

3 Light travels _____ than sound.

① fast   ② faster
③ fastest   ④ more fast
⑤ most fast

4 Jun is the most _____ boy that I have ever met.

① tall   ② fast
③ best   ④ busy
⑤ cheerful

5 What is the _____ animal on Earth?

① slow   ② slower
③ slowly   ④ slowest
⑤ most slow

6 다음 중 <u>not</u>이 들어갈 적절한 위치는?

My baby brother ① is ② as ③ tall ④ as ⑤ the sunflower.

(7–9) 빈칸에 들어갈 말로 알맞지 <u>않은</u> 것은?

7 The sun is _____ hotter than the moon.

① very   ② much
③ even   ④ far
⑤ a lot

8 Jin is 175cm tall, and Robert is 180cm tall.
= Jin is _____ Robert.

① shorter than   ② not taller than
③ less tall than   ④ not as tall as
⑤ much taller than

9 My bike is a lot _____ my sister's.

① newer than   ② thicker than
③ older than   ④ expensive than
⑤ heavier than

(10–11) 우리말을 영어로 바르게 옮긴 것을 고르시오.

10 뉴욕은 내가 방문한 곳 중 가장 바쁜 도시이다.

① No city is as busiest as New York.
② No city is the busiest city in New York.
③ New York is one of the busiest city that I visit.
④ New York is the busiest city I have ever visited.
⑤ New York is the busiest city in my visits.

11 나는 가능한 한 많이 걸으려고 노력한다.

① I try to walk as many as I can.
② I try to walk as much as I may.
③ I try to walk as possible as I can.
④ I try to walk as many as possible.
⑤ I try to walk as much as possible.

(12–13) 빈칸에 들어갈 말이 차례대로 짝지어진 것은?

12
· The concert hall became _____ and more crowded.
· The giant turtle lives _____ longer than man.

① more - more   ② more - much
③ more - many   ④ much - very
⑤ more - very

13
· What is the deepest lake _____ the world?
· Soccer is one of the most popular _____ in Korea.

① of - sport   ② in - sports
③ of - sports   ④ in - sport
⑤ at - sport

14 다음 주어진 문장과 같은 뜻의 문장은?

Soccer is not as exciting as baseball.

① Soccer is as not exciting as baseball.
② Soccer is more exciting than baseball.
③ Baseball is as exciting as soccer.
④ Baseball is not as exciting as soccer.
⑤ Baseball is more exciting than soccer.

15 밑줄 친 부분이 어법상 어색한 것은?

① He drove as slowly as he can.
② I walked even faster than him.
③ The temperature rose as high as 40°C.
④ Jupiter is 1,300 times bigger than Earth.
⑤ New York is one of the largest cities in the world.

16 밑줄 친 부분이 바르게 쓰인 것은?

① He is as wiser as you.

② What is the most expensive thing here?

③ The sweet the food is, the more we eat.

④ Please write to me as sooner as possible.

⑤ Paul is much interested in music than me.

(17–18) 두 문장의 빈칸에 공통으로 들어갈 말을 쓰시오.

17 · People travel abroad _____ often than before.

· The higher the kite flew, the _____ excited I got.

⇨ _____

18 · He played the flute _____ better than Eric.

· My brother eats twice as _____ as I eat.

⇨ _____

(19–20) 우리말과 의미가 같도록 ( ) 안의 말을 배열하시오.

19 한국 대중음악은 점점 더 인기를 얻고 있다.
(and, more, popular, more, Asia, in)

⇨ K-pop is getting _____
_____.

20 매머드의 상아는 코끼리의 것보다 훨씬 컸다.
(bigger, much, were, tusks, than, elephants')

⇨ The tusks of mammoths _____
_____.

21 다음 중 어법상 옳은 것을 고르시오.

① Read the book as loud as possible.

② Ann is the thinner of all the students.

③ He is one of the most famous scientist.

④ More you practice, the better you play the piano.

⑤ The sofa is very more comfortable than the bed.

22 밑줄 친 부분을 잘못 설명한 친구는?

① I weigh as more as Tom.

② This summer is hoter than last year.

③ The whale is biggest animal in the world.

④ Fruit is good for you than meat.

⑤ The more we have, more we want.

① 은혜: [as ~ as] 사이에 원급 much가 와야 해.

② 지수: hot의 비교급은 hotter를 써야 해.

③ 은비: 최상급 앞에는 the를 써야 해.

④ 지영: '더 좋다'는 more good이야.

⑤ 지은: [the + 비교급, the + 비교급] 구문이므로 the more로 써야 해.

(23–24) 주어진 문장과 의미가 같도록 ( ) 안의 말을 이용하여 빈칸을 채우시오.

23 Elephants live two times longer than bears. (as, long)

⇨ Elephants live _____

_____ bears.

24 Money is not as important as happiness. (than)

⇨ Happiness is _____

than money.

(25–26) 우리말과 의미가 같도록 ( ) 안의 말을 이용하여 문장을 완성하시오.

25 다이아몬드는 가장 단단한 광물이다. (hard)

⇨ Diamonds are _____ mineral.

26 우리가 더 많이 웃을수록, 우리는 더 행복해진다. (much, happy)

⇨ _____ we laugh,

_____ we become.

27 내 형의 영어 점수는 점점 더 좋아지고 있다. (good)

⇨ My brother's English grade is getting

_____ .

(28–29) 틀린 것이 있으면 고치고 이유를 설명하시오.

28 He did worst on this test than on the test before.

고치기: _____ ⇨ _____

이유: than 앞에는 bad의 (비교급, 최상급) 사용

29 It is one of the most popular game in the world.

고치기: _____ ⇨ _____

이유: '가장 ~한 (것, 것들) 중 하나'
　　 one of the 최상급 + (단수, 복수)명사

30 다음 조건을 이용하여 알맞게 영작하시오.

Brian은 우리 반에서 가장 말이 많은 학생이다.
조건 1: talkative, my class
조건 2: 9단어

⇨ _____

_____ .

한눈에 정리하는 Grammar Mapping

○ 빈칸에 알맞은 답을 보기에서 골라 넣어 grammar mapping 완성하기

원급		
의미	두 개의 대상을 비교하며 '~만큼 ~한 / ~하게'	
형태	A + as 원급 as + B	
응용표현	A + ① _____ + as 원급 as + B	A는 B보다 ~배 더 ~한 / ~하게
	as 원급 as ② _____ = 주어 can / could	가능한 한 ~한 / ~하게
	A + not as 원급 as + B	A는 B만큼 ~못한 / ~못하게

비교급		
의미	③ _____의 대상을 비교하며 '~보다 더 ~한 / ~하게'	
형태	A + 비교급 ④ _____ + B	
응용표현	⑤ _____, even, far, a lot, still + 비교급 + than	~보다 훨씬 더 ~한 / ~하게
	⑥ _____	점점 더 ~한 / ~하게
	the 비교급 (S + V), ⑦ _____ (S + V)	더 ~할수록 더 ~해지다

최상급		
의미	⑧ _____의 대상 중에 '가장 ~한 / ~하게'	
형태	A + the 최상급 ⑨ _____ + 대상	
응용표현	⑩ _____ of the 최상급 + 복수명사	가장 ~한 것들 중 하나
	the 최상급 + 명사 + 주어 ⑪ _____	지금껏 한 것 중 가장 ~한

보기	· possible	· 배수사	· much	· the 비교급
	· 두 개	· 셋 이상	· than	· in / of
	· one	· 비교급 and 비교급		· have / has ever p.p.

접속사

GP 39 시간 접속사

GP 40 이유 접속사

GP 41 조건 접속사

GP 42 양보 접속사

GP 43 명령문 and / or

GP 44 접속사 that

GP 45 상관접속사

- Grammar & Writing

- Actual Test

- 한눈에 정리하는 Grammar Mapping

시간 접속사

GP 39

두 문장 사이의 시간 관계를 나타내는 시간 접속사는 when, while, as, until, since 등이 있다. 이런 접속사가 이끄는 문장을 부사절이라고 한다.

	시간 부사절		주절
	접속사	주어 + 동사	주어 + 동사
~할 때	☆ When (As)	he goes fishing,	I will join him.
~하기 전에	Before	you take action,	you should think twice.
~한 후에	After	I packed my school bag,	I went to bed.
~하는 동안	While	kids sleep,	they grow the most.
~할 때까지	☆ Until	she says, "Yes,"	her dog won't eat.
~한 이후로	Since	I moved to this city,	I have made many friends.

The movie started **before** Eric arrived.
The old man makes a ho-ho-ho sound **when** he laughs.

- Upgrade •

시간 부사절의 시제
주절이 미래시제일 때에도 시간 부사절의 시제는 미래시제 대신 현재시제를 사용한다.
☆ We will get home *before* it **gets** (~~will get~~) dark.

이유 접속사

GP 40

두 문장 사이의 원인과 결과 관계를 나타내는 이유 접속사는 because, as, since 등이 있다.

	이유 부사절		주절
	접속사	주어 + 동사	주어 + 동사
~하기 때문에	☆ Because	he didn't sleep enough,	he had red eyes.
	As	I am under 19,	I can't watch the movie.
	Since	my dog has short legs,	it can't run fast.

I don't want to talk to him **because** he is not honest.
The hotel is popular **as** it has a nice view.

GP Practice

A ( ) 안에서 알맞은 것을 고르시오.

1 She talks a lot (when, before) she feels nervous.

2 He had to drive slowly (because, after) the road was bumpy.

3 I will meet her when the first snow (will fall, falls).

4 He tried to find the answer (since, before) he asked a question.

B 보기에서 알맞은 접속사를 골라 두 문장을 연결하시오. (한 번씩만 사용)

| 보기 | since | while | after | because |

1 _____ Ken was swimming, he lost his locker key.

2 I will do the dishes _____ we finish dinner tonight.

3 He has lived in London _____ he was five years old.

4 She drank a lot of water _____ she ate spicy food.

C 우리말과 의미가 같도록 ( ) 안의 말을 이용하여 문장을 완성하시오.

1 그녀는 색맹이기 때문에 몇몇 색깔을 구별하지 못해. (be, color-blind)

→ _____ _____ _____ _____, she can't see some colors.

2 재채기를 할 때는 입을 가려라. (sneeze)

→ Cover your mouth _____ _____ _____.

3 밤늦은 시간이었기 때문에, 모든 가게들이 문을 닫았다. (since, it)

→ _____ _____ _____ _____ at night, all the stores were closed.

4 그녀는 생크림으로 변할 때까지 우유를 저었어. (it, turn into)

→ She whipped the milk _____ _____ _____ _____ whipped cream.

D 밑줄 친 부분에 대한 설명을 체크하고 틀린 경우엔 바르게 고치시오. (맞으면 'O' 표시)

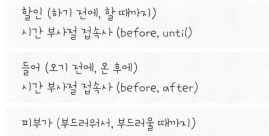

1	He will wait <u>before</u> the bike is on sale. → ( )	할인 (하기 전에, 할 때까지) 시간 부사절 접속사 (before, until)
2	Lock the door <u>before</u> you come in. → ( )	들어 (오기 전에, 온 후에) 시간 부사절 접속사 (before, after)
3	<u>Until</u> babies have soft skin, they look cute. → ( )	피부가 (부드러워서, 부드러울 때까지) 이유 부사절 접속사 (Because, Until)
4	I will call you when he <u>will arrive</u>. → ( )	'~할 때' 시간 (부사절, 주절)은 미래시제 대신 (현재, 미래)시제

조건 접속사

GP 41

두 문장 사이의 조건과 결과의 관계를 나타내는 접속사는 if, unless (= if ~ not) 등이 있다.

	조건 부사절		주절
	접속사	주어 + 동사	주어 + 동사
~한다면	☆ If	you take a walk,	you will feel better.
~하지 않으면	☆ Unless	we finish the meal,	we will get hungry soon.
	= If	we don't finish the meal,	we will get hungry soon.

My cat doesn't come to me **unless** it is hungry.
= My cat doesn't come to me **if** it is **not** hungry.

• Upgrade •

조건 부사절의 시제

주절이 미래시제일 때에도, 조건 부사절에서는 미래시제 대신 현재시제를 사용한다.

If she **reads** (~~will read~~) the book, she will find the answer.

양보 접속사

GP 42

두 문장 사이의 내용이 반대이거나 예상하지 못한 결과를 나타내는 양보 접속사는 though, although 등이 있다.

	양보 부사절		주절
	접속사	주어 + 동사	주어 + 동사
비록 ~이지만	☆ (Al)though	I practiced a lot,	I made a mistake.
	Even though	she is super rich,	she never wastes money.

Although the cap is not the right size, I will buy it.

명령문 and / or

GP 43

명령문(동사원형 ~),	and / or	주어 + 동사	
☆ Do your best,	and	you will succeed.	~해라, 그러면 ~할 것이다
☆ Water the plant,	or	it will die soon.	~해라, 그렇지 않으면 ~할 것이다

Do your best, **and** you will succeed.
= If you do your best, you will succeed.
Water the plant, **or** it will die soon.
= Unless you water the plant, it will die soon.

GP Practice

A ( ) 안에서 알맞은 것을 고르시오.

1 Please ring the bell (if, though) you need anything.

2 (If, Unless) you open your mind, you won't have any friends.

3 I will buy the shoes (if, unless) they are not too small.

4 My grandfather enjoys soccer (though, unless) he is old.

B 자연스러운 문장이 되도록 주절과 부사절을 연결하시오.

1 If I miss the bus, •   • Ⓐ my grandfather can't hear me.

2 Paul failed the test •   • Ⓑ I will take a taxi.

3 Unless I speak loudly, •   • Ⓒ or you can't swim in the pool.

4 Wear a swimsuit, •   • Ⓓ although he studied hard.

C 우리말과 의미가 같도록 ( ) 안의 말을 이용하여 문장을 완성하시오.

1 네가 그 음식을 빨리 먹지 않으면 상할 거야. (eat, quickly)

→ The food will rot ＿＿＿＿ ＿＿＿＿ ＿＿＿＿ ＿＿＿＿ ＿＿＿＿ ＿＿＿＿.

2 Evan은 한국어를 모르지만 한국 드라마를 좋아한다. (know Korean)

→ ＿＿＿＿ ＿＿＿＿ ＿＿＿＿ ＿＿＿＿ ＿＿＿＿, he loves Korean dramas.

3 일회용 컵을 적게 사용해라, 그러면 나무를 아낄 수 있어. (save trees)

→ Use fewer paper cups, ＿＿＿＿ ＿＿＿＿ ＿＿＿＿ ＿＿＿＿.

4 당신이 회원이 아니시면, 들어가실 수 없습니다. (unless, a member)

→ ＿＿＿＿ ＿＿＿＿ ＿＿＿＿ ＿＿＿＿ ＿＿＿＿, you can't get in.

D 밑줄 친 부분에 대한 설명을 체크하고 틀린 경우엔 바르게 고치시오. (맞으면 'O', 불필요하면 '삭제' 표시)

*S: 주어, V: 동사

1	If the meal smells good, it tastes bad. → ( )	좋은 냄새가 (나지만, 난다면) 접속사 (Although, If)
2	Unless I am <u>not</u> full, I will eat more. → ( )	unless는 (if, if ~ not)의 의미로 not과 동시에 (사용, 사용 불가)
3	If she <u>will do</u> her best, she will succeed. → ( )	'만약 ~한다면' 의미의 (부사절, 주절)에는 미래시제 대신 (미래, 현재)시제
4	Wear the goggles, <u>and</u> they will protect your eyes. → ( )	명령문 뒤에 (and S + V, or S + V)는 '~해라, (그러면, 그렇지 않으면) ~할 것이다'

접속사 that

GP 44

접속사 that이 이끄는 문장은 [that 주어 + 동사]의 형태로 '주어가 ~하는 것'으로 해석하고 문장에서 주어, 목적어, 보어로 쓰인다.

주어	동사	목적어 / 보어	
That penguins are birds	is	well known.	
It 〔가주어〕	is	well known	that penguins are birds. 〔진주어〕
I	know	that penguins are birds. 〔목적어〕	
The fact	is	that penguins are birds. 〔보어〕	

It is strange **that** it is snowing in May. (주어)

I expect **that** he will marry the woman. (목적어)

The problem is **that** we have too much homework. (보어)

상관접속사

GP 45

상관접속사는 두 개 이상의 어구가 짝을 이루어 문법적으로 동일한 성질의 두 요소를 연결하는 접속사이다.

both	A	and	B	A와 B 둘 다
either	A	or	B	A와 B 둘 중 하나
neither	A	nor	B	A와 B 둘 다 아닌
not only	A	but (also)	B	A뿐만 아니라 B도
=	B	as well as	A	

Her speech was **both** interesting **and** short.

I will give this ticket to **either** Eric **or** Allen.

He was **neither** rude **nor** unkind.

Not only his brothers **but also** Tim has blond hair.

• Upgrade •

상관접속사가 사용된 주어의 동사 일치

[both A and B]는 항상 복수취급하며, 나머지는 모두 B에 일치시킨다.

Neither Jane nor *her sisters* **are** shy.

GP Practice

A ( ) 안에서 알맞은 것을 고르시오.

1 (That, it) the airplane crashed is shocking.

2 She added neither salt (nor, or) sugar to the baby food.

3 (That, It) was sad that our team lost the final game.

4 I invited (either, both) Miranda and her husband.

5 Do you know (and, that) he is from Mexico?

B 두 문장을 상관접속사를 이용하여 한 문장으로 완성하시오.

1 You may eat it here. Or you can order takeout.

→ You may _____ eat here _____ order takeout.

2 The singer is famous in Asia. She is famous in Europe, too.

→ The singer is famous in Europe _____ in Asia.

3 The food was salty. It was also overcooked.

→ The food was _____ salty _____ overcooked.

C 우리말과 의미가 같도록 ( ) 안의 말을 이용하여 문장을 완성하시오.

1 아무도 그가 부자인 것을 몰랐어. (rich)

→ No one knew _____ _____ _____ _____.

2 엄마와 나 모두 볼에 보조개가 있어. (both)

→ _____ my mom _____ I have dimples.

3 비버가 일 년에 200그루 나무를 벨 수 있다는 것은 사실이야. (a beaver, cut down)

→ _____ is true _____ _____ _____ _____ _____ _____ 200 trees a year.

D 밑줄 친 부분에 대한 설명을 체크하고 틀린 경우엔 바르게 고치시오. (맞으면 'O' 표시)

*S: 주어, V: 동사

1	This was true that he passed the test. → ( )	가주어 ~ 진주어 (This, It) [that S + V]
2	He said and he would become a pilot. → ( )	주어 + say + 목적어 (and S + V, that S + V)
3	This bike is neither light or heavy. → ( )	[neither A (or, nor) B]는 A와 B (둘 중 하나, 둘 모두 아닌)의 의미
4	She as well as you talk fast. → ( )	주어 + 동사 [B as well as A] (A, B)에 동사 일치

A 우리말과 의미가 같도록 ( ) 안의 말을 배열하시오.

1 그는 장거리로 차를 탈 때 차멀미를 해. (he, rides, when, distances, long)

→ He gets carsick _____.

2 그 기계를 사용하기 전에 매뉴얼을 읽으세요. (use, before, the, machine, you)

→ Read the manual _____.

3 내 남동생은 내가 목소리를 높이지 않으면 말을 안 들어. (I, my, unless, voice, raise)

→ My younger brother doesn't listen _____.

4 비가 많이 왔지만, 우리는 즐거운 시간을 가졌다. (it, although, rained, a lot)

→ _____, we had a great time.

5 Emily와 Olivia 둘 다 생선회를 좋아하지 않아. (nor, Emily, Olivia, neither)

→ _____ likes raw fish.

6 우비를 입어라, 그렇지 않으면 비에 젖을 거야. (you, will, or, get wet)

→ Wear a raincoat, _____.

B 우리말과 의미가 같도록 ( ) 안의 말을 이용하여 문장을 완성하시오..

1 그 선생님은 친절하지는 않지만, 나는 그녀의 수업을 좋아해. (friendly)

→ _____ _____ _____

_____, I like her class.

2 다음(Next)을 클릭하기 전에 넌 이 버튼을 클릭해야 해. (click, "Next")

→ You need to click this button _____ _____ _____.

3 바나나가 나무에서 자라는 것이 아니라는 것을 알고 있니? (bananas, grow)

→ Do you know _____ _____ _____ on trees?

4 너는 집에 가든지 여기서 나를 기다리든지 해도 돼. (go home, wait for)

→ You can _____ _____ or _____

_____ _____ _____.

5 천장 창문이 있어서 나는 이 방이 마음에 들어. (it, have)

→ I like this room _____ _____ _____ a skylight.

6 손을 씻지 않으면, 너는 감기에 걸릴 수도 있어. (wash your hands)

→ _____ _____ _____ _____ _____, you

may catch a cold.

C 보기에서 알맞은 접속사를 골라 두 문장을 자연스럽게 연결하시오. (한 번씩만 사용)

| 보기 | while | if | even though | as well as |

1 Buy this bike online, and you will get 7% off.

→ _____, you will get 7% off.

2 She never starts talking. Others are speaking.

→ She never starts talking _____.

3 It is the rainy season. But the weather is fine these days.

→ _____, the weather is fine these days.

4 I have type O blood. My sister has type O blood, too.

→ _____ has type O blood.

D 그림에 맞게 두 문장을 선택한 다음, 알맞은 접속사로 연결하여 한 문장으로 쓰시오.

1 I can't use the Internet • • ① because • • ⓐ you came back.

2 Your dog kept waiting • • ② while • • ⓑ he was listening to music.

3 You will get one for free • • ③ if • • ⓒ you buy this shampoo.

4 He read a book • • ④ until • • ⓓ the Wi-Fi doesn't work well.

1 I can't use the Internet _____.

2 Your dog kept waiting _____.

3 You will get one for free _____.

4 He read a book _____.

(1–5) 빈칸에 들어갈 알맞은 말을 고르시오.

1

The boy hurt his leg _____ he was playing soccer.

① because   ② or   ③ before
④ while   ⑤ if

2

_____ I read the novel, I don't remember the story.

① When   ② Since   ③ As
④ Although   ⑤ Until

3

_____ you do your best, you will lose the game.

① If   ② And   ③ While
④ Unless   ⑤ So

4

Both my brother _____ I are left-handed.

① and   ② so   ③ or
④ as   ⑤ but

5

She knew _____ she could learn better by teaching others.

① when   ② as   ③ that
④ if   ⑤ but

6 밑줄 친 부분의 쓰임이 나머지와 <u>다른</u> 것을 고르시오.

① She wore a hat <u>since</u> it was cold.
② <u>Since</u> he was busy, he couldn't come.
③ I have known her <u>since</u> I was young.
④ I like Justin <u>since</u> he listens to me.
⑤ He looks friendly <u>since</u> he always smiles.

7 빈칸에 들어갈 말이 차례대로 짝지어진 것은?

We won't eat until you _____ home. If she _____ early, she will get a good seat.

① come - comes
② come - will come
③ will come - comes
④ came - came
⑤ will come - will come

8 빈칸에 들어갈 접속사가 나머지와 <u>다른</u> 것은?

① _____ he is late, he never runs.
② _____ she talks a lot, she is a good listener.
③ He did volunteer work _____ he was very busy.
④ I love summer _____ I enjoy water sports.
⑤ _____ he is an only son, he doesn't feel lonely.

(9-11) 다음 중 어법상 <u>어색한</u> 것은?

9 ① He came before the party ended.

② Even though my mom is from America, I am Korean.

③ Unless you buy that hat, I will buy it.

④ He sometimes talks while he sleeps.

⑤ As it was hot, he wore warm pants.

10 ① I will get some milk as I go shopping.

② If it will rain, we will stay inside.

③ I will call you after I arrive at the airport.

④ We will welcome you if you come again.

⑤ He will keep trying until he succeeds.

11 ① Either Olivia or Jane is telling a lie.

② Both you and he are 16 years old.

③ Neither he nor you have curly hair.

④ Not only she but also her mom is an early bird.

⑤ I as well as my brothers are tall.

(12-13) 빈칸에 공통으로 들어갈 말을 쓰시오.
(대문자와 소문자 적용)

12 · Either you _____ I must go.

· Wear a raincoat, _____ you will get wet in the rain.

⇨ _____

13 · _____ he speaks quietly, I can't hear him.

· Joey looked happy _____ she danced.

⇨ _____ , _____

14 밑줄 친 부분이 나머지와 <u>다르게</u> 쓰인 것을 고르시오.

① His face turns red <u>when</u> he is angry.

② I was painting the door <u>when</u> he came.

③ <u>When</u> I called, he was taking a shower.

④ <u>When</u> did Helen visit you?

⑤ I change my hair <u>when</u> I feel good.

15 밑줄 친 접속사가 나머지와 <u>다른</u> 의미로 쓰인 것은?

① He showed up <u>as</u> I needed his help.

② <u>As</u> he swims, he looks like a dolphin.

③ Turn off the gas <u>as</u> the soup boils.

④ I saw him <u>as</u> I passed his house.

⑤ <u>As</u> he had a great voice, he became a voice actor.

16 다음 중 틀린 부분을 잘못 설명한 사람은?

① Unless it isn't cold, we will go out.

율: unless 는 'if ~ not' 의미니까 not을 지우자.

② I will eat after I will finish the work.

진우: 시간부사절은 미래 대신에 현재시제지.

③ If you will get lost, just call me.

상민: 조건부사절은 미래 대신에 현재시제지.

④ Both Jessica or I like rock music.

지효: '둘 모두'는 [both A and B]야.

⑤ She is neither lazy or stupid.

수: '둘 모두 부정'할 때는 [neither A and B]야.

(17–19) 우리말과 의미가 같도록 빈칸에 알맞은 말을 쓰시오.

17 Paula는 작년에 중국뿐만 아니라 유럽도 여행했어.

⇨ Paula traveled to Europe _____

_____ to China last year.

18 우리는 다람쥐들이 입에 먹이를 저장할 수 있다는 것을 알아.

⇨ We know _____ a squirrel can save food in its mouth.

19 그 두 소녀는 똑같이 생겼지만, 그들은 자매가 아니야.

⇨ _____ the two girls look the same, they are not sisters.

(20–21) 두 문장의 의미가 같도록 빈칸에 알맞은 말을 쓰시오.

20 We checked the weather before we left home.

⇨ We left home _____ we checked the weather.

21 My uncle is not slim. He is not fat either.

⇨ My uncle is _____ slim nor fat.

22 다음 우리말을 영어로 잘못 옮긴 것은?

고래도 포유류이고, 돌고래도 포유류야.

① Both whales and dolphins are mammals.

② Either whales or dolphins are mammals.

③ Not only whales but also dolphins are mammals.

④ Whales are mammals, and dolphins are mammals, too.

⑤ Dolphins as well as whales are mammals.

23 어법상 어색한 것으로 짝지어진 것은?

> ⓐ Listen carefully, or you won't understand the rules.
> ⓑ Both you and your sister has your mom's eyes.
> ⓒ Jack said that loved Korean food.
> ⓓ As the runner started late, he came in first.
> ⓔ You can order either fish or meat.

① ⓐ, ⓒ   ② ⓑ, ⓒ, ⓔ   ③ ⓓ, ⓔ
④ ⓑ, ⓒ, ⓓ   ⑤ ⓒ, ⓓ, ⓔ

(24–25) 우리말과 의미가 같도록 ( ) 안의 말을 배열하시오.

24 동전을 넣으세요. 그러면 게임이 시작할 거예요.
(will, and, the, game, start)

⇨ Insert a coin, _____

_____.

25 그 보트가 균형을 잃으면 그것은 뒤집어 질 거야.
(loses, if, it, balance)

⇨ The boat will turn over _____

_____.

(26–27) 우리말과 의미가 같도록 ( ) 안의 말을 이용하여 문장을 완성하시오.

26 토크쇼에서 게스트는 "예" 또는 "아니요"로 대답했어.
(either)

⇨ On the talk show, the guest answered

_____.

27 보름달이 있었기 때문에 밤하늘이 밝았어.
(a full moon, since)

⇨ The night sky was bright _____

_____.

28 다음 조건을 이용하여 두 문장을 한 문장으로 쓰시오.

> Jim is not good at cooking.
> I am not good at cooking either.
> 조건 1: 상관접속사 사용
> 조건 2: 8 단어

⇨ _____

_____

(29–30) 틀린 것이 있으면 고치고 이유를 설명하시오.

29 Before winter will come, I will get you a warm jacket.

고치기: _____ ⇨ _____

이유: (시간, 조건) 부사절에서
미래시제 대신 (현재, 미래)시제 사용

30 Unless he doesn't wear a uniform, he doesn't look like a policeman.

고치기: _____ ⇨ _____
또는 _____ ⇨ _____

이유: unless는 (if, if ~ not)의 의미여서
not과 동시에 (사용, 사용 불가)

한눈에 정리하는 Grammar Mapping

빈칸에 알맞은 답을 보기에서 골라 넣어 grammar mapping 완성하기

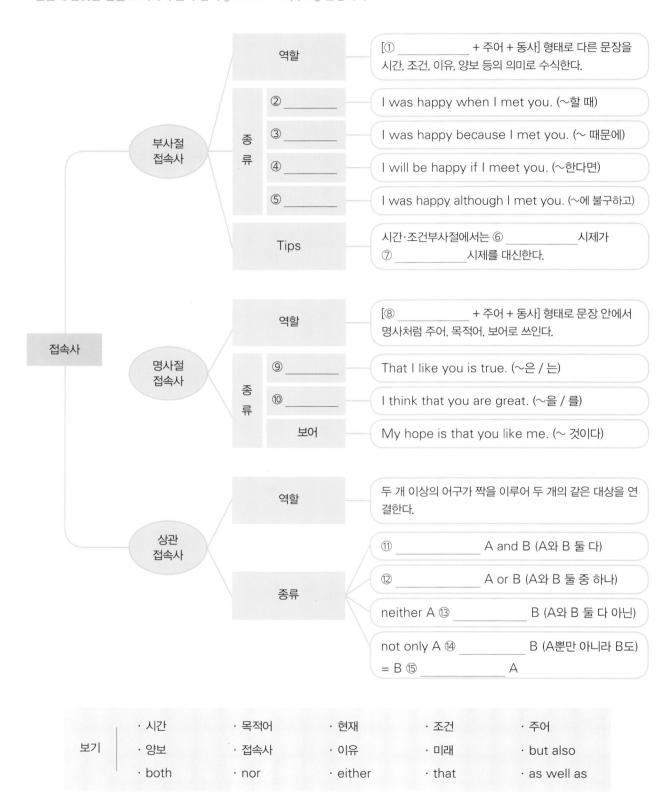

접속사

부사절 접속사

역할: [① _____ + 주어 + 동사] 형태로 다른 문장을 시간, 조건, 이유, 양보 등의 의미로 수식한다.

종류:
- ② _____ : I was happy when I met you. (~할 때)
- ③ _____ : I was happy because I met you. (~ 때문에)
- ④ _____ : I will be happy if I meet you. (~한다면)
- ⑤ _____ : I was happy although I met you. (~에 불구하고)

Tips: 시간·조건부사절에서는 ⑥ _____ 시제가 ⑦ _____ 시제를 대신한다.

명사절 접속사

역할: [⑧ _____ + 주어 + 동사] 형태로 문장 안에서 명사처럼 주어, 목적어, 보어로 쓰인다.

종류:
- ⑨ _____ : That I like you is true. (~은 / 는)
- ⑩ _____ : I think that you are great. (~을 / 를)
- **보어**: My hope is that you like me. (~ 것이다)

상관 접속사

역할: 두 개 이상의 어구가 짝을 이루어 두 개의 같은 대상을 연결한다.

종류:
- ⑪ _____ A and B (A와 B 둘 다)
- ⑫ _____ A or B (A와 B 둘 중 하나)
- neither A ⑬ _____ B (A와 B 둘 다 아닌)
- not only A ⑭ _____ B (A뿐만 아니라 B도) = B ⑮ _____ A

보기

· 시간	· 목적어	· 현재	· 조건	· 주어
· 양보	· 접속사	· 이유	· 미래	· but also
· both	· nor	· either	· that	· as well as

관계사

GP 46 관계대명사의 역할과 종류

GP 47 주격 관계대명사 who, which, that

GP 48 목적격 관계대명사 who(m), which, that

GP 49 소유격 관계대명사 whose

GP 50 관계대명사 that

GP 51 관계대명사 생략

GP 52 관계대명사 what

GP 53 관계부사 when, where, why, how

• Grammar & Writing

• Actual Test

• 한눈에 정리하는 Grammar Mapping

관계대명사의 역할과 종류

GP 46

관계대명사는 접속사와 대명사 역할을 동시에 하고 관계대명사가 이끄는 절은 앞에 나오는 명사(선행사)를 수식한다.
관계대명사는 수식을 받는 선행사와 관계대명사의 격에 따라 다음과 같이 나뉜다.

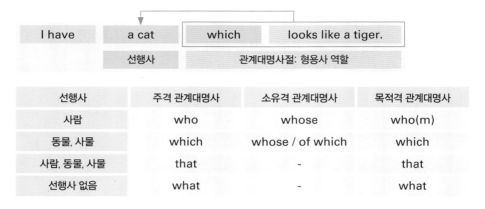

선행사	주격 관계대명사	소유격 관계대명사	목적격 관계대명사
사람	who	whose	who(m)
동물, 사물	which	whose / of which	which
사람, 동물, 사물	that	-	that
선행사 없음	what	-	what

주격 관계대명사 who, which, that

GP 47

주격 관계대명사는 주어 역할을 하고 바로 뒤에 동사가 온다.

My teacher chose *the book*. + It was written in English. <It = the book>
→ ☆ My teacher chose *the book* which (that) was written in English.

목적격 관계대명사 who(m), which, that

GP 48

목적격 관계대명사는 목적어 역할을 하고 바로 뒤에 주어와 동사가 온다.

He posted *a picture* on his blog. + He took it yesterday. <it = a picture>
→ ☆ He posted *a picture* which (that) he took yesterday on his blog.

GP Practice

A ( ) 안에서 알맞은 것을 고르시오.

1 Here are some tips (which, who) will be helpful for teens.

2 Amy is my friend (which, whom) I can trust.

3 He is the chef (who, whom) cooks Italian food well.

4 This is the sunflower (which, whom) I planted last year.

B 관계대명사를 이용하여 두 문장을 한 문장으로 쓰시오. (that 제외)

1 Monet is the painter. I like him the most.

→ Monet is the painter _____ the most.

2 We watched a movie. It was about the Korean War.

→ We watched a movie _____ about the Korean War.

3 The boy is looking for his dog. He lost it in the park.

→ The boy is looking for his dog _____ in the park.

C 우리말과 의미가 같도록 ( ) 안의 말을 이용하여 문장을 완성하시오.

1 나는 항상 늦는 사람들을 좋아하지 않는다. (late)

→ I don't like people _____ _____ _____ _____ .

2 선생님은 내가 보내는 메시지에 언제나 답장하신다. (send)

→ My teacher always replies to the messages _____ _____ _____ .

3 나는 주머니가 많은 재킷이 필요해요. (have)

→ I need a jacket _____ _____ _____ _____ .

4 Jessica가 그렸던 그 신사는 그녀의 할아버지이셔. (draw)

→ The gentleman _____ _____ _____ is her grandfather.

D 밑줄 친 부분에 대한 설명을 체크하고 틀린 경우엔 바르게 고치시오. (맞으면 'O', 불필요하면 '삭제' 표시)

*S: 주어, V: 동사

1	This is the drugstore <u>who</u> is open 24 hours a day. → ( )	선행사가 (사람, 사물) 관계대명사 (주격, 목적격) + V
2	Is he the actor <u>whom</u> you like? → ( )	선행사가 (사람, 사물) 관계대명사 (주격, 목적격) + S + V
3	She met a boy that <u>he</u> came from France. → ( )	(주격, 목적격) 관계대명사 뒤에 주격 대명사 (사용, 삭제)
4	He built the tower which I liked <u>it</u> a lot. → ( )	(주격, 목적격) 관계대명사 뒤에 목적격 대명사 (사용, 삭제)

소유격 관계대명사 whose

GP 49

소유격 관계대명사는 소유격 역할을 하며 바로 뒤에 명사가 온다.

접속사와 대명사	I know	a boy.	+	His	voice is soft.

관계대명사	I know	a boy	whose	voice is soft.

관계대명사가 소유격 역할을 하므로, 소유격 대명사 삭제

He is from *a country*. **+ Its** nature is very beautiful. <Its = a country's>
→ ☆ He is from *a country* **whose** nature is very beautiful.

> ○ Tip ○
> 관계대명사의 격과 어순 관계
> ① 선행사 + [주격 관계대명사 + 동사 ~]
> ② 선행사 + [목적격 관계대명사 + 주어 + 동사 ~]
> ③ 선행사 + [소유격 관계대명사 + 명사 + (주어) + 동사 ~]

관계대명사 that

GP 50

❶ 관계대명사 that은 소유격 형태가 없으며, 관계대명사 who, which 대신 쓸 수 있다.

주격	I like	the girl	that (who)	is dancing on the stage.

목적격	I like	the movie	that (which)	Alex made last year.

❷ 주로 관계대명사 that을 쓰는 경우

선행사			
[사람 + 사물], [사람 + 동물]			☆ Look at the boy and the cat that are running.
최상급, 서수			☆ I am the first girl that arrived here.
the very, the only	that	(주어) + 동사	☆ It is the very book that she wants.
the same, the last			This is the same bag that I lost.
(some, every, no) thing			There was nothing that she liked.

> ○ Tip ○
> [the very + 명사]: 바로 그 ~
> [the only + 명사]: 유일한 ~

GP Practice

A ( ) 안에서 알맞은 것을 고르시오. (복수 정답 가능)

1 He gave me everything (who, that, whom) he had.

2 Kate has a dog (which, whose, that) mouth is very big.

3 Dylan was the first boy (which, whose, that) arrived in the classroom.

4 Students must use the map (which, that, whose) they draw.

B 관계대명사를 이용하여 두 문장을 한 문장으로 쓰시오.

1 My sister likes a cat. Its fur is white.

→ My sister likes a cat _____ white.

2 This is the very robot. It understands my words.

→ This is the very robot _____ my words.

3 I need a big box. Its bottom is made of wood.

→ I need a big box _____ made of wood.

C 우리말과 의미가 같도록 ( ) 안의 말을 이용하여 문장을 완성하시오.

1 나는 새를 키우는 것이 취미인 소년을 인터뷰했다. (hobby)

→ I interviewed a boy _____ _____ _____ raising birds.

2 그녀는 비밀번호를 아는 유일한 사람이다. (only, know)

→ She is _____ _____ person _____ _____ the password.

3 이것이 Sandra가 직접 쓴 바로 그 편지이다. (very, write)

→ This is _____ _____ letter _____ _____ _____ herself.

4 그는 배터리가 더 오래 지속되는 노트북을 살 것이다. (battery, last)

→ He is going to buy a laptop _____ _____ _____ longer.

D 밑줄 친 부분에 대한 설명을 체크하고 틀린 경우엔 바르게 고치시오. (맞으면 'O', 불필요하면 '삭제' 표시)

*관대: 관계대명사

1	Give me the book <u>which</u> cover is red. → ( )	선행사 + (주격, 소유격) 관대 + 명사
2	I like movies <u>that</u> are about animals. → ( )	선행사 movies는 (사람, 사물)이므로 관대 (who, that)
3	It was the first job <u>which</u> he got. → ( )	서수 포함 선행사는 관대 (which, that) 사용
4	I helped the boy whose <u>his</u> leg broke. → ( )	(주격, 소유격) 관대 뒤에는 소유격 대명사 (사용, 삭제)

관계대명사 생략

GP 51

❶ 목적격 관계대명사 who(m), which, that은 생략할 수 있다.

선행사	목적격 관계대명사	주어 + 동사
the book	who(m), which, that	I bought yesterday

❷ 주격 관계대명사는 뒤에 be동사가 나올 때 같이 생략할 수 있다.

선행사	주격 관계대명사	be동사	~
the boys	who	are	singing a song

The man **(whom)** I met yesterday is a famous musician.
※ We have to recycle the cans **(which)** we used.
※ The girl **(who is)** giving a speech is my sister.
Titanic is a movie **(that is)** based on a real story.

• Upgrade •

전치사의 목적어로 관계대명사가 쓰일 경우 관계대명사절에 있는 전치사가 관계대명사 앞에 올 수 있다.
이때 관계대명사 that은 쓸 수 없고 목적격 관계대명사를 생략할 수도 없다.

I know the topic **which (that)** we will talk **about**.
= I know the topic **about which** we will talk. (전치사 + 관계대명사)
I know the topic **about that** we will talk. (X) (전치사 + 관계대명사 that (X))
I know the topic **about** we will talk. (X) (전치사 뒤 목적격 관계대명사 생략 (X))

관계대명사 what

GP 52

관계대명사 what은 선행사를 포함해서 the thing which (that)로 나타낼 수 있고 '~하는 것'으로 해석한다.

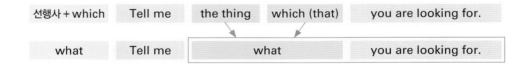

Can you show me **the thing which (that)** is in your pocket?
→ ※ Can you show me **what** is in your pocket?

GP Practice

A 밑줄 친 부분을 생략할 수 있으면 O, 생략할 수 없으면 X로 표시하시오.

1 Have you read the book <u>which</u> I gave you? _____

2 The girl <u>who</u> is wearing the blue skirt is your partner. _____

3 The artist <u>that</u> we met yesterday was very nice. _____

4 I bought the novel <u>which was</u> written in Spanish. _____

B 두 문장이 같은 의미를 갖도록 빈칸을 채우시오.

1 I will tell you all that I know.

→ I will tell you _____ I know.

2 She can't understand what he says in Japanese.

→ She can't understand anything _____ he says in Japanese.

3 The thing that he is listening to is a movie's soundtrack.

→ _____ he is listening to is a movie's soundtrack.

C 우리말과 의미가 같도록 ( ) 안의 말을 배열하시오.

1 내가 마시고 싶은 것은 한 잔의 물이다. (want, what, I, to drink)

→ _____ is a glass of water.

2 이곳이 우리가 지난주에 방문했던 그 병원이에요. (visited, we, the hospital)

→ This is _____ last week.

3 창가에 앉아 있는 남자분이 우리 선생님이다. (by the window, sitting, the man)

→ _____ is our teacher.

4 네가 Hans에 대해 들었던 것을 말해 줘. (about, heard, you, what, Hans)

→ Tell me _____ .

D 밑줄 친 부분에 대한 설명을 체크하고 틀린 경우엔 바르게 고치시오. (맞으면 'O' 표시)

*관대: 관계대명사

1	This is the software <u>what</u> I use a lot. → ( )	선행사가 있으므로 관대 (what, which) 사용
2	<u>The TV we bought</u> is broken. → ( )	선행사 + 목적격 관대 + 주어 + 동사 생략 (가능, 불가)
3	<u>That</u> is important is not money. → ( )	선행사가 없으므로 관대 (what, that) 사용
4	The girl <u>waving</u> at us is Jane. → ( )	선행사 + 주격 관대 + be동사 + 현재분사 생략 (가능, 불가)

관계부사 when, where, why, how

관계부사는 접속사와 부사 역할을 동시에 하고 관계부사가 이끄는 절은 앞에 나오는 명사(선행사)를 수식한다.
관계부사는 선행사에 따라 다음과 같이 나누고 [전치사 + 관계대명사] 형태로 바꿀 수 있다.

	선행사	관계부사	전치사 + 관계대명사
시간	the time, the day	when	at / in / on... which
장소	the place, the house	where	at / in / on... which
이유	the reason	why	for which
방법	the way	how	in which

❶ **when:** 시간을 나타내는 the time, the day, the year 등이 선행사일 때

9 o'clock is *the time*. + Our class starts **at the time**.

→ 9 o'clock is *the time* **when (at which)** our class starts.

❷ **where:** 장소를 나타내는 the place, the house, the city 등이 선행사일 때

This is *the park*. + I usually exercise **at the park**.

→ This is *the park* **where (at which)** I usually exercise.

❸ **why:** 이유를 나타내는 the reason이 선행사일 때

I don't know *the reason*. + He was absent **for the reason**.

→ I don't know *the reason* **why (for which)** he was absent.

❹ **how:** 방법을 나타내는 the way가 선행사일 때

This is *the way*. + He solved the puzzle **in the way**.

→ This is *the way* **how** he solved the puzzle. (×)

→ This is *the way* **in which** he solved the puzzle.

→ This is **the way (how)** he solved the puzzle.

> **Tip**
> 선행사 the way와 관계부사 how는 같이 쓸 수 없다.

GP Practice

A ( ) 안에서 알맞은 것을 고르시오. (복수 정답 가능)

1 Tell me the reason (why, where, when) you are angry.

2 I remember the day (why, where, when) we visited the museum.

3 Let's decide on the resort (when, where, how) we will stay tonight.

4 He wants to know (the way, how, the way how) we use chopsticks.

B 관계부사를 이용하여 두 문장을 한 문장으로 만드시오.

1 She often goes to the gallery. She feels comfortable in the gallery.

→ She often goes to the gallery, _____.

2 You will never know the reason. Your parents love you for that reason.

→ You will never know the reason _____.

3 Steve Jobs told us the way. He made Apple Computer in that way.

→ Steve Jobs told us _____.

C 우리말과 의미가 같도록 ( ) 안의 말을 배열하시오.

1 너는 Ann이 한국을 떠났던 날짜를 알고 있니? (left, Korea, the date, Ann, when)

→ Do you know _____?

2 이것은 에스키모인들이 서로 인사하는 방식이야. (Eskimos, greet, how)

→ This is _____ one another.

3 그 공원은 내가 자유시간을 보내는 장소이다. (spend, the place, I, where)

→ The park is _____ my free time.

4 우리는 지진이 발생하는 이유를 배웠다. (happen, earthquakes, the reason, why)

→ We learned _____.

D 밑줄 친 부분에 대한 설명을 체크하고 틀린 경우엔 바르게 고치시오. (맞으면 'O', 불필요하면 '삭제' 표시)

		선행사 + 관계부사	
1	Tell me the time <u>where</u> it will start. → ( )	(장소, 시간)	(where, when)
2	This is the way <u>how</u> I succeeded. → ( )	(방법, 이유)	(how, 없음)
3	I know the reason <u>why</u> he was absent. → ( )	(시간, 이유)	(when, why)
4	This is the office <u>when</u> she works. → ( )	(장소, 방법)	(where, how)

A 우리말과 의미가 같도록 ( ) 안의 말을 배열하시오.

1 그들은 커다란 정원이 있는 집에 산다. (has, a, which, big garden)

→ They live in a house _____ .

2 질문에 대답했던 남자아이를 기억하니? (question, the, answered, who)

→ Do you remember the boy _____ ?

3 우리가 지난달 방문했던 레스토랑은 지금 문을 닫았다. (visited, month, which, last, we)

→ The restaurant _____ is closed now.

4 내가 가르치고 싶은 것은 역사에 대한 진실이다. (I, teach, to, what, want)

→ _____ is the truth about history.

5 Jack은 페달이 고장 난 자전거를 고쳤어. (pedal, whose, broken, was)

→ Jack fixed the bicycle _____ .

6 네가 집에 돌아왔던 시간을 알려 줘. (home, when, you, back, came)

→ Let me know the time _____ .

B 우리말과 의미가 같도록 ( ) 안의 말을 이용하여 문장을 완성하시오.

1 Judy는 그 콘서트에 도착했던 마지막 사람이다. (arrive at)

→ Judy is the last person _____ _____ _____ _____ _____ .

2 내가 오늘 가르쳤던 공식은 꼭 외워야 한다. (teach)

→ You must memorize the formula _____ _____ _____ _____ .

3 이 동영상은 치즈케이크가 어떻게 만들어지는지 보여 준다. (be made)

→ This video clip shows _____ _____ _____ _____ .

4 너는 그들이 그 축제를 취소한 이유를 알고 있니? (cancel, festival)

→ Do you know the reason _____ _____ _____ _____ _____ ?

5 TV가 우리에게 보여 주는 것이 항상 사실은 아니다. (show)

→ _____ _____ _____ _____ is not always true.

6 그들은 한국에서 생산되는 차를 좋아한다. (be produced)

→ They like the cars _____ _____ _____ _____ .

C 그림 상황에 맞도록 주어진 말과 보기의 관계사를 이용하여 문장을 완성하시오.

long, is, tail

Korea, is, from

the, we, out, throw, garbage

| 보기 | which | whose | when |

1 The cat _____ is climbing the stairs.

2 I am learning taekwondo, _____ .

3 Saturday is the day _____ .

D 보기의 표현을 이용하여 주어진 문장을 완성하시오.

보기
· how we can keep our bodies warm
· which will surprise him
· whom many Koreans are proud of
· where my parents studied
· why the accident happened here

1 I must find out the reason _____ .

2 I want to go to the university _____ .

3 We are preparing a party _____ .

4 Could you explain to me _____ ?

5 Yuna Kim is a figure skater _____ .

(1–3) 빈칸에 들어갈 알맞은 말을 고르시오.

1
She works for a company _____ makes airplanes.

① who   ② whom
③ whose   ④ which
⑤ what

2
I chose glasses _____ frames are blue.
＊frames: 안경테

① what   ② where
③ whose   ④ who
⑤ when

3
He is the comedian _____ the children like a lot.

① which   ② whom
③ whose   ④ what
⑤ how

4 빈칸에 알맞지 <u>않은</u> 말을 고르시오.

Do you remember the teacher _____ I told you about?

① who   ② whose
③ whom   ④ 생략
⑤ that

(5–7) 두 문장의 빈칸에 공통으로 들어갈 말을 고르시오.

5
· The toys _____ are made by the company are safe.
· I know the man _____ is on this TV show.

① which   ② what   ③ that
④ whose   ⑤ how

6
· I forgot the day _____ our winter vacation started.
· Tell me the time _____ you were born.

① where   ② how   ③ why
④ when   ⑤ what

7
· _____ he says is always easy to understand.
· She saves _____ she earns.

① where   ② how   ③ why
④ when   ⑤ what

8 두 문장을 한 문장으로 바꿔 쓸 때 which가 들어갈 곳은?

· The dress is for Halloween.
· She bought the dress.

→ The dress __①__ __②__ __③__ __④__ __⑤__ Halloween.

9 밑줄 친 부분에서 생략된 말을 고르시오.

> The <u>girl sitting</u> next to Jack is his sister.

① who she is   ② who is

③ which is   ④ who

⑤ which

(10–11) 빈칸에 들어갈 말이 차례대로 짝지어진 것은?

10
> · Is there a restaurant _____ I can eat Vietnamese food?
> · She didn't understand _____ you said.

① where - what

② where - which

③ when - what

④ that - why

⑤ when - how

11
> · I don't know the reason _____ he doesn't eat cucumbers.
> · There is a lady _____ wants to see you.

① how - whom

② why - whom

③ why - who

④ that - whose

⑤ how - who

12 밑줄 친 부분이 바르게 쓰인 것은?

① I know the boy <u>whom</u> runs the blog.

② He is a hero <u>whose</u> we respect.

③ I saw the dog <u>whom</u> Jane bought.

④ He owns pictures <u>which</u> are famous to Koreans.

⑤ She looks after the babies <u>who</u> mothers work.

13 밑줄 친 부분이 어법상 어색한 것은?

① Now is the time <u>when</u> I need you.

② This is the reason <u>where</u> I am here.

③ I remember the place <u>where</u> I first met him.

④ Monday is the day <u>when</u> we get together.

⑤ He told me <u>how</u> he survived the war.

(14–15) 두 문장의 빈칸에 공통으로 들어갈 말을 쓰시오.

14
> · He showed me _____ he made the model plane.
> · This is _____ we can take care of nature.

⇨ _____

15
> · He is the very actor _____ the director wanted.
> · This is the highest mountain _____ I have ever climbed.

⇨ _____

(16–18) 우리말과 의미가 같도록 빈칸에 알맞은 말을 쓰시오.

16 마이다스라는 이름을 가진 왕이 있었다.

⇨ There was a king _____
name was Midas.

17 이 음식은 제가 주문했던 것이 아니에요.

⇨ This food is not _____
I ordered.

18 여기가 내가 살았던 집이에요.

⇨ This is the house _____
I lived.

19 다음 중 who가 다르게 쓰인 것을 고르시오.

① This is the man who lent me his phone.
② She teaches students who are very smart.
③ He knows who sent him the flowers.
④ We met the writer who wrote this novel.
⑤ I have a friend who is helping the poor in Africa.

20 다음 밑줄 친 부분 중 생략할 수 없는 것을 고르시오.

① This is a game which boys usually play.
② The man who is wearing a blue tie is my uncle.
③ My mom bought the skirt that I wanted.
④ I like a woman who has a sense of humor.
⑤ The robot which was designed by him is serving the food.

21 다음 중 that이 들어갈 수 없는 문장은?

① I like anyone _____ is polite to people.
② What is the best film _____ you have ever seen?
③ The police recorded _____ she said.
④ He wrote a novel _____ is about his childhood.
⑤ My son got the job _____ he wanted.

22 다음 중 빈칸에 들어갈 말이 나머지와 다른 것은?

① The picture _____ he painted looks real.
② Where is the milk _____ was in the fridge?
③ Animals _____ have big ears are sensitive.
④ I enjoyed the music _____ he played for me.
⑤ Tom is reading a book _____ author is Hemingway.

(23-24) 우리말과 의미가 같도록 ( ) 안의 말을 배열하시오.

23 그는 축구를 하고 있는 소년들의 사진을 찍고 있다.
(that, are, boys, soccer, playing)

⇨ He is taking a picture of _____

_____ .

24 여기는 내 부모님이 결혼했던 장소이다.
(married, where, parents, my, got)

⇨ This is the place _____

_____ .

(25-27) 보기에서 알맞은 관계사를 골라 두 문장을 연결하
시오. (중복 사용 불가)

보기 | who   which   what   when   how

25 Do you know the store?
It sells recycled bags.

⇨ Do you know the store _____

_____ ?

26 I want to see the thing.
He is making it.

⇨ I want to see _____

_____ .

27 I get up at 7 o'clock.
The alarm clock goes off at 7.

⇨ I get up at 7 o'clock _____

_____ .

(28-29) 틀린 것이 있으면 고치고 이유를 설명하시오.

28 What is the most interesting book that
you have read it?

고치기: _____ ⇨ _____

이유: (주격, 목적격) 관계대명사 뒤에는
목적격 대명사 (사용, 삭제)

29 I want to know the way how you cook
Italian food.

고치기: _____ ⇨ _____

이유: 선행사 the way와 관계부사 how는 같이
(쓸 수 있다, 쓸 수 없다)

30 다음 조건을 이용하여 알맞게 영작하시오.

이것은 그가 북극에서 찍었던 사진이다.
조건 1: take, the Arctic
조건 2: 10단어, 관계대명사 사용

⇨ _____

_____ .

한눈에 정리하는 Grammar Mapping

빈칸에 알맞은 답을 보기에서 골라 넣어 grammar mapping 완성하기

*S: 주어, V: 동사

관계사

① _____	관계대명사 ⟨S⟩ + ⟨V⟩
	관계부사 ⟨S⟩ + ⟨V⟩

관계대명사

역할: [접속사 + 대명사] 역할을 하면서 형용사처럼 명사를 수식한다.

종류

주격 관계대명사

선행사	+	주격 관계대명사	
② _____	+	who	+ ③ _____
사물 / 동물	+	which	
사람 / 사물 / 동물	+	that	

a girl who dances well

목적격 관계대명사

선행사	+	목적격 관계대명사	
사람	+	who(m)	+ ⑥ _____
사물 / 동물	+	④ _____	
⑤ _____	+	that	

a girl whom Tim likes

소유격 관계대명사

선행사	+	소유격 관계대명사	
사람	+	whose	+ ⑧ _____
사물 / 동물	+	⑦ _____	+ (S) + V

a girl whose voice is soft

that: 소유격 형태는 없고 선행사가 [사람 + 사물], 서수, 최상급 등일 때 쓴다.

what: 선행사를 포함하는 관계대명사로 '⑨ _____'으로 해석하며 앞에 수식하는 선행사가 ⑩ _____.

관계대명사 생략
- ⑪ _____ 관계대명사 생략
- [주격 관계대명사 + be동사] 생략

관계부사

역할: [접속사 + 부사] 역할을 하면서 형용사처럼 명사를 수식한다.

종류
- **when**: the time(⑫ _____) + when 주어 + 동사
- **where**: the place(⑬ _____) + where 주어 + 동사
- **why**: the reason(⑭ _____) + why 주어 + 동사
- **how**: the way(⑮ _____) + how 주어 + 동사
  (the way, how 둘 중 하나 반드시 ⑯ _____)

Tips: 관계부사 = ⑰ _____ + 관계대명사
where = (in / on / at) + which

보기

· 명사	· 목적격	· 선행사	· 생략	· 장소	· 시간
· 전치사	· 이유	· 방법	· 없다	· ~하는 것	· 사람
· 사람 / 사물 / 동물	· V	· S + V	· whose	· which	

164

가정법

GP 54 가정법 과거

GP 55 단순 조건문과 가정법 과거

GP 56 I wish + 가정법 과거

GP 57 as if + 가정법 과거

- Grammar & Writing

- Actual Test

- 한눈에 정리하는 Grammar Mapping

가정법 과거

가정법 과거는 현재 사실과 반대되는 상황을 나타내거나 실현 불가능한 것을 가정할 때 사용한다.

❶ 가정법 과거

★ If he **got up** early, he **would** not **be** late for class.
If you **were** invisible, what **would** you **do**?

> **Tip**
> 가정법 과거에서 If절의 be동사는 주어의 인칭과 단복수에 상관없이 were를 사용한다.

❷ 가정법 과거의 직설법 전환: 가정법 과거는 직설법 현재시제로 전환

★ If I **had** enough time, I **would visit** you.
  → ★ As I **don't have** enough time, I **won't visit** you.

• Upgrade •

가정법 과거완료: 과거 사실을 반대로 가정할 때 사용하는 표현

[If + 주어 + had p.p. ~, 주어 + would / could / might + have p.p. ~.]

If I **had hurried**, I **could have taken** the bus.

단순 조건문과 가정법 과거

단순 조건문은 말하는 내용이 실현 가능성이 있을 때 사용하고 가정법 과거는 현재 사실을 반대로 나타내거나
실현 가능성이 없는 일을 나타낼 때 사용하는 표현이다.

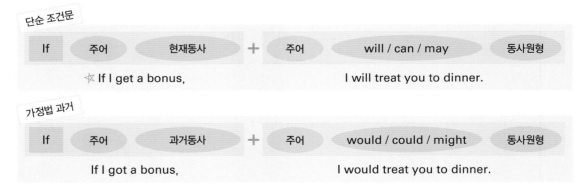

If I **win** the lottery, I **will travel** around the world. (단순 조건문)
If I **won** the lottery, I **would travel** around the world. (가정법 과거)

GP Practice

A ( ) 안에서 알맞은 것을 고르고 조건문인지 가정법인지 표시하시오.

1 If she (studies, studied) hard, she would get good grades.　　(조건문, 가정법)

2 If you (are, were) in trouble, I will help you out.　　(조건문, 가정법)

3 If you leave now, you (will, would) get there on time.　　(조건문, 가정법)

4 If I had more time, I (will, would) stay longer.　　(조건문, 가정법)

B 다음 문장을 가정법 문장으로 바꿔 쓰시오.

1 As I don't have a ticket, I can't go to the concert.

　→ If I _____ a ticket, I _____ to the concert.

2 As I don't see you, I can't say hello to you.

　→ If I _____ you, I _____ hello to you.

3 As Harry is sick, he can't go out and play.

　→ If Harry _____ sick, he _____ out and play.

C 우리말과 의미가 같도록 ( ) 안의 말을 이용하여 문장을 완성하시오.

1 선생님이 조금 더 천천히 말씀하시면, 나는 더 잘 이해할 텐데. (speak, understand)

　→ If my teacher _____ more slowly, I _____ _____ him better.

2 내가 타임머신이 있다면, 나는 나의 미래를 방문할 텐데. (have, visit)

　→ If I _____ a time machine, I _____ _____ the future.

3 저 가수가 다른 노래를 한다면, 모두들 더 좋아할 텐데. (sing, another, enjoy)

　→ If the singer _____ _____ _____, everyone _____

　_____ themselves more.

D 밑줄 친 부분에 대한 설명을 체크하고 틀린 경우엔 바르게 고치시오. (맞으면 'O' 표시)

*S: 주어, R: 동사원형

	문장	설명
1	If he <u>bothers</u> me, he would get punished. → ( )	실현 가능성 (있는, 없는) 가정법 If + S + (과거, 현재)동사, S + (will, would) + R
2	If I <u>took</u> a taxi, I will arrive on time. → ( )	실현 가능성 (있는, 없는) 조건문 If + S + (과거, 현재)동사, S + (will, would) + R
3	If I <u>am</u> 20 years old, I could vote. → ( )	실현 가능성 (있는, 없는) 가정법 If + S + (am, were), S + (can, could) + R
4	If he asks me, I <u>will</u> tell him the truth. → ( )	실현 가능성 (있는, 없는) 조건문 If + S + (과거, 현재)동사, S + (will, would) + R

I wish + 가정법 과거

GP 56

I wish + 가정법 과거는 현재에 이루기 힘든 것을 소망할 때 사용한다.

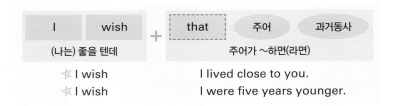

❶ I wish + 가정법 과거

I wish I **could speak** English well.

I wish I **didn't have to go** to school.

❷ I wish + 가정법 과거의 직설법 전환: I am sorry + 직설법 현재

☆ I **wish** you **didn't make** so much noise.

→ ☆ I **am sorry** you **make** so much noise.

I wish it **stopped** raining.

→ I am sorry it **doesn't stop** raining.

as if + 가정법 과거

GP 57

as if + 가정법 과거는 현재 사실의 반대를 가정할 때 사용한다.

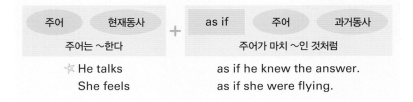

❶ as if + 가정법 과거

She acts **as if** she **were** my mother.

He talks **as if** he **had** a girlfriend.

❷ as if + 가정법 과거의 직설법 전환: In fact, + 직설법 현재

☆ She treats me **as if** I **were** a baby.

→ ☆ In **fact**, I **am not** a baby.

He talks **as if** he **could fix** the car himself.

→ **In fact**, he **can't fix** the car himself.

GP Practice

A ( ) 안에서 알맞은 것을 고르시오.

1 I wish there (aren't, weren't) so many people in the mall.

2 I feel as if I (am, were) alone in the world.

3 I wish I (am, were) outgoing like Emma.

4 My friend speaks as if he (travels, traveled) to Europe.

B 다음 문장을 가정법 문장으로 바꿔 쓰시오.

1 In fact, my friend is not ill now.

→ My friend looks as if she _____ ill.

2 I am sorry I don't carry lotion with me.

→ I wish I _____ lotion with me.

3 I am sorry I don't know how to play the violin.

→ I wish I _____ how to play the violin.

C 우리말과 의미가 같도록 ( ) 안의 말을 이용하여 문장을 완성하시오.

1 그 가난한 남자는 마치 백만장자인 것처럼 생활한다. (be)

→ The poor man lives _____ _____ _____ _____ a millionaire.

2 이야기할 가까운 친구가 있으면 좋을 텐데. (have)

→ _____ _____ _____ _____ a close friend to talk with.

3 Liz는 마치 발레리나인 것처럼 걷는다. (be)

→ Liz walks _____ _____ _____ _____ a ballerina.

4 내가 그녀의 이름을 기억하면 좋을 텐데. (remember)

→ _____ _____ _____ _____ _____ .

D 밑줄 친 부분에 대한 설명을 체크하고 틀린 경우엔 바르게 고치시오. (맞으면 'O' 표시)

*S: 주어

1	He looks as if he <u>is</u> 10 years younger. → ( )	현재 (사실, 사실의 반대)처럼 as if + S + (현재, 과거)동사
2	Robert talks as if he <u>did</u> the work alone. → ( )	현재 (사실, 사실의 반대)처럼 as if + S + (현재, 과거)동사
3	I wish it <u>doesn't</u> snow so much. → ( )	현재에 이루기 힘든 소망은 I wish + S + (현재, 과거)동사
4	I wish he <u>opens</u> his mind to others. → ( )	현재에 이루기 힘든 소망은 I wish + S + (현재, 과거)동사

A   우리말과 의미가 같도록 ( ) 안의 말을 배열하시오.

1 나의 개가 좀 더 작았더라면, 개집에 넣어서 다닐 텐데. (take, would, were, if, my dog)

→ _____ smaller, I _____ him in a carrier.

2 내가 시험에 통과하면, 오늘 저녁을 살게. (treat, pass, will)

→ If I _____ the exam, I _____ you to dinner.

3 그는 이것이 처음 식사인 것처럼 음식을 먹는다. (it, if, his first meal, were, as)

→ He eats food _____ .

4 미세먼지가 사라지면 좋을 텐데. (the fine dust, wish, disappeared)

→ I _____ .

5 내가 수영을 배우면, 스노클링 클럽에 참여할 수 있을 텐데. (join, learned, could, if, I)

→ _____ how to swim, I _____ the snorkeling club.

6 나는 그의 음식을 좋아하는 것처럼 행동하지만, 사실은 안 좋아해. (liked, as, if, I, food, his)

→ I act _____ , but I don't actually like it.

B   우리말과 의미가 같도록 ( ) 안의 말을 이용하여 문장을 완성하시오.

1 만약 네가 이 기회를 놓친다면, 너는 그것을 후회할 것이다. (miss, chance, regret) (＊실현 가능성 있을 때)

→ If you _____ _____ _____ , you _____ _____ it.

2 그 영화가 조금 덜 무서우면, 나는 영화를 즐길 텐데. (less scary, enjoy)

→ If the movie _____ _____ _____ , I _____ _____ it.

3 내 동생은 내 설명을 이해한 것처럼 고개를 끄덕인다. (understand)

→ My sister nodded her head _____ _____ _____
my explanation.

4 만약 네가 물을 무서워하지 않으면, 바다 아래 광경도 볼 수 있을 텐데. (be afraid of)

→ If you _____ _____ _____ _____ _____ ,
you _____ _____ the beautiful view underwater.

5 나는 오늘 너무 행복하다. 그들도 똑같이 느끼면 좋을 텐데. (can feel)

→ I feel very happy today. _____ _____ _____ _____
_____ the same way.

6 그녀는 나를 모르는 것처럼 행동한다. (know)

→ She acts _____ _____ _____ _____ me.

C 그림 상황에 맞도록 주어진 말을 이용하여 문장을 완성하시오.

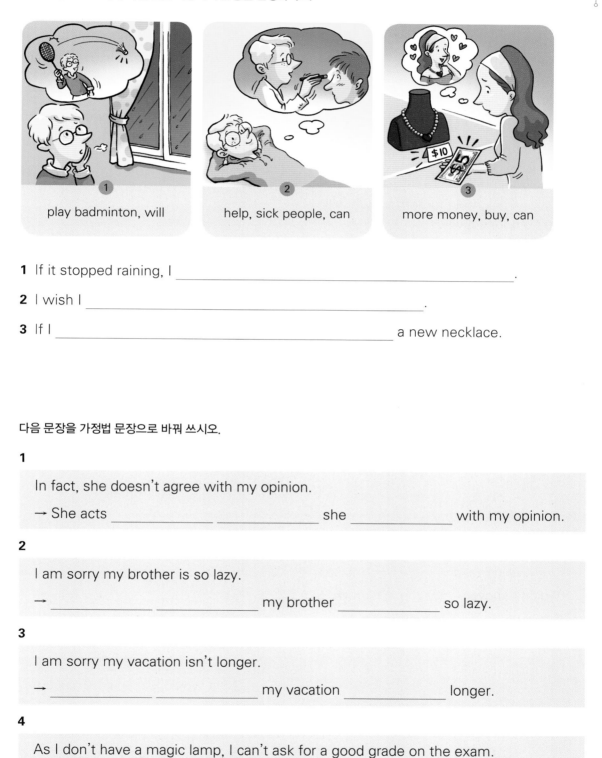

play badminton, will

help, sick people, can

more money, buy, can

1 If it stopped raining, I _____.

2 I wish I _____.

3 If I _____ a new necklace.

D 다음 문장을 가정법 문장으로 바꿔 쓰시오.

1

In fact, she doesn't agree with my opinion.

→ She acts _____ _____ she _____ with my opinion.

2

I am sorry my brother is so lazy.

→ _____ _____ my brother _____ so lazy.

3

I am sorry my vacation isn't longer.

→ _____ _____ my vacation _____ longer.

4

As I don't have a magic lamp, I can't ask for a good grade on the exam.

→ If I _____ a magic lamp, I _____ _____ for a good grade on the exam.

(1–5) 빈칸에 들어갈 알맞은 말을 고르시오.

1

If she _____ every morning, she would be healthier.

① will jog   ② doesn't jog

③ jogged   ④ jogs

⑤ didn't jog

2

If it _____ cold tomorrow, we will do outdoor activities.

① isn't   ② weren't

③ wasn't   ④ aren't

⑤ will not be

3

If I didn't have homework, I _____ shopping.

① did go   ② can go

③ went   ④ could go

⑤ go

4

She doesn't know the secret. But she talks as if she _____ it.

① didn't know   ② doesn't know

③ knows   ④ will know

⑤ knew

5

I'm sorry you don't give me any help. I wish you _____ me some help.

① don't give   ② didn't give

③ had given   ④ gave

⑤ give

(6–7) 다음 대화를 완성할 때 적절한 것은?

6

A: I want to buy this camera.

B: You have one already. If I were you, I _____ it.

① would buy   ② would not buy

③ will not buy   ④ didn't buy

⑤ don't buy

7

A: If you _____ a lot of money, what would you do?

B: I would travel to Europe.

① had   ② will have

③ have   ④ had had

⑤ would have

8 밑줄 친 부분이 어법상 어색한 것은?

① I wish I <u>were</u> as tall as you.

② He <u>would</u> join us if he has time.

③ If my friends were with me, I <u>wouldn't</u> be nervous.

④ If it <u>rained</u>, I couldn't take a walk.

⑤ She walks as if she <u>were wearing</u> a tight skirt.

9 밑줄 친 부분이 바르게 쓰인 것은?

① I wish I have an umbrella now.

② Don't talk as if you are a baby.

③ I won't buy that if I were you.

④ I wish my sister will be nice to me.

⑤ How would you feel if you lost the game?

(12–13) 빈칸에 들어갈 말이 차례대로 짝지어진 것은?

12
I can't find your house because it is dark.
→ I _____ your house if it _____ dark.

① found - wouldn't be

② could find - wouldn't be

③ found - weren't

④ could find - weren't

⑤ couldn't find - weren't

(10–11) 우리말을 영어로 가장 바르게 옮긴 것은?

10
그녀는 마치 박스가 가벼운 것처럼 옮긴다.

① She carries the box as if it will be light.

② She carries the box as if it were light.

③ She carries the box as if it is light.

④ She carries the box as if it had been light.

⑤ She carries the box like it was light.

13
· If I had a garden, I _____ many flowers.

· I wish I _____ the phone numbers of the idol group members.

① would plant - knew

② planted - knew

③ planted - would know

④ would plant - will know

⑤ would plant - know

11
내 친구가 바쁘지 않으면 좋을 텐데.

① I wish my friend isn't busy.

② I wished my friend weren't busy.

③ I wish my friend will not be busy.

④ I wish my friend weren't busy.

⑤ I wish my friend was not busy.

14 밑줄 친 if의 쓰임이 나머지와 다른 것은?

① If the hat were cheaper, I would buy it.

② What would you say if you were me?

③ I will help you if you need my help.

④ If I knew it, I would let you know.

⑤ She could win the game if she weren't sick.

(15–16) 두 문장에 공통으로 들어갈 말을 빈칸에 쓰시오.

15　· She acts as if she _____ sick now.
　　· I wish I _____ wise like my dad.

⇨ _____

16　· I am so busy, so I wish I _____
　　two more hours in a day.
　　· I would pick you up if I _____ a
　　car.

⇨ _____

(17–18) 우리말과 의미가 같도록 ( ) 안의 말을 배열하시오.

17　고양이가 말을 할 수 있다면 우리에게 무슨 말을 할까?
　　(they, speak, if, could)

⇨ What would cats say to us _____
_____ ?

18　그녀는 원어민인 것처럼 영어를 유창하게 말한다.
　　(a native speaker, as, she, if, were)

⇨ She speaks English fluently _____
_____ .

(19–20) 주어진 문장을 가정법으로 바꾸시오.

19　As I am not dressed up, I can't enter
　　to see the concert.

⇨ If I _____ ,
I _____ to see the
concert.

20　In fact, the children are not police
　　officers.

⇨ The children act _____
_____ police officers.

21　주어진 문장과 같은 뜻의 문장은?

We would be happy if the teacher
didn't move to another school.

① As we aren't happy, the teacher
　doesn't move to another school.

② As the teacher moves to another
　school, we aren't happy.

③ As the teacher doesn't move to
　another school, we aren't happy.

④ As the teacher moved to another
　school, we weren't happy.

⑤ We were happy, because the teacher
　didn't move to another school.

22 어법상 <u>어색한</u> 것으로 짝지어진 것은?

> ⓐ If it snowed a lot, we can go skiing.
> ⓑ I wish I could find a quiet place.
> ⓒ If it is not hot, I would play tennis.
> ⓓ They treat her as if she were a star.
> ⓔ I wish I have a driver's license.

① ⓐ, ⓑ   ② ⓑ, ⓒ
③ ⓐ, ⓒ, ⓔ   ④ ⓒ, ⓓ
⑤ ⓓ, ⓔ

(23–25) 주어진 단어를 알맞게 고쳐 빈칸을 채우시오.

23 She doesn't have a cell phone now. If she _____ a cell phone, she would call him. (have)

24 I don't live near the beach. I wish I _____ near the beach. (live)

25 Today is not Sunday. But, I feel as if today _____ Sunday. (be)

26 우리말과 의미가 같도록 ( ) 안의 말을 이용하여 문장을 완성하시오.

> 내가 귀여운 강아지를 갖고 있다면 좋을 텐데. (have)

⇨ I _____ a cute puppy.

27 내가 너라면 '빅 세일'을 기다릴 텐데. (be, wait for)

⇨ If I _____ you, I _____ _____ the big sale.

(28–29) 틀린 것이 있으면 고치고 이유를 설명하시오.

28 The kid is talking to the doll as if the doll is a human.

고치기: _____ ⇨ _____
이유: 현재 (사실, 사실의 반대)처럼 일 때
　　　 as if + S + (현재, 과거)동사

29 What will you do first if you were stuck in an elevator?

고치기: _____ ⇨ _____
이유: 실현 가능성 (있는, 없는) 가정법은
　　　 [If + S + 과거동사, S + (will, would) + 동사원형]

30 다음 조건을 이용하여 알맞게 영작하시오.

> 내게 Emily 같은 언니가 한 명 있으면 좋을 텐데.
> 조건 1: wish, older sister
> 조건 2: 9단어

⇨ _____

한눈에 정리하는 Grammar Mapping

빈칸에 알맞은 답을 보기에서 골라 넣어 grammar mapping 완성하기

가정법

| 쓰임 | 실제 사실과 ① _____ 상황 또는 실현 불가능한 일을 가정 |

가정법 과거

| 형태 | [If + 주어 + ② _____] + [주어 + ③ _____ + 동사원형]
(be동사 → were) |
| 의미 | 만약 ~한다면, ~할 텐데
If I were a bird, I could fly to you. |

단순 조건절

| 형태 | [If + 주어 + ④ _____] + [주어 + 조동사 현재 + 동사원형] |
| 의미 | 만약 ~하면, ~할 거다
If you work hard, you will succeed. |

I wish

| 형태 | I wish + [주어 + 과거동사] |
| 의미 | (사실의 반대 상황이면) ⑤ _____
I wish I knew the answer. |

as if

| 형태 | 주어 + 현재동사 + [as if 주어 + 과거동사] |
| 의미 | (사실의 반대 상황) ⑥ _____
He talks as if he were my brother. |

보기
- 반대되는
- 과거동사
- 마치 ~인 것처럼
- 현재동사
- 좋을 텐데
- 조동사 과거

A 3-level grammar embodiment project:
visualizing grammar and writing practice

Level **2**

Grammar
ViSTA
workbook

DARAKWON

Grammar ViSTA
workbook

Level 2

A 3-level grammar embodiment project: visualizing grammar and writing practice

DARAKWON

목차

Chapter 01 문장의 형태   004

- 문법패턴 빈칸 채우기   004
- Unit 01 동사 + 보어   008
- Unit 02 수여동사 + 간접목적어 + 직접목적어   010
  수여동사 + 직접목적어 + 전치사 + 간접목적어
- Unit 03 동사 + 목적어 + 목적격보어   012
- Unit 04 사역·지각동사 + 목적어 + 목적격보어   014
- Error Correction   016
- Sentence Writing   017

Chapter 02 시제   018

- 문법패턴 빈칸 채우기   018
- Unit 05 현재완료·과거와 현재완료   020
- Unit 06 현재완료 용법   022
- Error Correction   024
- Sentence Writing   025

Chapter 03 조동사   026

- 문법패턴 빈칸 채우기   026
- Unit 07 can, may, will   029
- Unit 08 must, have to, should   031
- Unit 09 had better, used to, would like to   033
- Error Correction   035
- Sentence Writing   036

Chapter 04 수동태   037

- 문법패턴 빈칸 채우기   037
- Unit 10 능동태와 수동태   040
- Unit 11 수동태의 시제와 여러 형태   042
- Unit 12 동사구 수동태·by 이외의 전치사를 쓰는 수동태   044
- Error Correction   046
- Sentence Writing   047

Chapter 05 to부정사   048

- 문법패턴 빈칸 채우기   048
- Unit 13 to부정사의 명사적 쓰임   052
- Unit 14 to부정사의 형용사적 쓰임   054
- Unit 15 to부정사의 부사적 쓰임   056
- Unit 16 to부정사의 의미상 주어·to부정사를 이용한 구문   058
- Error Correction   060
- Sentence Writing   061

Chapter 06 동명사   062

- 문법패턴 빈칸 채우기   062
- Unit 17 동명사의 명사적·관용적 쓰임   064
- Unit 18 동명사와 to부정사   066
- Error Correction   068
- Sentence Writing   069

Chapter 07 분사 070

- 문법패턴 빈칸 채우기 070
- Unit 19 현재분사와 과거분사·분사의 형용사적 쓰임 073
- Unit 20 감정을 나타내는 분사·현재분사와 동명사 075
- Unit 21 분사구문 077
- Error Correction 079
- Sentence Writing 080

Chapter 08 대명사 081

- 문법패턴 빈칸 채우기 081
- Unit 22 재귀대명사 084
- Unit 23 부정대명사 one, another, other(s) 086
- Unit 24 부정대명사 all, both, each, every 088
- Error Correction 090
- Sentence Writing 091

Chapter 09 비교표현 092

- 문법패턴 빈칸 채우기 092
- Unit 25 원급, 비교급, 최상급 094
- Unit 26 원급, 비교급, 최상급을 이용한 표현 096
- Error Correction 098
- Sentence Writing 099

Chapter 10 접속사 100

- 문법패턴 빈칸 채우기 100
- Unit 27 시간 접속사·이유 접속사 103
- Unit 28 조건 접속사·양보 접속사·명령문 and / or 105
- Unit 29 접속사 that·상관접속사 107
- Error Correction 109
- Sentence Writing 110

Chapter 11 관계사 111

- 문법패턴 빈칸 채우기 111
- Unit 30 관계대명사의 역할과 종류 115
  주격과 목적격 관계대명사
- Unit 31 소유격 관계대명사·관계대명사 that 117
- Unit 32 관계대명사 생략·관계대명사 what 119
- Unit 33 관계부사 when, where, why, how 121
- Error Correction 123
- Sentence Writing 124

Chapter 12 가정법 125

- 문법패턴 빈칸 채우기 125
- Unit 34 가정법 과거와 단순 조건문 127
- Unit 35 I wish와 as if 가정법 과거 129
- Error Correction 131
- Sentence Writing 132

도전! 필수구문 156 133

GP 01 동사 + 보어

*본 교재 GP 참조

[주어 + 동사 + 보어]로 이루어진 문장을 2형식 문장이라고 한다. 2형식은 동사 다음에 주어를 설명해 주는 주격보어를 필요로 한다.

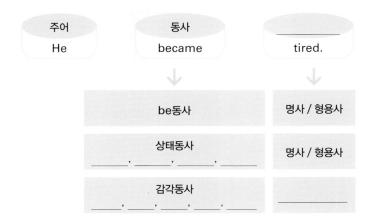

❶ be동사

The cat's eyes **are** *blue*.

My grandfather **was** *a photographer*.

❷ 상태동사

☆ He **became** *a sports hero*.

The weather **is getting** *cold*.

❸ 감각동사

☆ Your bag **looks** *fashionable*.

The movie **sounds** *very interesting*.

> ○ Tip ○
>
> ① 1형식 문장
> [주어 + 동사 + (수식어)]
> · Andy went to school.
>
> ② 3형식 문장
> [주어 + 동사 + 목적어]
> · I like spicy soup.

• Upgrade 1 •

감각동사의 의미

look	feel	smell	sound	taste

• Upgrade 2 •

감각동사 + _____
· It **looks** *exciting*.
· It **smells** *sweet*.

감각동사 + like + _____
· It **looks** _____ *a clock*.
· It **smells** _____ *fish* but **tastes** _____ *chicken*.

GP 02 수여동사 + 간접목적어 + 직접목적어

[주어 + 수여동사 + 간접목적어 + 직접목적어]로 이루어진 문장을 4형식 문장이라고 하고 '~에게 ~을 해 주다'라고 해석한다.

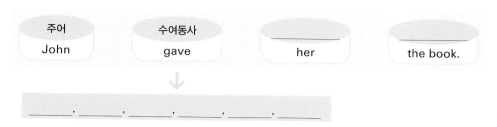

주어	수여동사		
John	gave	her	the book.

_____, _____, _____, _____, _____, _____

I **gave** *my brother* a game coupon.
He **showed** *me* his sister's picture.
The man **made** *his son* a toy car.

GP 03 수여동사 + 직접목적어 + 전치사 + 간접목적어

4형식 문장은 전치사 to, for, of를 이용하여 같은 의미의 3형식 문장으로 바꿔 쓸 수 있다.

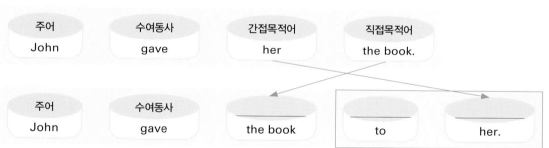

주어	수여동사	간접목적어	직접목적어
John	gave	her	the book.

주어	수여동사			
John	gave	the book	to	her.

❶ _____를 이용한 문장 전환: give, send, tell, _____, _____, _____ …
Mr. Brown **taught** *us* math. (4형식)
→ ☆ Mr. Brown **taught** math _____ *us*. (3형식)

❷ _____를 이용한 문장 전환:
make, buy, _____, _____, _____ …
Mary **bought** *her kids* some cookies. (4형식)
→ ☆ Mary **bought** some cookies _____ *her kids*. (3형식)

❸ _____를 이용한 문장 전환: ask…
☆ He **asked** *his doctor* two questions. (4형식)
→ He **asked** two questions _____ *his doctor*. (3형식)

◦ **Tip** ◦

수여동사의 의미

	3형식 동사	4형식 동사
tell		
teach		
write		
bring		
make		
buy		
cook		
find		
get		

[주어 + 동사 + 목적어 + 목적격보어]로 이루어진 문장을 5형식 문장이라고 한다. 5형식은 동작의 대상이 되는 목적어와 그 목적어를 설명하는 목적격보어를 필요로 한다.

주어	동사	____	____
Tom	made	his son	brave.

make, _____, _____, elect	_____
_____, _____, find, leave	_____
_____, _____, _____, advise, allow	_____

❶ 목적격보어로 _____ 를 쓰는 동사: _____, call, name, _____ …

People **called** him *a hero*. (그를 영웅이라고)

They **named** their daughter *Ann*.

☆ We **elected** him *chairman of our club*.

❷ 목적격보어로 _____ 를 쓰는 동사: make, keep, _____, _____ …

Tom **made** me *happy*. (나를 행복하게)

☆ We must **keep** our room *clean*.

I **found** the sofa very *comfortable*.

❸ 목적격보어로 _____ 를 쓰는 동사: want, tell, ask, expect, _____, _____ …

☆ I **want** him *to exercise every day*. (그가 매일 운동하기를)

She **asked** me *to buy her dinner*. (나에게 저녁을 사달라고)

He **allowed** his daughter *to watch TV*. (그의 딸이 TV 보는 것을)

• Upgrade •

4형식 문장 vs. 5형식 문장

_____ 문장	He **made** his son *a chair*. (his son ≠ a chair)	그의 아들에게 의자를
_____ 문장	He **made** his son *a doctor*. (his son = a doctor)	그의 아들을 의사로

5형식 문장의 동사가 사역동사와 지각동사일 때는 목적격보어로 동사원형을 쓴다. 다만 지각동사는 [동사원형 + -ing]를 쓸 수도 있다.

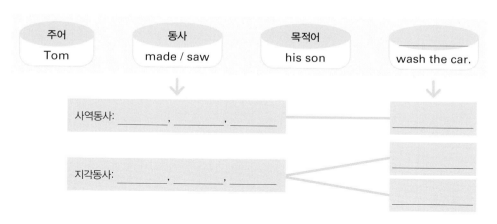

주어	동사	목적어	
Tom	made / saw	his son	wash the car.

사역동사: _____ , _____ , _____

지각동사: _____ , _____ , _____

❶ **사역동사**: _____ , _____ , _____ ...

✯ She **made** him *clean the bedroom*.

✯ I **had** my brother *do his homework*.

✯ My mom didn't **let** me *watch horror movies*.

❷ **지각동사**: see, _____ , hear, _____ , feel, _____ ...

✯ I **saw** her *draw (drawing) a picture*.

✯ We **heard** a parrot *say (saying) hello*.

   She **felt** something *crawl (crawling) on her back*.

○ **Tip** ○

사역동사는 '~하게 하다, 시키다'의 의미로 남이 어떤 동작을 하게끔 하는 동사이다.
지각동사는 사람의 감각 기관을 통해 보고, 듣고, 느끼는 것을 나타내는 동사이다.

• Upgrade •

❶ **get**

get은 5형식 문장에서 '_____ '의 의미로 쓰이고 목적격보어로 _____ 를 취한다.

He **got** us *to bring our own towels*.

(= He **had** us _____ *our own towels*.)

❷ **help**

help가 5형식 문장에서 '~하는 것을 돕다'의 의미로 쓰이고 목적격보어로 _____ 나 _____ 모두 취할 수 있다.

The teacher **helped** me *to choose a career*.

The teacher **helped** me _____ *a career*.

A　( ) 안에서 알맞은 것을 고르시오.

1 The waitress was very (friend, friendly).

2 The pie on the table tastes (sweet, sweetly).

3 I think this rose smells (bad, badly).

4 Does this computer work (good, well)?

5 My father's hair began to turn (gray, grayness).

6 I usually feel (sleep, sleepy) after lunch.

7 Paul remained (silent, silently) during the conversation.

B　보기의 단어를 이용하여 빈칸을 채우시오.

보기 |　　feel　　　　get　　　　look　　　　smell　　　　walk

1 I think the eggs _____ rotten now.

2 Do these boots _____ good on me?

3 It _____ hotter and hotter these days.

4 I _____ bored, so I surfed the Internet.

5 We _____ happily on the beach last week.

C　보기에서 알맞은 단어를 골라 대화를 완성하시오.

보기 |　　nice　　　　tired　　　　terrible　　　　a singer

1 A: How was your trip last week?

　　B: Unfortunately, it was _____ .

2 A: Do I look like a movie star?

　　B: Let me see. You look like _____ .

3 A: Tony, the chicken soup is ready.

　　B: Wow, it smells _____ . I can't wait!

4 A: What happened to you?

　　B: I stayed up all night, so I feel _____ .

D 우리말과 의미가 같도록 ( ) 안의 말을 배열하시오.

1 그 버스 기사님은 늘 활기차 보이신다. (energetic, looks, always)

→ The bus driver _____ .

2 축구 팬 한 명이 운동장을 가로질러 뛰었다. (ran, the, across, field)

→ A soccer fan _____ .

3 눈보라가 친 후에 도로가 매우 미끄러워졌다. (slippery, became, roads, the)

→ After the snowstorm, _____ .

4 엄마가 고기를 조리대 위에 두었는데 그것이 곧 상해버렸다. (bad, it, went)

→ Mom left meat on the counter, and _____ quickly.

5 나는 내 공책에 스티커를 붙였다. (a, my, on, put, sticker, notebook)

→ I _____ .

6 이 스프는 몹시 쓴맛이 나. 스프에 무엇을 넣었니? (bitter, this, very, tastes, soup)

→ _____ . What did you put in it?

E 우리말과 의미가 같도록 ( ) 안의 말을 이용하여 문장을 완성하시오.

1 이 빵과 치즈에서 이상한 냄새가 났다. (strange)

→ This bread and cheese _____ _____ .

2 그 레모네이드는 신맛이 나지 않았다. (sour)

→ The lemonade _____ _____ _____ .

3 너의 아빠와 엄마는 선생님처럼 보였어. (teachers)

→ Your mom and dad _____ _____ _____ .

4 그의 얼굴은 그 뉴스에 창백하게 변했어. (pale)

→ _____ _____ _____ at the news.

5 할머니의 옛날이야기는 항상 무섭게 들려. (scary)

→ Grandma's old story _____ _____ .

6 그녀는 그 음악을 듣고 우울하게 느꼈어. (gloomy)

→ _____ _____ _____ after listening to the music.

A ( ) 안에서 알맞은 것을 고르시오.

1 Lucy teaches math (to, for, of) her sister.

2 A friend of mine gave his USB (to, for, of) me.

3 The clown made a balloon dog (to, for, of) the kid.

4 Mary promised to cook pasta (to, for, of) me.

5 The reporter asked some questions (to, for, of) the singer.

6 She brought a piece of cake (to, for, of) me this morning.

7 He sent troops (to, for, of) Vietnam.

B 보기와 같이 밑줄 친 부분의 해석과 문장의 형식을 고르시오.

*직목: 직접목적어, 간목: 간접목적어

		직목　　간목	형식
보기	He gave <u>the runner</u> a bottle of water.	(~을·를, <u>~에게</u>)	(3형식, <u>4형식</u>)
	He gave <u>a bottle of water</u> to the runner.	(<u>~을·를</u>, ~에게)	(<u>3형식</u>, 4형식)
1	He bought <u>some socks</u> for me.	(~을·를, ~에게)	(3형식, 4형식)
2	Will she lend <u>me</u> her earphones?	(~을·를, ~에게)	(3형식, 4형식)
3	The coach gave <u>us</u> time to rest.	(~을·를, ~에게)	(3형식, 4형식)
4	I asked a <u>favor</u> of my homeroom teacher.	(~을·를, ~에게)	(3형식, 4형식)
5	I found <u>her</u> a seat in the theater.	(~을·를, ~에게)	(3형식, 4형식)
6	Ray cooked <u>ramen</u> for his parents.	(~을·를, ~에게)	(3형식, 4형식)

C 두 문장이 같은 의미를 갖도록 빈칸을 채우시오.

1 Pass the chilli sauce to me.

→ Pass _____ _____ _____ _____.

2 Andy bought his friend a baseball glove.

→ Andy bought _____ _____ _____ _____.

3 She brought me a lunchbox.

→ She brought _____ _____ _____ _____.

4 I made my brother lemonade.

→ I made _____ _____ _____ _____.

D 우리말과 의미가 같도록 ( ) 안의 말을 배열하시오.

1 그 위성은 지구로 화성의 사진을 보냈다. (pictures of Mars, sent, the Earth, to)

→ The satellite _____ .

2 그 선생님은 학생들에게 색종이를 건네주었다. (colored, handed, her pupils, paper)

→ The teacher _____ .

3 Emily는 나에게 몇 가지 개인적인 질문을 했다. (me, some, asked, private questions)

→ Emily _____ .

4 그 피아니스트에게 힘찬 박수를 보냅시다. (the, give, pianist, a big hand)

→ Let's _____ .

5 한 부자가 가난한 사람들을 위해 집을 지어 줬다. (houses, people, for, built, poor)

→ A rich man _____ .

6 우리는 보안 요원에게 우리의 신분증을 보여 줘야 한다. (our, show, ID cards, the guard)

→ We must _____ .

E 우리말과 의미가 같도록 ( ) 안의 말을 이용하여 문장을 완성하시오.

1 나는 그에게 내 전자사전을 주었다. (electronic dictionary)

→ I _____ _____ _____ _____ _____ .

2 Oliver는 나에게 사과 편지를 써 주었어. (a letter of apology)

→ Oliver _____ _____ _____ _____ _____ .

3 Paul은 그의 동생에게 운전하는 법을 가르쳐 주었다. (how to drive)

→ Paul _____ _____ _____ _____ _____ .

4 나는 그 환자들에게 노란색 튤립을 보내고 싶어요. (tulips, the patients)

→ I want to _____ _____ _____ _____ _____ .

5 그는 그의 아이들에게 로봇 장난감을 사 주었다. (robot toys, his children)

→ He _____ _____ _____ _____ _____ .

6 그 이웃사람이 우리에게 잃어버린 강아지를 찾아 줬다. (our lost puppy)

→ The neighbor _____ _____ _____ _____ _____ .

A ( ) 안에서 알맞은 것을 고르시오.

1 I found her advice (helpful, helpfully).

2 She told him (water, to water) the plant.

3 My brother always calls (me, my) Tinker Bell.

4 He expected the guests (bring, to bring) their own food.

5 We elected (him, his) president of our school.

6 The owner ordered his dog (sit, to sit) down.

7 They asked us (take off, to take off) our shoes in the temple.

8 The difficult times made people (strong, strongly).

B 보기와 같이 목적어와 목적격보어 관계인 밑줄 친 부분을 해석하시오.

	주어 + 동사	목적어 + 목적격보어	
보기 ǀ We want people to save water.	우리는 원해	사람들이 물을 아끼기를	
1 The police told him to stop.	경찰이 말했어	_____ 에게	_____ 라고
2 He asked us to stand up.	그는 부탁했어	_____ 에게	_____ 달라고
3 She allowed me to drink a coke.	그녀는 허락했어	_____ 가	_____ 는 것을
4 Ava advised me to eat vegetables.	Ava는 충고했어	_____ 에게	_____ 라고

C 보기의 표현 중 알맞은 것을 골라 문장을 완성하시오.

보기	· fantastic	· warm for me	· to eat less salt
	· to play in the sand	· a walking dictionary	

1 Please keep this pizza _____ .

2 The doctor advised him _____ .

3 We called the smart girl _____ .

4 She allowed the kids _____ .

5 South Asians found Korean dramas _____ .

D 우리말과 의미가 같도록 ( ) 안의 말을 배열하시오.

1 우리는 그 소문이 거짓임을 알았다. (the, false, rumor, found)

→ We _____ .

2 내가 완벽할 것이라고 기대하지는 마. (to, me, expect, perfect, be)

→ Don't _____ .

3 그는 그의 강아지에게 Superpower라고 이름 지었다. (his, dog, named, Superpower)

→ He _____ .

4 늑대는 아기 돼지들에게 문을 열라고 말했다. (to, told, open, the door, the baby pigs)

→ The wolf _____ .

5 언니는 내가 온라인으로 옷을 사기를 원한다. (to, online, me, buy, wants, clothes)

→ My sister _____ .

6 구술시험은 학생들을 계속 긴장시킬 것이다. (make, the students, nervous)

→ The oral exam will _____ .

E 우리말과 의미가 같도록 ( ) 안의 말을 이용하여 문장을 완성하시오.

1 그들은 Tom을 책벌레라고 불렀다. (call, a bookworm)

→ They _____ _____ _____ _____ .

2 달콤한 사탕은 사람들을 덜 피곤하게 만든다. (make, less tired)

→ Sweet candies _____ _____ _____ _____ .

3 그녀는 경찰에게 그녀를 도와달라고 요청했다. (ask, the police)

→ She _____ _____ _____ _____ .

4 아이들은 그 상자가 비었다는 것을 알았다. (find, empty)

→ The kids _____ _____ _____ .

5 엄마는 아빠가 컴퓨터를 끄기를 원하셨다. (want, the computer)

→ Mom _____ _____ _____ _____ .

6 여동생은 내가 그녀의 베개를 사용하는 것을 허락하지 않았다. (allow, her pillow)

→ My sister _____ _____ _____ _____ .

A ( ) 안에서 알맞은 것을 고르시오.

1 The hot bath made me (feel, to feel) relaxed.

2 I helped my brother (wash, washed) the dog.

3 She didn't watch the pot (to boil, boil).

4 I heard someone (to knock, knocking) on the door.

5 I am very busy now. Please let me (go, to go).

6 The lady had her kid (pick, to pick) up his trash.

7 Mr. Robin asked the police (helping, to help) him.

B ( ) 안의 단어를 이용하여 빈칸을 채우시오.

1 We saw some balloons _____ in the air. (fly)

2 The comedian made everyone _____. (smile)

3 She expects them _____ on time. (be)

4 Jessica helped him _____ the driving test. (pass)

5 I watched them _____ a mobile game. (play)

6 My mom let me _____ to the pajama party. (go)

7 The teacher had me _____ after school. (stay)

C 보기의 표현 중 알맞은 것을 골라 문장을 완성하시오.

보기	· cry (crying) in the street	· shaking a bit
	· run around the house	· burning in the yard
	· to clean up after the party	· read an English newspaper

1 She let the dog _____.

2 The tourist felt the tower _____.

3 Mr. Donner had us _____.

4 I heard a cat _____.

5 Did you smell something _____?

6 He got the children _____.

D 우리말과 의미가 같도록 ( ) 안의 말을 배열하시오.

1 내가 점심값을 지불해도 될까요? (me, for, pay, let, lunch)

→ Will you ＿＿＿＿＿＿＿＿＿＿＿＿＿＿＿＿＿＿＿＿＿＿＿＿＿＿＿＿ ?

2 우리는 기차가 역을 떠나는 것을 보았다. (the train, the station, leaving, watched)

→ We ＿＿＿＿＿＿＿＿＿＿＿＿＿＿＿＿＿＿＿＿＿＿＿＿ .

3 많은 비로 인해 사람들은 집에 머물렀다. (at, stay, home, made, people)

→ The heavy rain ＿＿＿＿＿＿＿＿＿＿＿＿＿＿＿＿＿＿＿＿＿＿ .

4 소녀들은 밴드가 재즈 음악 연주하는 것을 들었다. (play, jazz, heard, music, the band)

→ The girls ＿＿＿＿＿＿＿＿＿＿＿＿＿＿＿＿＿＿＿＿ .

5 한 소년이 그녀가 짐 옮기는 것을 도와주었다. (to, her, her, carry, helped, luggage)

→ A boy ＿＿＿＿＿＿＿＿＿＿＿＿＿＿＿＿＿＿＿ .

6 엄마는 나에게 빨래를 널라고 했다. (me, the, out, had, hang, laundry)

→ My mom ＿＿＿＿＿＿＿＿＿＿＿＿＿＿＿＿＿＿ .

E 우리말과 의미가 같도록 ( ) 안의 말을 이용하여 문장을 완성하시오.

1 나는 누군가 내 어깨를 만지는 것을 느꼈다. (feel, touch)

→ I ＿＿＿＿＿＿＿＿ ＿＿＿＿＿＿＿＿ ＿＿＿＿＿＿＿ my shoulder.

2 너는 낯선 사람이 문에 서 있는 것을 보았니? (see, a stranger)

→ Did you ＿＿＿＿＿＿＿ ＿＿＿＿＿＿＿ ＿＿＿＿＿＿＿ at the door?

3 Darcy는 우리가 그의 이야기를 믿게 했어. (have, believe)

→ Darcy ＿＿＿＿＿＿＿ ＿＿＿＿＿＿＿ ＿＿＿＿＿＿＿ ＿＿＿＿＿＿＿ .

4 나는 내 형이 잠꼬대 하는 것을 들었다. (hear, talk)

→ I ＿＿＿＿＿＿＿ ＿＿＿＿＿＿＿ ＿＿＿＿＿＿＿ in his sleep.

5 우리 반장은 우리에게 쓰레기를 밖에 내놓으라고 했다. (get, take out)

→ Our class president ＿＿＿＿＿ ＿＿＿＿＿ ＿＿＿＿＿ ＿＿＿＿＿ the garbage.

6 아빠는 내 친구가 이번 주말에 나와 함께 있는 것을 허락할 것이다. (let, stay)

→ Dad will ＿＿＿＿＿＿＿ ＿＿＿＿＿＿＿ ＿＿＿＿＿＿＿ with me this weekend.

Error Correction

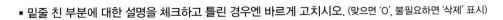

▪ 밑줄 친 부분에 대한 설명을 체크하고 틀린 경우엔 바르게 고치시오. (맞으면 'O', 불필요하면 '삭제' 표시)

*직목: 직접목적어, 간목: 간접목적어

1	He became <u>like</u> a sports hero. (→)	상태동사 become + 주격보어 (like + 명사, 명사)
2	Your bag <u>looks fashionable</u>. (→)	감각동사 look + (형용사, 부사) 감각동사 look like + (형용사, 명사)
3	Mr. Brown taught math <u>for us</u>. (→)	가르치다 (~를 ~에게, ~에게 ~를) teach + (직목 + to + 간목, 직목 + for + 간목)
4	Mary bought some cookies <u>of</u> her kids. (→)	사주다 (~를 ~에게, ~에게 ~를) buy + (직목 + for + 간목, 직목 + of + 간목)
5	He asked <u>his doctor two questions</u>. (→)	묻다 (~를 ~에게, ~에게 ~를) ask + (간목 + 직목, 직목 + 간목)
6	We elected <u>his</u> chairman of our club. (→)	elect + 목적어 + 목적격보어 (목적격, 소유격)
7	We must keep our room <u>cleanly</u>. (→)	keep + 목적어 + 목적격보어 (형용사, 부사)
8	I want him <u>to exercise</u> every day. (→)	want + 목적어 + 목적격보어 (to + 동사원형, 동사원형)
9	She made him <u>cleaning</u> the bedroom. (→)	make + 목적어 + 목적격보어 (동사원형 + -ing, 동사원형)
10	I had my brother <u>do</u> his homework. (→)	have + 목적어 + 목적격보어 (to + 동사원형, 동사원형)
11	My mom didn't let me <u>to watch</u> horror movies. (→)	let + 목적어 + 목적격보어 (to + 동사원형, 동사원형)
12	I saw her <u>to draw</u> a picture. (→)	see + 목적어 + 목적격보어 (to + 동사원형, 동사원형)
13	We heard a parrot <u>saying</u> hello. (→)	hear + 목적어 + 목적격보어 (to + 동사원형, 동사원형 + -ing)

Sentence writing

▪ 주어진 단어를 알맞게 이용하여 우리말과 의미가 같도록 영작하시오.

1	become, sports	그는 / 되었다 / 스포츠 영웅이 →
2	look, fashionable	너의 가방은 / ~해 보인다 / 유행하는 →
3	teach, math	Brown 씨가 / 가르쳤다 / 수학을 / 우리에게 →
4	buy, cookies	Mary는 / 사주었다 / 약간의 쿠키를 / 그녀의 아이들에게 →
5	ask, questions	그는 / 물었다 / 그의 의사에게 / 두 가지 질문을 →
6	elect, chairman	우리는 / 선출했다 / 그를 / 우리 클럽의 회장으로 →
7	keep, clean	우리는 / 유지해야 한다 / 우리 방을 / 깨끗하게 →
8	want, exercise	나는 / 원한다 / 그가 / 매일 운동하기를 →
9	make, clean	그녀는 / 시켰다 / 그가 / 침실을 청소하도록 →
10	have, do	나는 / 시켰다 / 내 동생이 / 숙제를 하도록 →
11	let, watch	엄마는 / 허락하지 않았다 / 내가 / 공포영화 보는 것을 →
12	see, draw	나는 / 보았다 / 그녀가 / 그림을 그리는 것을 →
13	a parrot, hear	우리는 / 들었다 / 앵무새 한 마리가 / "Hello"라고 말하는 것을 →

문법패턴 빈칸 채우기

GP 06 현재완료

현재완료는 [＿＿＿＿＿＿＿＿ + ＿＿＿＿＿＿＿＿]의 형태로 나타낸다. ＿＿＿＿＿＿＿에 발생한 일이 ＿＿＿＿＿＿＿
까지 영향을 미치거나 현재와 관련성을 가질 때 쓴다.

형태	주어	have / has	과거분사(p.p.)	
부정문	주어	have / has	not	과거분사(p.p.)
의문사				
의문문	have / has	주어	과거분사(p.p.)	~?

I **have read** the novel.

☆ Oliver **has** never **seen** snow in Sydney.

☆ A: **Have** you ever **heard** of moving stones?　　　B: Yes, I have. / ☆ No, I haven't.

　A: How long **has** she **been** asleep?　　　　　　B: For eight hours.

GP 07 과거와 현재완료

과거는 현재와의 관련성 없이 지나간 과거의 상황만을 나타내지만 현재완료는 과거와 관련이 있는 현재의 상황을 나타낸다.

☆ He lost the key.

☆ He has lost the key.

❶ 과거

　　She **lived** in London. (현재는 어디에 살고 있는지 모름)

❷ 현재완료

　　She ＿＿＿＿＿＿＿＿ ＿＿＿＿＿＿＿＿ in London for 12 years.

　　(현재까지 런던에 살고 있음)

　　[She **started to live** in London 12 years ago. + She still **lives** in London now.]

Tip

주로 ＿＿＿＿＿＿＿＿ 와 함께 쓰는 표현
yesterday, last night, then, [~ ago],
[in + 과거 연도], when...

주로 ＿＿＿＿＿＿＿＿ 와 함께 쓰는 표현
just, already, before, twice, since...

현재완료는 의미에 따라 보통 4가지 방법으로 해석한다.

완료	have / has	과거분사(p.p.)	+	_____, _____, _____

☆ My sister has just come back home. (과거에 시작해서 지금 막) ~했다

경험	have / has	과거분사(p.p.)	+	_____, _____, _____, ~ times

☆ Have you ever traveled by ship?　(과거부터 지금까지) ~한 적이 있다

계속	have / has	과거분사(p.p.)	+	_____, _____, how long

☆ He has lived in Paris for two years.　(과거부터 지금까지) 계속 ~해 오고 있다

결과	have / has	과거분사(p.p.)	—	lose, go, leave, close

☆ She has lost interest in music.　(과거에) ~해서 (그 결과로 지금) ~하다

❶ _____

Peter **has** just **arrived** at the station.

The ice in my drink **has** already **melted**.

❷ _____

I **have** never **lived** alone.

☆ She **has watched** the movie ten times.

❸ _____

He **has had** a cold for three days.

☆ You **have grown** a lot since I last saw you.

❹ _____

Lucas **has bought** a USB online.

He **has gone** to America.

• Upgrade •

[have been to] vs. [have gone to]

[have been to + 장소 명사]: _____ (경험)

[have gone to + 장소 명사]: _____ (결과)

☆ She **has been to** London. She is here now.

☆ She **has gone to** London. She isn't here now.

○ **Tip** ○

① [주어 + 완료시제] + [since + _____]
　~해오고 있다　　~시점부터 계속

② [주어 + 완료시제] + [for + 기간]
　~해오고 있다　　~ 동안 계속

A 보기와 같이 영향을 미치는 시점에 밑줄을 긋고 ( ) 안에서 알맞은 것을 고르시오.

> 보기 | I (lost, have lost) my cell phone yesterday.　　　　(과거에만, 현재까지) 영향

1 He (broke, has broken) his glasses last night.　　　　(과거에만, 현재까지) 영향

2 Three years (passed, have passed) since we met.　　　　(과거에만, 현재까지) 영향

3 When (did you go, have you gone) to the festival?　　　　(과거에만, 현재까지) 영향

4 I (didn't meet, have never met) a TV star in my life.　　　　(과거에만, 현재까지) 영향

5 My family (moved, have moved) to Busan in 2009.　　　　(과거에만, 현재까지) 영향

6 (Did, Have) you ever met each other before?　　　　(과거에만, 현재까지) 영향

7 (When, How long) have you known her?　　　　(과거에만, 현재까지) 영향

8 She (has learned, learned) yoga two years ago.　　　　(과거에만, 현재까지) 영향

9 I (read, have read) his book three times so far.　　　　(과거에만, 현재까지) 영향

10 We (got, have gotten) five millimeters of rain yesterday.　　　　(과거에만, 현재까지) 영향

B 주어진 단어를 이용하여 빈칸을 채우시오.

1 A: Mike _____ the vase, and it is still broken. (break)

　　B: Mike has broken the vase.

2 A: Do you know the story of the noble?

　　B: No, I don't. I _____ _____ _____ it. (never, read)

3 A: _____ _____ _____ busy lately? (be)

　　B: Yes, I have. But I won't be busy after this project.

4 A: Do you have any candy?

　　B: Sorry. I don't. I _____ _____ _____ all my candy. (just, eat)

5 A: How long have you known each other?

　　B: For five years. We _____ for the first time five years ago. (meet)

6 A: _____ _____ _____ _____ all day? (where, be)

　　B: I went swimming with my cousin.

7 A: Can I talk to Mr. Chae?

　　B: I am sorry. He is not here. He _____ _____ _____

　　Daegu. (go, to)

C 우리말과 의미가 같도록 ( ) 안의 말을 배열하시오.

1 Ray가 지금 막 나한테 전화했어. (just, called, has, me)

→ Ray _____ .

2 그는 어젯밤에 손을 베었어. (his, cut, last, night, finger)

→ He _____ .

3 그녀는 어젯밤부터 지금까지 잠을 안 잤어. (slept, has, since, not, last, night)

→ She _____ .

4 최근에 어떻게 지내고 있니? (been, how, you, have)

→ _____ lately?

5 우리 오빠가 내 새 재킷을 벌써 입어버렸어. (worn, already, has, new, my, jacket)

→ My brother _____ .

6 아이들은 아직 놀이를 끝내지 않았다. (yet, finished, playing, haven't)

→ The children _____ .

7 나는 두 달 전에 그 케이블카를 탔어. (that cable car, ago, rode, two months)

→ I _____ .

D 우리말과 의미가 같도록 ( ) 안의 말을 이용하여 문장을 완성하시오.

1 나는 그 아이돌 그룹이 데뷔한 이래로 그들을 좋아해 왔지. (love, idol)

→ I _____ _____ _____ _____ since their debut.

2 그는 작년에 인공지능에 관한 TV 프로그램을 만들었어. (make)

→ He _____ _____ _____ _____ about AI last year.

3 나는 아직 그 영화를 보지 못했다. (watch, film)

→ I _____ _____ _____ _____ yet.

4 우리는 막 그 그룹 프로젝트를 끝냈다. (project, just, finish)

→ We _____ _____ _____ _____ .

5 백년전쟁은 1337년부터 1453년까지 116년 동안 지속되었어. (last)

→ The Hundred Years' War _____ _____ _____ _____ from 1337 to 1453.

6 그는 2004년 올림픽에서 두 개의 금메달을 땄어. (win, medals)

→ He _____ _____ _____ _____ at the 2004 Olympics.

A 주어진 단어를 이용하여 빈칸을 채우시오.

1 Brian _____ just _____ from his middle school. (graduate)

2 _____ you ever _____ the sunrise before? (see)

3 The apple tree _____ _____ _____ _____ this year. (grow a lot)

4 Mary _____ _____ at the mall three times this month. (shop)

5 We _____ _____ Dokdo once. (visit)

6 The patient _____ _____ in the hospital since last week. (be)

7 Jacob _____ never _____ his country. (leave)

8 How many times _____ she _____ you today? (call)

B 두 문장이 같은 의미를 갖도록 빈칸을 채우시오.

1 I began to study English two years ago, and I still study it.

→ I _____ _____ English _____ two years.

2 My sister was sick yesterday, and she is sick now.

→ My sister _____ _____ _____ since yesterday.

3 Katherine went to Mexico, and she is not here now.

→ Katherine _____ _____ _____ Mexico.

4 They began to sell the concert tickets. They don't have the tickets any more.

→ They _____ _____ all the concert tickets.

5 The astronaut went to the moon. He is now on the Earth.

→ The astronaut _____ _____ _____ the moon.

C 보기에서 알맞은 단어를 골라 현재완료로 고쳐 문장을 완성하시오.

보기 |　　collect　　　　work　　　　see　　　　teach　　　　play

1 I _____ _____ coupons since March.

2 The kids _____ never _____ together before.

3 I _____ never _____ such a beautiful lake.

4 How long _____ he _____ math?

5 She _____ _____ at the company for 10 years.

D 우리말과 의미가 같도록 ( ) 안의 말을 배열하시오.

1 이 엘리베이터는 이번 달에 지금까지 두 번 고장 났어. (broken, has, times, two)

→ The elevator _____ this month.

2 그 소년들이 두 시간째 퍼즐 놀이를 해 왔어. (worked on, the puzzle, have, for, two)

→ They _____ hours.

3 그는 지금 길을 잃었어. (his, has, lost, way)

→ He _____.

4 너 오늘 벌써 초콜릿바를 다섯 개 먹었어. (already, eaten, chocolate bars, five, have)

→ You _____ today.

5 지난주부터 더 추워지고 있어. (become, since, last, has, week, colder)

→ It _____.

6 뉴욕에 가 본 적 있으세요? (you, been, ever, to, have)

→ _____ New York?

7 그 발명가는 지금까지 437개의 품목을 발명해 왔어. (invented, 437 items, has, so far)

→ The inventor _____.

E 우리말과 의미가 같도록 ( ) 안의 말을 이용하여 문장을 완성하시오.

1 이 단어를 들어 본 적 있니? 한국어야? (hear, ever)

→ _____ _____ _____ _____ ?

Is it a Korean word?

2 나는 그 책을 세 번 읽었다. (three times)

→ I _____ _____ _____ _____.

3 우리는 12년 동안 서로 알고 지내 왔다. (know, each other, for)

→ We _____ _____ _____ _____.

4 Jane은 지난 10월 이래로 스페인어를 공부해 왔어. (Spanish, October)

→ Jane _____ _____ _____ _____.

5 이 리조트에 머문 지 얼마나 오래 되었나요? (how long, stay)

→ _____ _____ _____ at this resort?

6 Lisa는 캐나다로 돌아가버렸어. 그녀가 보고 싶어. (go back, Canada)

→ Lisa _____ _____ _____. I miss her a lot.

Error Correction

■ 밑줄 친 부분에 대한 설명을 체크하고 틀린 경우엔 바르게 고치시오. (맞으면 'O' 표시)

*p.p.: 과거분사

1 Oliver <u>never has seen</u> snow in Sydney.
   (→ 　　　　　　　　　　　　)

현재완료 부정문 어순은
(never + has + p.p., has + never + p.p.)

2 <u>Have you</u> ever heard of moving stones?
   (→ 　　　　　　　　　　　　)

현재완료 의문문 어순은
(Did + 주어 + have, Have + 주어) + p.p. ~?

3 No, I <u>have</u>.
   (→ 　　　　　　　　　　　　)

현재완료 질문에 대한 현재완료 부정의 대답은
No, I + (have, haven't).

4 He <u>has lost</u> the key two days ago.
   (→ 　　　　　　　　　　　　)

ago는 (과거, 과거부터 현재까지) 부사로
(과거, 현재완료)시제와 함께 쓰임

5 He <u>has lost</u> the key. (He can't find it anywhere.)
   (→ 　　　　　　　　　　　　)

(과거, 현재완료)시제

6 My sister has just <u>came</u> back home.
   (→ 　　　　　　　　　　　　)

(온 적이 있다, 방금 막 왔다)
(has + just + p.p., just + 과거동사)

7 Have you ever <u>travel</u> by ship?
   (→ 　　　　　　　　　　　　)

현재완료 의문문은
Have + you + (동사원형, p.p.) ~?

8 He has lived in Paris <u>since</u> two years.
   (→ 　　　　　　　　　　　　)

(~ 동안 계속, ~부터 계속) 의미
(since, for) + (기간, 시점)

9 She <u>have</u> lost interest in music.
   (→ 　　　　　　　　　　　　)

(잃어버렸다, 잃어버리고 지금 없다)
3인칭 단수 주어 + (have, has) + p.p.

10 She has <u>watch</u> the movie ten times.
   (→ 　　　　　　　　　　　　)

(본 적 있다, 방금 막 봤다)
주어 + (have + p.p., have + 동사원형)

11 You <u>grew</u> a lot since I last saw you.
   (→ 　　　　　　　　　　　　)

어떤 시점부터 계속 (해 왔다, 했다)
주어 + (과거, 완료)시제 + since 과거시점

12 She <u>has been</u> to London. (She is here now.)
   (→ 　　　　　　　　　　　　)

(~에 가 본 적 있다, ~으로 가버렸다)
have + (gone, been) + to 장소

13 She <u>has gone</u> to London. (She isn't here now.)
   (→ 　　　　　　　　　　　　)

(~에 가 본 적 있다, ~으로 가버렸다)
have + (gone, been) + to 장소

Sentence writing

▪ 주어진 단어를 알맞게 이용하여 우리말과 의미가 같도록 영작하시오.

1	never, Sydney	Oliver는 / 본 적이 없다 / 눈을 / 시드니에서 →
2	hear of, moving stones	너는 / 들어 본 적 있니 / 움직이는 돌들에 대해? →
3	have	아니, / 나는 / 한 적이 없다 (현재완료 질문에 대한 대답) →
4	lose, ago	그는 / 잃어버렸다 / 그 열쇠를 / 이틀 전에 →
5	lose	그는 / 잃어버렸다 / 그 열쇠를 (그래서 지금은 없다.) →
6	come back	나의 언니가 / 이제 막 돌아왔다 / 집에 →
7	ever, by ship	너는 / 여행해 본 적 있니 / 배를 타고? →
8	have, Paris	그는 / 살아 왔다 / 파리에서 / (과거부터 현재까지) 2년 동안 →
9	lose interest	그녀는 / 잃어버렸다 / 관심을 / 음악에 대한 (그래서 지금도 없다.) →
10	watch, ten times	그녀는 / 봐 왔다 / 그 영화를 / 열 번 →
11	grow, a lot, last	너는 / 많이 자랐구나 / 내가 마지막으로 / 너를 본 이후로 →
12	be, London	그녀는 / 가 본 적이 있다 / 런던에 →
13	go, London	그녀는 / 가버렸다 / 런던으로 (그래서 지금 여기 없다.) →

문법패턴 빈칸 채우기 ✏

GP 09 can, may, will

❶ can / could

can		
능력, 가능	_____	✷ She can read people's minds. = She is able to read people's minds.
허락	_____	You can take a break.
요청, 부탁	_____	Can (Could) you deliver the pizza here?

could		
can의 과거	~할 수 있었다	I could not answer your call yesterday.
요청, 부탁	~해 주시겠어요?	Could (Can) you deliver the pizza here?

• Upgrade •

can(~할 수 있다)의 과거와 미래 표현

❶ 과거: could, _____   He was able to find the answer.

❷ 미래: _____   ✷ He will be able to find the answer.

❷ may / might

may		
허락	_____	You may use my eraser. May (Can) I see your student ID card?
불확실한 추측	_____	✷ The bird may look ugly, but it is very clever.

might		
may의 과거	~해도 된다	She said her son might eat some ice cream.
불확실한 추측	~일지도 모른다	The bird might look ugly, but it is very clever.

❸ will / would

will		
예정	_____	We will be 17 years old next year. = We are going to be 17 years old next year.
의지	_____	✷ I will keep my promise.
요청, 부탁	_____	Will you wait a minute, please?

would		
will의 과거	~일 것이다	He thought she would buy shoes for him.
요청, 부탁	~해 주시겠어요?	Would you wait a minute, please?

❶ must

	must	
의무		You must write your name on the report.
강한 추측		☆ The rumor must be false.

	must not	
금지		☆ You must not tell the secret to anyone else.

We **must** slow down at the crosswalk. (= have to)

She didn't have breakfast. She **must** be hungry now.

You **must not** wake the baby.

❷ have to

	have to	
의무		He has to read the book before class.

	don't have to	
불필요		We don't have to climb the stairs.

She **has to** feed her dog. (= must)

Robert **had to** take out the garbage.

☆ You **will have to** hurry.

☆ She **doesn't have to** get up early on Sundays.

○ Tip ○

[must not] vs. [don't have to]

① must not: _____

　You must not go there.

② don't have to: _____

　You don't have to go there.

❸ should

	should	
충고, 조언 (긍정)		You should get a haircut.

	should not ~해서는 안 된다	
충고, 조언 (부정)		We should not use bad words.

The model is too skinny. She **should** eat more.

You **shouldn't** play the guitar at this hour.

❶ had better

	had better	
강한 충고 (긍정)	_____	☆ You had better turn off your cell phone.
강한 충고 (부정)	～하지 않는 게 낫겠다	☆ Jack had better not eat junk food.

We **had better** wait and see.

You **had better not** waste your time.

❷ used to

	used to	
과거의 습관	_____	☆ My brother used to collect rocks.
과거의 상태	_____	☆ The president used to be an actor.
과거의 습관	didn't use to ～하지 않곤 했다	He didn't use to cook at home.

(1) **과거의 습관**: ～하곤 했다 (= _____)

We **used to** play hide-and-seek together.

We **would** play hide-and-seek together.

She **didn't use to** like living here.

> **○ Tip ○**
> 조동사 would는 과거의 습관을 나타내어 _____ 를 대신할 수 있으나 _____ 에는 사용하지 않는다.

(2) **과거의 상태**: ～이었다

There **used to** be a bridge over there.

There ~~would~~ be a bridge over there. (X)

❸ would like to

	would like to	
소망	_____	☆ I would like to travel to Europe.

Would you like to leave a message?

A ( ) 안에서 알맞은 것을 고르시오.

1 He could (caught, catch) the first train.

2 (Will, May) you open the window, please?

3 I knew it (will, would) snow that afternoon.

4 She (doesn't may, may not) be interested in you.

5 (Can, Might) I ask your phone number?

6 (Does he can, Can he) speak Chinese?

7 The president will (makes, make) a speech tomorrow.

B 밑줄 친 부분의 의미를 보기에서 골라 해당 번호를 쓰시오. (중복 사용 가능)

보기 ┃ ① 의지, 미래 ② 허락 ③ 약한 추측 ④ 요청, 부탁	의미
1 I won't break our promise.	
2 You may remember me.	
3 Could you feed my cat this afternoon?	
4 You may leave the table if you are full.	
5 We will repair the broken door.	

C 두 문장이 같아지도록 보기에서 알맞은 단어를 골라 빈칸을 채우시오. (한 번씩만 사용)

보기 ┃   may   can   will   would   may not

1 Are you able to lift this heavy box?

→ _____ you lift this heavy box?

2 You can stay at Jane's house this Saturday.

→ You _____ stay at Jane's house this Saturday.

3 Are you going to paint the roof of your house alone?

→ _____ you paint the roof of your house alone?

4 It is possible that Tom won't come to school today.

→ Tom _____ come to school today.

5 Could you show me your ticket, sir?

→ _____ you show me your ticket, sir?

D 우리말과 의미가 같도록 ( ) 안의 말을 배열하시오.

1 이 자전거는 Austin 것일지도 몰라. (belong, may, to, Austin, this bike)

→ _____ .

2 너는 얼마나 오래 숨을 참을 수 있니? (hold, can, your breath, you)

→ How long _____ ?

3 내가 이 샌들을 신어 봐도 될까요? (these sandals, try, can, on, I)

→ _____ ?

4 Jane이 오디션에 합격할 것이라고 생각했어. (would, Jane, pass, the audition)

→ I thought that _____ .

5 내 콘서트에 네 친구를 데리고 와도 좋아. (take, may, your friends, my concert, to)

→ You _____ .

6 올해는 장미를 심을 건가요? (going, plant, are, to, you, roses)

→ _____ this year?

E 우리말과 의미가 같도록 ( ) 안의 말을 이용하여 문장을 완성하시오.

1 아마도 그는 답을 모르는 것일지도 몰라. (know, may)

→ He _____ _____ _____ _____ _____ .

2 줄을 서 주시겠습니까? (stand in line, would)

→ _____ _____ _____ _____ _____ ?

3 그는 강을 헤엄쳐서 건너갈 수 있었다. (able)

→ _____ _____ _____ _____ across the river.

4 신사 숙녀 여러분, 집중해 주시겠습니까? (may, have, attention)

→ Ladies and gentlemen, _____ _____ _____ _____

_____ , please?

5 우리 아빠는 베트남 음식을 잘 할 수 있으셔. (Vietnamese dishes, cook)

→ My dad _____ _____ _____ _____ _____ .

6 내가 성공하기 전까지 오래 걸리지는 않을 거야. (take, will)

→ It _____ _____ _____ _____ before I succeed.

A ( ) 안에서 알맞은 것을 고르시오.

1 He will (must, have to) cancel his trip to Japan tomorrow.

2 You (should, have to) not look down on the poor.

3 Your mom (must is, must be) good at cooking.

4 Did you (have to, had to) wait long?

5 Zoo animals don't (must, have to) fight over food.

6 He sat on his glasses by mistake. They (should, must) be broken.

7 Should I (save, saved) money for the future?

8 Brian (has to, have to) look after his sister.

B 밑줄 친 부분의 의미를 보기에서 골라 번호를 쓰고, 해석을 쓰시오.

보기 |	① 강한 추측	② 금지	③ 의무	④ 불필요	의미	해석
1 We don't <u>have to</u> run.					___	___
2 People <u>should help</u> each other.					___	___
3 I <u>didn't have to explain</u> again.					___	___
4 He <u>must be</u> your dad. He has your eyes.					___	___
5 You <u>must not waste</u> water.					___	___

C 두 문장이 같아지도록 보기에서 알맞은 말을 골라 빈칸을 채우시오. (한 번씩만 사용)

보기 |	must	should not	have to	don't have to

1 How long must I stay here?

→ How long do I _____ stay here?

2 I am sure that he is a pilot.

→ He _____ be a pilot.

3 You must not bring food from the outside into the theater.

→ You _____ bring food from the outside into the theater.

4 It is not necessary to wear a raincoat.

→ You _____ wear a raincoat.

D 우리말과 의미가 같도록 ( ) 안의 말을 배열하시오.

1 우리는 스쿨존에서 운전을 빠르게 하면 안 돼. (should, drive, we, not, fast)

→ _____ in the school zone.

2 그 빵집은 인기가 많은 것이 분명해. (the, must, popular, be, bakery)

→ _____.

3 나는 에어컨을 켤 필요가 없었어. 날씨가 선선했거든. (turn, I, have, didn't, to, on)

→ _____ the air conditioner. It was cool.

4 그녀는 꿀벌에 관한 보고서를 써야만 하나요? (write, does, she, have, a report, to)

→ _____ on honeybees?

5 너는 캠프에서 다른 사람들과 방을 같이 써야 할 거야. (share, have to, will, room, a)

→ You _____ with others at the camp.

6 여러분은 45분 내로 시험을 끝마쳐야 합니다. (finish, must, in, you, the, test)

→ _____ 45 minutes.

E 우리말과 의미가 같도록 ( ) 안의 말을 이용하여 문장을 완성하시오.

1 그 새는 새장 안에서 분명히 외로울 거야. (must, lonely, cage)

→ The bird _____ _____ _____ _____ _____ .

2 너는 너의 보스에게 사실을 말씀드려야 해. (should, the truth, to)

→ You _____ _____ _____ _____ _____ _____ .

3 우리는 은행에 자주 갈 필요가 없어. (have)

→ We _____ _____ _____ _____ to the bank often.

4 그는 초콜릿 케이크를 만들기 위해 초콜릿을 녹여야만 했다. (have to, melt)

→ He _____ _____ _____ _____ to make a chocolate cake.

5 아이들은 식당에서 뛰어다니면 안 돼. (should, run around)

→ Kids _____ _____ _____ _____ in restaurants.

6 일본에서는 운전자들이 도로의 왼쪽에서 운전해야 해? (must, drive)

→ _____ _____ _____ on the left side of the road in Japan?

A ( ) 안에서 알맞은 것을 고르시오.

1 You (have, had) better not run on the escalator.

2 We would like (join, to join) you on your camping trip.

3 She (uses, used) to have a rabbit as a pet.

4 I (had not better, had better not) wear this cap.

5 What would you like (to wearing, to wear) to the party?

6 There used to (being, be) a big hill in the middle of town.

B 밑줄 친 부분을 어법상 알맞게 고쳐 쓰시오.

1 You had better <u>to follow</u> her advice.   (→   )

2 There <u>would be</u> many tigers in Korea.   (→   )

3 When <u>would you like visiting</u> me?   (→   )

4 Jane <u>uses to</u> live in Italy.   (→   )

5 We <u>don't had better</u> take pictures here.   (→   )

6 I used to <u>eating</u> street food every day, but now I don't.   (→   )

C 두 문장이 같아지도록 보기의 말을 이용하여 문장을 완성하시오. (한 번씩만 사용)

> 보기 | would like to   had better   had better not   used to

1 I think you should walk from here.

→ You _____ from here.

2 I want to meet the writer in person.

→ I _____ the writer in person.

3 She was a doctor. Now she has become a singer.

→ She _____ a doctor.

4 You should not believe his story.

→ You _____ his story.

D 보기에서 알맞은 말을 골라 대화를 완성하시오. (한 번씩만 사용)

보기 | would like to   had better   had better not   used to

1 A: I am gaining too much weight these days.

B: Oh, you _____ eat snacks between meals.

2 A: Was this town busy ten years ago?

B: No, this town _____ be very quiet at that time.

3 A: What can I do for you, sir?

B: I _____ leave a message for Dr. Smith.

4 A: Should I wear the yellow shirt or this pink one?

B: You _____ choose the pink one. It will go well with your pants.

E 우리말과 의미가 같도록 ( ) 안의 말을 배열하시오.

1 Darcy는 이전에 곱슬머리를 가졌었어. (have, used, curly, to, hair)

→ Darcy _____.

2 우리는 예전에는 아침을 거하게 먹곤 했었지. (heavy meals, breakfast, for, would, eat)

→ We _____.

3 놀이공원에서 무엇을 가장 먼저 타고 싶으세요? (ride, would, like, you, what, to, first)

→ _____ at the amusement park?

4 우리 집에 네 애완동물을 데리고 오지 않는 것이 낫겠어. (bring, not, had, better)

→ You _____ your pet to my house.

F 우리말과 의미가 같도록 ( ) 안의 말을 이용하여 문장을 완성하시오

1 길모퉁이에 오래된 서점이 하나 있었지. (bookstore)

→ There _____ _____ _____ _____ _____ around the corner.

2 너는 그 강아지를 혼자 두는 것이 낫겠다. (leave, alone)

→ You _____ _____ _____ _____ _____ _____.

3 차를 조금 더 드시겠어요? (to, more tea)

→ _____ _____ _____ _____ _____ _____ ?

4 아빠하고 나하고 일요일마다 도서관에 가곤 했었지. (the library)

→ Dad and I _____ _____ _____ _____ _____ every Sunday.

Error Correction

▪ 밑줄 친 부분에 대한 설명을 체크하고 틀린 경우엔 바르게 고치시오. (맞으면 'O' 표시)

1	She can <u>reads</u> people's minds. (→)	조동사 + (동사원형, 현재동사)
2	He will <u>can</u> find the answer. (→)	[조동사 + 조동사]는 (가능, 불가능)하므로 can은 (be going to, be able to)로 대체
3	The bird <u>will</u> look ugly, but it is very clever. (→)	'~일지도 모른다'처럼 (의지, 약한 추측)을·를 의미하면, 조동사 (will, may) 사용
4	I <u>may</u> keep my promise. (→)	'~하겠다'처럼 (의지, 약한 추측)을·를 의미하면, 조동사 (will, may) 사용
5	The rumor <u>must false</u>. (→)	조동사 + (형용사, be + 형용사)
6	You <u>don't must</u> tell the secret to anyone else. (→)	조동사의 부정형은 (don't + 조동사, 조동사 + not)
7	You will <u>must</u> hurry. (→)	[조동사 + 조동사]는 (가능, 불가능)하므로 must는 (have to, should)로 대체
8	She <u>has not to</u> get up early on Sundays. (→)	(~하면 안 돼, ~할 필요 없다)는 (have not to, don't have to)
9	You <u>have</u> better turn off your cell phone. (→)	'~하는 게 낫다'처럼 (충고, 허락)을·를 의미하면, (have, had) better + 동사원형
10	Jack <u>had not better</u> eat junk food. (→)	had better의 부정형은 (had better not, had not better)
11	My brother used to <u>collect</u> rocks. (→)	과거의 (상태, 습관)을·를 의미하면, used to + (과거동사, 동사원형)
12	The president <u>would</u> be an actor. (→)	과거의 (상태, 습관)을·를 의미하면, (would, used to) + 동사원형
13	I <u>would like travel</u> to Europe. (→)	'~하고 싶다'를 의미하면, would like + (동사원형, to + 동사원형)

Sentence writing

■ 주어진 단어를 알맞게 이용하여 우리말과 의미가 같도록 영작하시오.

1	read, minds	그녀는 / ~할 수 있다 / 사람들의 마음을 읽다 →
2	able, find	그는 / ~할 수 있을 거다 / 답을 찾다 →
3	look, ugly	그 새는 / ~일지도 모른다 / 추하게 보이다 / 그러나 매우 영리하다 →
4	keep	나는 / ~하겠다 / 내 약속을 지키다 →
5	rumor, must	그 소문은 / 틀림없이 ~일 거다 / 거짓인 →
6	must, anyone else	너는 / ~해서는 안 된다 / 그 비밀을 말하다 / 다른 사람들에게 →
7	hurry	너는 / ~해야만 할 거다 / 서두르다 →
8	have to, get up	그녀는 / ~할 필요가 없다 / 일찍 일어나다 / 일요일에 →
9	turn off	여러분은 / ~하는 게 낫다 / 여러분의 휴대폰을 끄다 →
10	eat, junk food	Jack은 / ~하지 않는 게 낫다 / 정크푸드를 먹다 →
11	used, collect	우리 오빠는 / (예전에) ~하곤 했다 / 돌을 수집하다 →
12	used, be	그 대통령은 / (예전에) ~이었다 / 배우이다 →
13	would like	나는 / ~하고 싶다 / 유럽으로 여행하다 →

문법패턴 빈칸 채우기

GP 12 능동태와 수동태

능동태는 주어가 동작을 직접 행하는 것으로 '(주어가) _____'란 의미이다. 수동태는 주어가 동작의 영향을 받거나 당하는 형태로 '(주어가) _____'란 의미이다.

주어	동사	목적어
He	made	a chair.

❸   ❷   ❶

주어			by 행위자
A chair	was	made	by him.

수동태를 만드는 방법

❶ 능동태의 _____를 수동태의 _____로 쓴다.

❷ 능동태의 동사를 _____ 형태로 바꾼다.

❸ 능동태의 주어를 _____ 형태로 바꾼다.

He **broke** the window. (능동태)

→ The window _____ him. (수동태)

A lot of girls **love** the singer. (능동태)

→ ☆ The singer _____ a lot of girls. (수동태)

• Upgrade •

수동태로 쓸 수 없는 동사

❶ 목적어를 갖지 않는 자동사

_____(도착하다), _____(오르다), _____(발생하다), appear(나타나다), look(~해 보이다)...

We arrived at the airport in time.

→ The airport ~~was arrived by~~ us in time. (×)

❷ 상태나 소유를 나타내는 타동사

_____(가지다), meet(만나다), _____(닮다), belong to(속하다)...

We have a nice garden.

→ A nice garden ~~is had by~~ us. (×)

수동태의 시제는 be동사의 현재·과거·미래·진행시제 형태로 나타낸다.

현재시제	_____	과거분사	The soup is cooked by him.
과거시제	_____	과거분사	The soup was cooked by him.
미래시제	_____	과거분사	The soup will be cooked by him.
진행시제	_____	과거분사	The soup is being cooked by him.

The Olympic Games _____ **held** every four years.　(~되다)

☆ All her fans _____ **invited** by the actress.　(~되었다)

☆ This program _____ **used** by college students.　(~될 것이다)

☆ My car _____ **washed** by Sam.　(~되는 중이다)

☆ Dinner _____ **prepared** in the kitchen by my dad.　(~되는 중이었다)

부정문		주어	be동사	_____	과거분사	The ring was not found.
의문문	_____ _____				과거분사 ~?	Was the ring found?
	_____ _____ _____				과거분사 ~?	When was the ring found?
조동사		주어	조동사	_____	과거분사	The ring must be found.

❶ 부정문

He didn't write the book.

→ ☆ The book _____ by him.

❷ 의문문

Did Fred design the building?

→ ☆ **Was** the building **designed** by Fred?

When did King Sejong create Hangeul?

→ ☆ _____ _____ Hangeul _____ by King Sejong?

> ∘ **Tip** ∘
>
> 의문사가 주어인 문장의 수동태
> [By whom + be동사 + 주어 + 과거분사 ~?]
> · Who wrote the book?
> → _____ was the book written?

❸ 조동사 수동태

☆ The rules **should** _____ followed by people.

두 개 이상의 단어로 이루어진 동사구는 하나의 단어 개념으로 생각하고 수동태로 바꾼다.

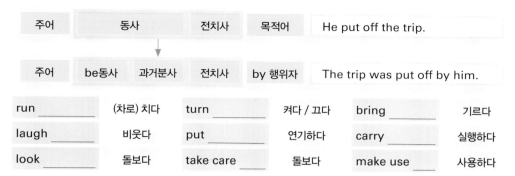

| 주어 | 동사 | 전치사 | 목적어 | He put off the trip. |

| 주어 | be동사 | 과거분사 | 전치사 | by 행위자 | The trip was put off by him. |

run _____	(차로) 치다	turn _____	켜다 / 끄다	bring _____	기르다
laugh _____	비웃다	put _____	연기하다	carry _____	실행하다
look _____	돌보다	take care _____	돌보다	make use _____	사용하다

He **turned on** the music app.

→ ☆ The music app **was turned on** by him.

The mother eagle **took care of** the egg.

→ ☆ The egg _____ by the mother eagle.

수동태에서 행위자를 나타내는 전치사 by 대신 다른 전치사가 쓰일 수도 있다.

| 주어 | be동사 | 과거분사 | by | Cheese is made by him. |
| | | | 기타 전치사 | Cheese is made from milk. |

be interested _____	~에 관심이 있다	be worried _____	~에 걱정하다
be covered with	~로 덮여 있다	be filled _____	~로 가득 차 있다
be satisfied _____	~에 만족하다	be pleased _____	~에 기뻐하다
be surprised _____	~에 놀라다	be made _____	~로 만들어지다
be known _____	~에게 알려져 있다	be known _____	~로 유명하다

Chris **is interested** _____ space research.

☆ We **are satisfied** _____ the English class.

☆ K-pop **is known** _____ many teenagers in Asia.

• Upgrade •

[by + 행위자]의 _____ : 행위자가 일반인이거나 불분명하고 중요하지 않을 때는 _____ 한다.

The dollar is used all over the world (by people).

My laptop computer was stolen (by someone).

A ( ) 안에서 알맞은 것을 고르시오.

1 Diamonds (cut, are cut) by lasers.

2 No one (hurt, was hurt) in the accident.

3 The car crash (happened, was happened) last night.

4 A pepperoni pizza (ordered, was ordered) by my teacher.

5 The robot (carried, was carried) the box to the door.

6 Zombies (appeared, was appeared) in my dream last night.

7 Strawberries (grow, are grown) by Ryan's family every summer.

B 주어진 동사를 이용하여 문장을 완성하고 주어와 동사의 의미 관계를 고르시오.

		주어와 동사의 의미 관계
1 The love letter _____ in 1872.	write	주어가 (썼다, 쓰여졌다)
2 Baseball _____ six times a week.	play	주어가 (경기하다, 경기되다)
3 The farmer _____ the fence green.	paint	주어가 (칠했다, 칠이 되었다)
4 I _____ a little birdhouse.	make	주어가 (만들었다, 만들어졌다)
5 The Colosseum _____ in 70 A.D.	build	주어가 (지었다, 지어졌다)
6 My father _____ in Pohang.	bring up	주어가 (키웠다, 키워졌다)

C 두 문장의 의미가 같도록 문장을 완성하시오.

1 The team celebrates a victory every year.

→ _____ by the team every year.

2 Peter invited us to his birthday party.

→ _____ to his birthday party by Peter.

3 My aunt laid the baby in the stroller.

→ _____ in the stroller by my aunt.

4 Many people around the world love Korean culture.

→ _____ by many people around the world.

5 The mail carrier delivers a package every morning.

→ _____ by the mail carrier every morning.

D 우리말과 의미가 같도록 ( ) 안의 말을 배열하시오.

1 에티켓은 집에서 가르쳐진다. (is, in the home, etiquette, taught)

→ _____.

2 이 거대한 성은 노예에 의해 지어졌다. (by, was, this, built, great, slaves, castle)

→ _____.

3 Jimmie는 오토바이 사고로 부상당했다. (a, in, was, injured, accident, motorcycle)

→ Jimmie _____.

4 Teens 잡지는 십대들에 의해 발행된다. (is, by, magazine, published, teenagers)

→ *Teens* _____.

5 그 나무는 일요일마다 아빠에 의해 손질된다. (by, the, dad, are, trees, trimmed, my)

→ _____ on Sundays.

6 부케가 신부에 의해 공중으로 던져졌다. (in, the, the, was, air, tossed, bouquet)

→ _____ by the bride.

E 우리말과 의미가 같도록 ( ) 안의 말을 이용하여 문장을 완성하시오.

1 모든 사람은 평등하게 태어난다. (bear)

→ All people _____ _____ equal.

2 코카콜라는 전 세계에서 광고된다. (advertise)

→ Coca-Cola _____ _____ all over the world.

3 수백만 개의 이메일이 매일 보내진다. (send)

→ Millions of e-mails _____ _____ every day.

4 그 쥐는 복잡한 미로에 놓여졌다. (rat, place)

→ _____ _____ _____ in a complex maze.

5 이 사진은 전혀 포토샵 되지 않았어. (Photoshop)

→ _____ _____ _____ not _____ at all.

6 뜨거운 커피는 큰 머그잔에 제공되었다. (serve)

→ _____ _____ _____ in large mugs.

A ( ) 안에서 알맞은 것을 고르시오.

1 (Did, Was) breakfast served at the hotel?

2 Tree branches (are cutting, are being cut) now.

3 (Whom, By whom) was the memo written?

4 (Does, Is) the machine move the heavy boxes?

5 The milk and the flour (do not be mixed, were not mixed) well.

6 The old lady will (help, be helped) by the volunteers.

7 Salt should (be not added, not be added) to the soup.

B 다음 문장이 수동태가 되도록 빈칸에 알맞은 말을 쓰시오.

1 Did she buy these black jeans?

→ _____ these black jeans _____ by her?

2 He was changing the light bulbs.

→ The light bulbs _____ _____ _____ by him.

3 Can we solve the math problem?

→ _____ the math problem _____ _____ by us?

4 Who saw the accident?

→ _____ _____ the accident _____ ?

5 The boy is reading a science book.

→ A science book _____ _____ _____ by the boy.

C 다음 문장이 능동태가 되도록 빈칸에 알맞은 말을 쓰시오.

1 Was the cup dropped by Bill? → _____ Bill _____ the cup?

2 The pudding was not made by Alice.

→ Alice _____ _____ _____ the pudding.

3 The puzzle could be solved by the boy.

→ The boy _____ _____ the puzzle.

4 By whom was the cart pulled? → Who _____ the cart?

5 The test papers are being collected by Jasmine.

→ Jasmine _____ _____ the test papers.

D 우리말과 의미가 같도록 ( ) 안의 말을 배열하시오.

1 다음 올림픽은 어디에서 개최되니? (be, will, held, where, the next Olympics)

→ _____ ?

2 스카프의 얼룩을 제거할 수 없었다. (be, not, could, removed)

→ The stain on the scarf _____ .

3 그 소포가 언제 배송되었니? (the package, when, delivered, was)

→ _____ ?

4 Tony는 다음주에 고용될 예정이다. (is, be, to, next, hired, going, week)

→ Tony _____ .

5 길거리가 비에 의해 씻겨지고 있었어. (rain, were, washed, the, by, being)

→ The streets _____ .

6 이 꽃은 영어로 뭐라고 불려지니? (this flower, what, called, is)

→ _____ in English?

E 우리말과 의미가 같도록 ( ) 안의 말을 이용하여 문장을 완성하시오.

1 편지에 우표가 붙여지지 않았다. (put)

→ A stamp _____ _____ _____ on the letter.

2 누구에 의해 그 에세이는 편집되었니? (edit)

→ _____ _____ _____ the essay _____ ?

3 아이들이 연을 날리고 있었다. (fly)

→ The kites _____ _____ _____ by children.

4 로봇이 그 마루를 청소했니? (clean, the floor)

→ _____ _____ _____ _____ by the robot?

5 많은 돈이 그 프로젝트에 쓰일 것이다. (spend, money)

→ A lot of _____ _____ _____ on the project.

6 그 증인이 지금 질문을 당하는 중이야. (question)

→ The witness _____ _____ _____ .

A   ( ) 안에서 알맞은 것을 고르시오.

1 The roof is covered (on, with) white snow.

2 My grandparents are looked (after, with) by my family.

3 People nowadays are interested (in, of) Arabic.

4 The teacher was surprised (to, at) my answers.

5 The clown is being laughed (to, at) by everybody.

6 To some people, Hungary is known (to, for) its spicy food.

B   주어진 동사를 이용하여 빈칸을 채우시오. (현재시제 사용)

1 tire   We _____ very _____ _____ fast food.

2 fill   The sky _____ _____ _____ dark clouds.

3 worry   People _____ _____ _____ global warming.

4 satisfy   Tiffany _____ _____ _____ her boyfriend's gift.

5 please   They _____ _____ _____ their new apartment.

6 know   Your nickname _____ _____ _____ Internet users.

7 know   Seoul _____ well _____ _____ its traditional palaces.

C   두 문장의 의미가 같도록 문장을 완성하시오.

1 We turned off the heater.

   → The heater _____ by us.

2 The plan was laughed at by scientists.

   → Scientists _____ .

3 He will look for spelling errors in the report.

   → Spelling errors _____ in the report by him.

4 The volume should be turned down by her.

   → She should _____ .

5 The nurse is taking care of his patients.

   → His patients _____ by the nurse.

D 우리말과 의미가 같도록 ( ) 안의 말을 배열하시오.

1 내일 태양의 일부가 달에 의해 가려질 거야. (covered, the moon, be, will, by)

→ A part of the sun _____ tomorrow.

2 내 옷장은 예쁜 분홍색 옷들로 채워져 있다. (is, with, cute, filled, clothes, pink)

→ My closet _____.

3 보트가 파도에 의해 밀려나가는 중이야. (is, the, boat, pushed away, being)

→ _____ by the waves.

4 그녀는 얼굴의 여드름이 걱정이다. (is, the, about, she, pimples, worried)

→ _____ on her face.

5 Ray는 삼촌에 의해 농장에서 길러졌다. (by, up, was, his, uncle, brought)

→ Ray _____ on a farm.

6 하와이는 아름다운 해변들로 잘 알려져 있다. (is, its, for, known, beautiful, beaches)

→ Hawaii _____.

E 우리말과 의미가 같도록 ( ) 안의 말을 이용하여 문장을 완성하시오.

1 나는 그녀의 행동에 실망이다. (disappoint, behavior)

→ I _____ _____ _____ _____ _____.

2 그 가족의 뒷이야기는 사람들에게 알려져 있지 않아. (know)

→ The story behind the family _____ _____ _____ _____.

3 그녀의 딸은 우주탐사에 관심이 많다. (interest, space exploration)

→ Her daughter _____ _____ _____ _____.

4 그 제비는 흥부의 보살핌을 받았다. (take care of, Heungbu)

→ The swallow _____ _____ _____ _____.

5 아빠는 월급 인상에 기뻐하셨다. (please, the pay raise)

→ My father _____ _____ _____ _____.

6 내 사랑니는 이번 주 금요일에 뽑힐 것이다. (pull out, wisdom tooth)

→ _____ _____ _____ _____ _____

_____ this Friday.

Error Correction

■ 밑줄 친 부분에 대한 설명을 체크하고 틀린 경우엔 바르게 고치시오. (맞으면 'O' 표시)

*p.p.: 과거분사

1. The singer <u>loves</u> by a lot of girls.
(→   )

   가수가 (사랑하다, 사랑받다)이므로
   (동사, be동사 + p.p.)

2. All her fans were invited <u>at</u> the actress.
(→   )

   수동태의 행위자는
   (by + 행위자, at + 행위자)

3. This program <u>will is used</u> by college students.
(→   )

   조동사 수동태는
   will + (is + p.p., be + p.p.)

4. My car is <u>be</u> washed by Sam.
(→   )

   현재진행형 수동태는
   am / is / are + (be + p.p., being + p.p.)

5. Dinner <u>was being prepared</u> in the kitchen by my dad. (→   )

   과거진행형 수동태는
   was / were + (be + p.p., being + p.p.)

6. The book <u>not was written</u> by him.
(→   )

   수동태 부정문은
   (be동사 + not, not + be동사) + p.p.

7. Was the building <u>design</u> by Fred?
(→   )

   수동태 의문문은
   (Be동사 + 주어 + p.p., Did + 주어 + 동사원형)~?

8. <u>When Hangeul was created</u> by King Sejong?
(→   )

   의문사가 있는 의문문의 수동태는
   의문사 + (be동사 + 주어, 주어 + be동사) + p.p.

9. The rules should be <u>follow</u> by people.
(→   )

   조동사 수동태는
   should + (is + p.p., be + p.p.)

10. The music app <u>was turned</u> by him.
(→   )

   동사구 turn on(켜다)의 수동태는
   be동사 + (turned, turned on)

11. The egg <u>took care of</u> by the mother eagle.
(→   )

   그 알이 (보살폈다, 보살펴졌다)이므로
   was + (동사원형, p.p.)

12. We are satisfied <u>for</u> the English class.
(→   )

   '~에 만족하다'는
   be동사 + satisfied (for, with)

13. K-pop is known <u>to</u> most teenagers in Asia.
(→   )

   '~에게 알려져 있다'는
   be동사 + known + (to, for, as)

Sentence writing

▪ 주어진 단어를 알맞게 이용하여 우리말과 의미가 같도록 영작하시오.

1　　love, a lot of　　　그 가수는 / 사랑을 받는다 / 많은 소녀들에 의해
　　　　　　　　　　　　→

2　　invite, fans　　　그녀의 모든 팬들은 / 초대되었다 / 그 여배우에 의해
　　　　　　　　　　　　→

3　　use, college students　　이 프로그램은 / 사용될 것이다 / 대학생들에 의해
　　　　　　　　　　　　→

4　　wash, car　　　내 차는 / 세차되고 있다 / Sam에 의해
　　　　　　　　　　　　→

5　　prepare, dinner　　저녁식사가 / 준비되고 있었다 / 부엌에서 / 아빠에 의해
　　　　　　　　　　　　→

6　　write, book　　　그 책은 / 쓰여지지 않았다 / 그에 의해
　　　　　　　　　　　　→

7　　design, building　　그 건물은 / 디자인되었니 / Fred에 의해?
　　　　　　　　　　　　→

8　　create, King Sejong　　언제 / 한글은 / 창제되었니 / 세종대왕에 의해?
　　　　　　　　　　　　→

9　　follow, rules　　　그 규칙들은 / 지켜져야 한다 / 사람들에 의해
　　　　　　　　　　　　→

10　　turn on, music app　　그 음악 앱은 / 켜졌다 / 그에 의해
　　　　　　　　　　　　→

11　　the egg, take care of　　그 알은 / 돌봐졌다 / 엄마 독수리에 의해
　　　　　　　　　　　　→

12　　satisfy, English class　　우리는 / 만족하고 있다 / 그 영어 수업에
　　　　　　　　　　　　→

13　　know, teenagers　　K-pop은 / 알려져 있다 / 대부분의 십대들에게 / 아시아에서
　　　　　　　　　　　　→

문법패턴 빈칸 채우기 ✏

GP 17 to부정사의 명사적 쓰임

'~하는 것'의 의미를 가지며 문장에서 명사처럼 주어, 목적어, 보어 역할을 한다.

주어	동사	목적어 / 보어	
To master English	is	difficult.	
It		is	difficult	to master English.
Andrew	decided	to master English.	
My goal	is	to master English.	

❶ _____ 역할: ~하는 것은

To **invent** a flying car is my dream.

= ☆ It is my dream **to invent** a flying car.

❷ _____ 역할: ~하는 것을

They wanted **to stay** together.

☆ My friends promised **to keep** my secret.

❸ _____ 역할: ~하는 것이다

My plan is **to draw** cartoons.

His job is **to help** the homeless.

> ○ Tip ○
> to부정사 주어가 길면 문장 앞에 가주어
> it을 쓰고 뒤에 진주어 to부정사를 쓴다.

• Upgrade •

to부정사의 부정은 to부정사 앞에 _____ 이나 _____ 를 쓴다.

He promised _____ **to be** late again.

❹ **의문사 + to부정사**: to부정사가 의문사와 같이 쓰여 주어, 목적어, 보어 역할을 한다.

_____		무엇을 ~할지	_____		언제 ~할지
_____	to부정사	누가 (누구를) ~할지	_____	to부정사	어디서 ~할지
_____		어떤 것을 ~할지	_____		어떻게 ~할지

I don't know	what to do next.	의문사 + to부정사 ──────┐
=	what I should do next	의문사 + _____

The child didn't know **how to open** the bottle.

☆ Please don't tell me **when to study**.

Let's talk about _____ for our vacation.

(= **where we should go** for our vacation)

'_____'의 의미를 가지며 _____처럼 명사를 수식한다. 이때 to부정사는 명사 _____에 위치한다.

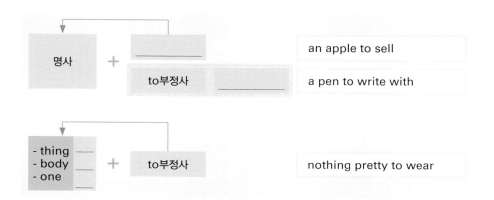

| 명사 | + | _____ | | an apple to sell |
| | | to부정사 | _____ | a pen to write with |

| - thing
- body
- one | + | to부정사 | nothing pretty to wear |

❶ 명사 + [to부정사]

I bought *a book* _____. (← read a book)

I have *a lot of homework* _____. (← do a lot of homework)

❷ 명사 + [to부정사 + 전치사]

I need *a chair* _____. (← sit on a chair)

☆ She bought *a house* _____. (← live in a house)

> **Tip**
>
> [명사 + to부정사 + 전치사]
> 수식하는 명사가 to부정사에
> 이어지는 전치사의 목적어인
> 경우 전치사가 필요하다.
> · paper to write _____
> · a pencil to write _____
> · a friend to play _____
> · something to talk _____

❸ [-thing / -body / -one + 형용사] + [to부정사]

I need *something delicious* to eat.

☆ Do you have *anything cold* to drink?

• Upgrade •

[be동사 + to부정사] 용법

be동사 뒤에 to부정사가 와서 주어의 상태에 대해서 보충 설명하는 형용사 역할을 한다. 이때 to부정사는 예정, 가능, 의무, 운명, 의도 등의 의미를 가진다.

❶ 예정 (_____) The movie **is to start** soon.

❷ 가능 (_____) No stars **were to be seen** in the night sky.

❸ 의무 (_____) You **are to bring** your own food.

❹ 운명 (_____) The soldier **was never to return** again.

❺ 의도 (_____) If you **are to help** me, please be quiet.

'∼하기 위해, ∼해서, ∼하기에, ∼하다니' 등의 의미를 가지며 문장에서 _____ 처럼 동사, 형용사, 문장을 수식한다.

_____	주어 + 동사 ∼		to부정사	He ran to catch the bus.
_____	주어 + 동사	_____	to부정사	I am happy to see you again.
_____	주어 + 동사	형용사	to부정사	The house is easy to build.
_____	주어 + _____ ∼		to부정사	Jane must be kind to help me.
_____	주어 + (무의지) 동사 ∼		to부정사	She lived to be 85 years old.

❶ 목적: _____ (∼하다)

Cathy *got up* early **to go** to school on time.

☆ I *work out* every day **to stay** healthy.

❷ 감정의 원인: _____ (∼한 감정이 들다)

☆ He was *surprised* **to hear** the news.

　Julie felt *scared* **to walk** into the dark woods.

❸ 형용사 수식: _____ (∼한 상태이다)

The dance was *easy* **to learn**.

❹ 판단의 근거: _____ (∼이겠다)

☆ You *must* be popular **to have** so many fans.

❺ 결과: ∼해서, (결국) _____

James *grew up* **to be** a world-famous photographer.

The army fought hard *only* **to lose** the battle.

• Upgrade •

결과를 나타내는 대표적 표현 (무의지 동사)

❶ grow up + to부정사: 자라서 ∼가 되다

❷ live + to부정사: 살아서 ∼가 되다

❸ wake up + to부정사: 깨어나서 ∼하게 되다

> ○ Tip ○
> **감정을 나타내는 형용사**
> happy, glad, sad, pleased, bored, scared, disappointed, surprised, shocked…

to부정사의 행위자를 의미상 주어라고 한다. 의미상 주어는 to부정사 앞에 [_____ + 목적격] 또는
[성품을 나타내는 형용사 + _____ + 목적격]의 형태로 쓴다.

Who solved?

의미상 주어	It	was	easy		to solve the mystery.
_____ 목적격	It	was	easy	_____ him	to solve the mystery.
_____ 목적격	It	was	wise	_____ him	to solve the mystery.

성품형용사
칭찬: _____, _____, _____, polite, brave
비난: _____, _____, _____, rude, cruel

☆ It is hard _____ **me** *to study* all night.
The dog is not easy _____ **you** *to train*.

☆ It was brave _____ **the firefighter** *to save* the boy.
It was nice _____ **her** *to take care* of the lost cat.

---

to부정사를 이용한 구문에는 [형용사 / 부사 + enough + to부정사]와 [too + 형용사 / 부사 + to부정사] 등이 있다.

❶ enough to

| 주어 + 동사 | 형용사 / 부사 | _____ | _____ _____ | | …할 만큼 충분히 ~하다 |
| 주어 + 동사 | _____ | 형용사 / 부사 | _____ _____ _____ _____ | | 매우 ~해서 …할 수 있다 |

☆ He is **strong enough to lift** the wooden box.
→ ☆ He is _____
lift the wooden box.

❷ too ~ to

| 주어 + 동사 | _____ | 형용사 / 부사 | _____ _____ | | …하기엔 너무 ~하다 |
| 주어 + 동사 | _____ | 형용사 / 부사 | _____ _____ _____ _____ | | 너무 ~해서 …할 수 없다 |

☆ Cathy was **too tired to wake up** at six.
→ ☆ Cathy was _____
wake up at six.

A ( ) 안에서 알맞은 것을 고르시오.

1 To (stand, stands) in line is important.

2 (It, This) was fun to play soccer after school.

3 To travel different planets (is, are) my future dream.

4 He learned (which, how) to snowboard from his cousin.

5 We promised (to not, not to) break the rules again.

6 I feel really tired today. I don't want (to move, move) an inch.

7 My dream is to (be, is) a cheerleader.

B 다음 문장을 가주어(It)와, 진주어(to부정사)를 이용하여 바꿔 쓰시오.

1 To download the travel app is necessary.

→ _____ is necessary _____.

2 To understand baby talk is not easy.

→ _____ is not easy _____.

3 To take a break every hour is important.

→ _____ is important _____.

4 To buy the cheaper bike was a good choice.

→ _____ was a good choice _____.

C 보기에서 알맞은 말을 골라 [의문사 + to부정사]로 바꿔 문장을 완성하시오.

보기 | stay   stop   bring   fold

1 소풍갈 때 무엇을 가져가야 하는지 알아?

→ Do you know _____ to the picnic?

2 우리는 미술시간에 개구리 종이접기 방법을 배웠어요.

→ We learned _____ a paper frog in art class.

3 이번 여름휴가 동안 어디에서 잠을 잘지를 결정합시다.

→ Let's decide _____ this summer vacation.

4 그는 언제 말하는 것을 멈춰야 하는지를 몰라.

→ He doesn't know _____ talking.

D 우리말과 의미가 같도록 ( ) 안의 말을 배열하시오.

1 나의 새해 결심은 엄마에게 말대꾸하지 않는 것이야. (to, not, talk back)

→ My new year's resolution is _____ to my mom.

2 좋은 부모는 언제 말할지와 언제 들을지를 알지. (to, when, talk, listen, to, when)

→ A good parent knows _____ and _____.

3 너는 수영을 언제 배운 거니? (learn, swim, to, how)

→ When did you _____?

4 그 퀴즈를 푸는 것은 쉽지 않았다. (easy, the quiz, solve, to, not, was)

→ It _____.

5 나는 저녁에 아이스크림을 먹지 않기로 결심했다. (decided, not, eat, ice cream, to)

→ I _____ in the evening.

6 나는 엄마를 PC방에서 만날 것을 예상하지 않았어. (expect, see, my mom, to)

→ I didn't _____ at the Internet café.

E 우리말과 의미가 같도록 ( ) 안의 말을 이용하여 문장을 완성하시오.

1 내 직업은 교복을 디자인하는 것이다. (design, uniforms)

→ My job is _____ _____ _____ _____.

2 그 군인들은 나라를 지키기 위해 노력했다. (try, protect)

→ The soldiers _____ _____ _____ _____ _____.

3 오후 3시에 네 강아지 산책시키는 것을 잊으면 안 된다. (forget, walk)

→ Don't _____ _____ _____ the puppy at 3 p.m.

4 당신이 학생들을 가르치기 위해서는 인내심이 필요하지요. (patience, teach)

→ You need _____ _____ _____ _____.

5 지진을 예측하는 것은 불가능해. (impossible, predict)

→ It is _____ _____ _____ earthquakes.

6 당신의 이름 철자를 어떻게 쓰는지 말해 주세요. (spell, name)

→ Please tell me _____ _____ _____ _____.

A   ( ) 안의 말을 이용하여 빈칸을 채우시오.

1 There are _____ _____ _____. (rules, follow)

2 It is _____ _____ _____ goodbye. (time, say)

3 I have some _____ _____ _____ you. (pictures, show)

4 Fall is the _____ _____ _____ _____ books. (best season, read)

5 There are _____ _____ _____ _____ you. (many people, help)

6 We are planning something _____ _____ _____ you. (great, surprise)

B   보기와 같이 주어진 표현을 이용하여 빈칸을 채우시오.

보기	의자 위에 앉다 to sit on a chair	She gave me a chair. I sat on it. → She gave me a chair to sit on.
집 안에서 살다 to live _____ a house	**1** Reina designed a house. She will live in it. → Reina designed a house _____ _____ _____.
박스 안에서 자다 to sleep _____ a box	**2** The cat found a box. The cat slept in it. → The cat found a box _____ _____ _____.
종이 위에 쓰다 to write _____ paper	**3** Please give me a piece of paper. I will write on it. → Please give me a piece of paper _____ _____ _____.
장난감을 갖고 놀다 to play _____ a toy	**4** I gave the baby a toy. He played with it. → I gave the baby a toy _____ _____ _____.

C   밑줄 친 부분의 해석을 쓰고, 해당하는 쓰임의 번호를 보기에서 골라 쓰시오.

보기 | ① 가능 ② 운명 ③ 의무 ④ 예정 ⑤ 의도		
1 You are to leave for the train now.	해석 _____	쓰임 ___
2 If you are to succeed, don't waste time.	해석 _____	쓰임 ___
3 The tower was to be seen from here.	해석 _____	쓰임 ___
4 She was never to return home.	해석 _____	쓰임 ___
5 She is to arrive here soon.	해석 _____	쓰임 ___

D 우리말과 의미가 같도록 ( ) 안의 말을 배열하시오.

1 그는 혼자서 세계 여행을 할 용기가 있었어. (to, travel, around, courage, the world)

→ He had _____ alone.

2 나는 화를 낼 이유가 없었어. (no, reason, get, to, angry)

→ I had _____.

3 우리는 머무를 멋진 호텔을 찾아냈어. (hotel, a, great, stay, to, at)

→ We found _____.

4 엄마는 잠자리에서 말해 줄 많은 이야기를 알고 있다. (stories, bedtime, tell, many, to)

→ Mom knows _____.

5 너는 걱정할 것이 없단다. (nothing, worry, to, about)

→ You have _____.

6 우리는 다음달에 뉴욕으로 이사 갈 예정이야. (move, to, New York, to, are)

→ We _____ next month.

E 우리말과 의미가 같도록 ( ) 안의 말을 이용하여 문장을 완성하시오.

1 버려야 할 것들이 많아. (things, throw away)

→ There are _____ _____ _____.

2 우리는 낭비할 시간이 없어. (time, waste)

→ We don't have _____ _____ _____.

3 나는 엄마를 기쁘게 해 드릴 가장 쉬운 방법을 알고 있어. (way, please)

→ I know _____ _____ _____ _____ my mom.

4 그녀는 올해 달성해야 할 목표가 하나 있다. (a goal, achieve)

→ She has _____ _____ _____ this year.

5 너는 이 기회를 잡아야 해. (grab, chance)

→ You are _____ _____ _____.

6 나는 너에게 말할 놀라운 무언가가 있어. (amazing, tell)

→ I have _____ _____ _____ you.

7 그는 같이 일할 파트너를 찾고 있는 중이야. (a partner, work)

→ He is looking for _____ _____ _____ _____.

A 보기의 단어를 이용하여 문장을 완성하시오.

보기 | stay   repair   come   learn   reach

1 Physics is very hard _____ .

2 We felt happy _____ at home all day.

3 The cat must be hungry _____ to me.

4 He did his best _____ the broken window.

5 She was excited _____ the top of the mountain.

B 밑줄 친 부분의 해석을 쓰고, 해당하는 쓰임의 번호를 보기에서 골라 쓰시오.

보기	① 목적 (~하기 위해) ② 감정의 원인 (~하게 되어) ③ 형용사 수식 (~하기에) ④ 결과 (결국 ~하다) ⑤ 판단의 근거 (~하는 것을 보니)		
1 She went out <u>to get fresh air.</u>	해석 _____	쓰임 _____
2 He grew up <u>to be a dancer.</u>	해석 _____	쓰임 _____
3 I was happy <u>to hear the news.</u>	해석 _____	쓰임 _____
4 The quiz was easy <u>to solve.</u>	해석 _____	쓰임 _____
5 It must be lonely <u>to live alone.</u>	해석 _____	쓰임 _____

C 주어진 to부정사가 각 문장에 들어갈 알맞은 위치를 고르시오.

1 그 어린 소녀는 자라서 과학자가 되었지.

    → The little girl (①) grew up (②) a scientist (③).   (to be)

2 그는 그 메시지를 듣고 놀랐어.

    → He (①) was surprised (②) the message (③).   (to hear)

3 그녀가 농구를 저렇게 하는 것을 보니 아플 리가 없어.

    → She (①) can't be (②) sick (③) basketball like that.   (to play)

4 그 호수는 들어가서 수영하기에 너무 차가워.

    → The lake (①) was (②) too cold (③) in.   (to swim)

5 우리는 점심을 먹기 위해 푸드코트에 갔어.

    → We (①) went (②) to the food court (③) lunch.   (to have)

D 우리말과 의미가 같도록 ( ) 안의 말을 배열하시오.

1 그는 근육을 키우기 위해서 운동했어. (worked out, muscle, build, to)

→ He _____.

2 그 어려운 책을 이해하는 것을 보니 영리한 것이 분명해. (smart, be, understand, to)

→ You must _____ such a difficult book.

3 지금 무대에서 연설할 준비가 되셨습니까? (you, are, ready, make, to, a speech)

→ _____ on the stage now?

4 나는 내 그림을 보여 주게 되어 자랑스러웠어. (proud, painting, my, to, was, show)

→ I _____.

5 그 물고기는 산란을 하기 위해 강으로 돌아가. (the river, to, return, breed, to)

→ The fish _____.

6 그 소년은 자라서 그 나라의 대통령이 되었지. (grew up, be, president, to, the)

→ The boy _____ of the country.

E 우리말과 의미가 같도록 ( ) 안의 말을 이용하여 문장을 완성하시오.

1 독일어는 배우기가 어려워. (difficult, learn)

→ German is _____ _____ _____.

2 Brian은 그의 옛집에서 이사 나가는 것이 슬펐어. (sad, move)

→ Brian was _____ _____ _____ out of his old house.

3 그 상자를 열어 보았지만 아무것도 없다는 것을 알았다. (find, only)

→ I opened the box _____ _____ _____ that there was nothing in it.

4 나의 개는 Daniel의 고양이를 보고 매우 겁을 먹었다. (frightened, see)

→ My dog _____ _____ _____ _____ Daniel's cat.

5 그녀는 잊어버리지 않기 위해 비밀번호를 적어 뒀어. (the password, forget)

→ She wrote down _____ _____ _____ _____ it.

6 간호사가 내게 주사를 놓기 위해 내 옷소매를 걷어올렸어. (roll up, sleeve, give)

→ The nurse _____ _____ _____ _____ _____ _____

me a shot.

A 보기와 같이 밑줄 친 부분의 해석을 쓰시오.

보기 | It was stupid of you to forget her name. 해석 네가 잊는 것

1 It was kind of her to take care of you.
해석 _____ 가 _____ 는 것

2 The movie is too scary for Nick to watch.
해석 _____ 이 _____ 기에

3 Spaghetti was hard for him to cook.
해석 _____ 가 _____ 하기에

4 It takes one hour for me to go to school.
해석 _____ 가 _____ 는 것

B 보기와 같이 ( ) 안의 단어가 의미상의 주어가 되도록 고쳐 쓰고 그 이유를 고르시오.

보기	It was very nice of you to help me. (you)	성품형용사 + 의미상 주어 (있음, 없음) + (for, of) 목적격

1 It is hard _____ to speak all day. (I) (있음, 없음) + (for, of) 목적격

2 It is foolish _____ to say that. (she) (있음, 없음) + (for, of) 목적격

3 It is necessary _____ to study English. (we) (있음, 없음) + (for, of) 목적격

4 It was silly _____ to tell a lie. (they) (있음, 없음) + (for, of) 목적격

5 This box is too heavy _____ to lift. (he) (있음, 없음) + (for, of) 목적격

6 It is strange _____ not to eat dinner. (you) (있음, 없음) + (for, of) 목적격

C 두 문장이 같은 의미를 갖도록 빈칸을 채우시오.

1 I am so hungry that I can't sleep.

→ I am _____ _____ _____ _____ .

2 He was so smart that he could answer the question.

→ He was _____ _____ _____ _____ the question.

3 The soldier was so careless that he lost his gun.

→ The soldier was _____ _____ _____ _____ his gun.

4 The book was so difficult that I couldn't understand it.

→ The book was _____ _____ for me _____ .

5 Sally was so kind that she showed me around the house.

→ Sally was _____ _____ _____ me around the house.

D 우리말과 의미가 같도록 ( ) 안의 말을 배열하시오.

1 이 곰 인형은 그 꼬마가 안기에 너무 커. (too, to, big, hold, for, the kid)

→ This teddy bear is _____ .

2 그는 매우 배가 불러서 더 먹을 수가 없었어. (so, he, full, that, eat, could, not)

→ He was _____ any more.

3 당신이 당신의 책들을 기부하다니 관대하시군요. (generous, you, to, of, donate)

→ It was _____ your books.

4 십대들이 그들의 꿈을 따르는 것은 중요해. (teens, for, important, follow, to)

→ It is _____ their dreams.

5 그가 진실을 알기까지 오랜 시간이 걸렸어. (him, learn, for, to)

→ It took a long time _____ the truth.

6 그 만화영화는 성인들이 보기에 흥미로워. (interesting, to, for, watch, adults)

→ The animated movie was _____ .

E 우리말과 의미가 같도록 ( ) 안의 말을 이용하여 문장을 완성하시오.

1 네가 버스를 잘못 타다니 부주의했구나. (take)

→ It was careless _____ _____ _____ the wrong bus.

2 우리가 환경을 보호하는 것은 필요한 일이다. (protect)

→ It is necessary _____ _____ _____ _____ the environment.

3 그 규칙들은 내가 따르기에 너무 엄격해. (strict, follow)

→ The rules are _____ _____ _____ _____ .

4 그 어린 소녀는 침대 아래에 숨을 만큼 충분히 작았다. (hide, small)

→ The little girl was _____ _____ _____ under the bed.

5 그는 매우 아파서 일을 하러 갈 수 없었어. (so, that, sick)

→ He was _____ _____ _____ _____

_____ to work.

6 그 텐트는 매우 커서 열 명이 들어가서 잘 수 있어. (so, that, big)

→ The tent is _____ _____ _____ _____

_____ _____ in it.

Error Correction

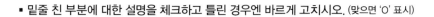

▪ 밑줄 친 부분에 대한 설명을 체크하고 틀린 경우엔 바르게 고치시오. (맞으면 'O' 표시)

1	<u>This</u> is my dream to invent a flying car. (→)	to부정사의 주어가 길면 문장 앞에 (가주어, 진주어)인 (This, It)을 사용
2	My friends promised <u>keep</u> my secret. (→)	주어 + promise + 목적어 (to부정사, 동사원형)
3	Please don't tell me when <u>study</u>. (→)	'언제 공부할지를'이므로 when + (동사원형, to부정사)
4	She bought a house to <u>live</u>. (→)	(live a house, live in a house)이므로 명사 + to부정사 + 전치사 (in, 없음)
5	Do you have <u>cold anything</u> to drink? (→)	-thing으로 끝나는 명사 수식은 (명사 + 형용사, 형용사 + 명사) + to부정사
6	I work out every day <u>stay</u> healthy. (→)	건강을 유지하기 위해(결과, 목적), 운동하는 것이므로 (동사원형, to부정사)
7	He was <u>surprise</u> to hear the news. (→)	뉴스를 들어서(감정 원인, 목적) 놀라게 된 것이므로 (동사, 감정형용사) + to부정사
8	You must be popular <u>have</u> so many fans. (→)	팬이 많아서(형용사 수식, 판단의 근거) 유명한 것이므로 (동사원형, to부정사)
9	It is hard <u>of</u> me to study all night. (→)	성품형용사가 (있으면, 없으면) 의미상 주어는 (of, for) + 목적격
10	It was brave <u>for</u> the firefighter to save the boy. (→)	성품형용사가 (있으면, 없으면) 의미상 주어는 (of, for) + 목적격
11	He is <u>enough strong</u> to lift the wooden box. (→)	(~하기 충분한, ~하기엔 너무 ~한)이므로 (enough + 형용사, 형용사 + enough) + to부정사
12	He is so strong that he <u>can</u> lift the wooden box. (→)	'매우 ~해서 ~할 수 있다'는 so + 형용사 + that + 주어 + (can, can't)
13	Cathy was <u>tired too</u> to wake up at six. (→)	(~하기 충분한, ~하기엔 너무 ~한)이므로 (too + 형용사, 형용사 + too) + to부정사

■ 주어진 단어를 알맞게 이용하여 우리말과 의미가 같도록 영작하시오.

1 it, invent, flying car

나의 꿈이다 / 발명하는 것은 / 날아다니는 차를

→

2 promise, keep

내 친구들은 약속했다 / 내 비밀을 지키는 것을

→

3 tell me, when

제발 제게 말하지 말아요 / 언제 공부해야 할지를

→

4 buy, live

그녀는 구매했다 / 집을 / (안에서) 살

→

5 cold, anything

너는 가지고 있니 / 무언가 차가운 것을 / 마실?

→

6 work out, healthy

나는 매일 운동을 한다 / 건강을 유지하기 위해

→

7 surprised, hear

그는 놀랐다 / 그 소식을 듣게 되어서

→

8 must be, fans

너는 유명한 것이 틀림없다 / 그렇게 많은 팬을 가졌으니

→

9 hard, all night

어렵다 / 내가 공부하는 것은 / 밤새

→

10 firefighter, save

용감했다 / 소방관이 구한 것은 / 그 소년을

→

11 lift, wooden

그는 충분히 힘이 세다 / 나무상자를 들기에

→

12 so, that

그는 매우 힘이 세다 / 그래서 그는 나무상자를 들 수 있다

→

13 wake up

Cathy는 너무 피곤했다 / 여섯 시에 일어나기에

→

GP 22 동명사의 명사적 쓰임

[_____] 형태로 '_____'의 의미이다. 문장에서 _____ 처럼 주어, 목적어, 보어 역할을 한다.

주어	동사	목적어 / 보어
☆ Watching musicals	is	fun.
☆ She	enjoys	singing loudly.
☆ I	am interested in	making robots.
☆ His hobby	is	taking pictures.

❶ _____ 역할: ~하는 것은

☆ _____ is good for the brain.

= **To use** chopsticks is good for the brain.

❷ _____ 역할: ~하는 것을

She *finished* **packing** her bag for the trip.　　　(_____의 목적어)

I was excited *about* **seeing** a whale in the ocean.　(_____의 목적어)

❸ _____ 역할: ~하는 것이다

The best part of camping is **meeting** new people.

> **Tip**
>
> 동명사 주어는 to부정사로 바꿔 쓸 수 있고, 항상 단수 취급을 한다.

• Upgrade •

동명사의 부정은 동명사 앞에 _____이나 _____를 쓴다.

We are sorry for _____ **answering** your questions.

GP 23 동명사의 관용적 쓰임

go -ing	~하러 가다	_____ -ing	~하느라 바쁘다
how / what about -ing	~하는 것이 어때?	spend 시간 / 돈 (in) -ing	~하는 데 ~을 소비하다
_____ -ing	~을 고대하다	_____ (in) -ing	~하는 데 어려움이 있다

He **is busy** study**ing** for the final exam.

How about go**ing** to a seafood buffet for dinner?

❶ 동명사를 목적어로 취하는 동사

Don't *give up* **climbing** to the top of the mountain.

James *avoided* **looking** into her eyes.

❷ to부정사를 목적어로 취하는 동사

Daniel *is planning* **to build** his own house.

❸ 동명사와 부정사를 모두 목적어로 갖고 의미 변화가 없는 동사

☆ Jane *began* **dancing** on the stage. = Jane *began* _____ on the stage.

❹ 동명사와 부정사를 모두 목적어로 갖지만 의미 차이가 있는 동사

☆ I *remember* **visiting** the museum before. (_____)

☆ *Remember* **to hand in** your report tomorrow. (_____)

☆ She *forgot* **meeting** you last year. (_____)

☆ Don't *forget* **to bring** your lunch today. (_____)

☆ We *tried* **solving** the puzzle for fun. (_____)

☆ We *tried* **to solve** the puzzle to win a prize. (_____)

• Upgrade •

❶ stop + 동명사: _____ (동명사가 stop의 목적어)

☆ He *stopped* **drinking** water.

❷ stop + to부정사 _____ (to부정사의 부사적 쓰임)

He *stopped* **to drink** water.

A ( ) 안의 단어를 알맞은 형태로 바꿔 빈칸을 채우시오.

1 _____ good neighbors is important. (have)

2 My dog kept _____ the ducks at my grandma's house. (chase)

3 He finally gave up _____ the whole pizza. (finish)

4 She learned English by _____ American dramas. (watch)

5 My son practiced _____ the drums for the festival. (play)

6 Did you have trouble _____ my house? (find)

B 밑줄 친 부분의 해석을 쓰고, 해당하는 쓰임의 번호를 보기에서 골라 쓰시오.

보기	① 주어 (~하는 것은) ③ 전치사의 목적어 (~하는 것을)	② 동사의 목적어 (~하는 것을) ④ 보어 (~하는 것이다)		
1 Jason avoids <u>eating</u> too much meat.	해석 _____	것을	쓰임 ___
2 She is interested in <u>living</u> on the island.	해석 _____	것을	쓰임 ___
3 <u>Keeping</u> your promises is important.	해석 _____	것은	쓰임 ___
4 His job is <u>designing</u> tall buildings.	해석 _____	것이다	쓰임 ___
5 Do you feel like <u>eating out</u> tonight?	해석 _____	것을	쓰임 ___

C 보기와 같이 두 문장을 한 문장으로 바꿔 쓰시오.

보기	We watched a horror movie. We enjoyed it. → We enjoyed <u>watching a horror movie</u>.

1 He collects model trains. It is his hobby.

→ His hobby is _____ _____ _____ .

2 She expressed her feelings. She was good at it.

→ She was good at _____ _____ _____ .

3 She will meet Tom at 2 p.m. It is her plan.

→ _____ _____ _____ is her plan.

4 Can you imagine it? You walk on a cloud.

→ Can you imagine _____ ?

D   우리말과 의미가 같도록 ( ) 안의 말을 배열하시오.

1 그 로봇청소기는 무언가에 부딪칠 때까지 계속 움직여. (cleaner, moving, keeps)

→ The robot ＿＿＿＿＿＿＿＿＿＿＿＿＿＿＿＿＿ until it hits something.

2 다음번 기차를 타는 것이 어때? (how, taking, about)

→ ＿＿＿＿＿＿＿＿＿＿＿＿＿＿＿＿＿ the next train?

3 당신은 그 대도시 여행하는 것을 즐기셨나요? (enjoy, did, you, traveling)

→ ＿＿＿＿＿＿＿＿＿＿＿＿＿＿＿＿＿ around the big city?

4 영화를 보는 동안 휴대폰을 꺼 주시겠습니까? (mind, your, turning off, phone)

→ Would you ＿＿＿＿＿＿＿＿＿＿＿＿＿ during the movie?

5 목표를 세우는 것은 성공의 첫 발걸음이지. (a goal, setting, is, the, step, first)

→ ＿＿＿＿＿＿＿＿＿＿＿＿＿＿＿＿＿ to success.

6 나는 아침형 인간이 아니야. 일찍 일어나는 것이 힘들어. (difficulty, getting up, have)

→ I am not an early bird. I ＿＿＿＿＿＿＿＿＿＿＿＿ early.

7 그의 문제는 다른 사람의 말을 주의 깊게 듣지 않는다는 것이야. (listening, others, to, not)

→ His problem is ＿＿＿＿＿＿＿＿＿＿＿＿＿＿ carefully.

E   우리말과 의미가 같도록 ( ) 안의 말을 이용하여 문장을 완성하시오.

1 나는 그의 농담에 웃음을 멈출 수가 없었어. (laugh at)

→ I couldn't ＿＿＿＿ ＿＿＿＿ ＿＿＿＿ ＿＿＿＿ .

2 좋은 딸이 되는 것은 어려운 일이 아니야. (be)

→ ＿＿＿＿ ＿＿＿＿ ＿＿＿＿ ＿＿＿＿ is not difficult.

3 오늘 아침에 널 귀찮게 해서 미안해. (bother)

→ I am sorry for ＿＿＿＿ ＿＿＿＿ ＿＿＿＿ ＿＿＿＿ .

4 그는 거의 일 년을 그 그림을 그리며 보냈어. (draw)

→ He ＿＿＿＿ almost a year ＿＿＿＿ ＿＿＿＿ ＿＿＿＿ .

5 나의 부모님은 파티룸을 장식하시느라 바쁘셔. (decorate)

→ ＿＿＿＿ ＿＿＿＿ ＿＿＿＿ ＿＿＿＿ ＿＿＿＿ the party room.

6 내 취미는 음식 사진을 찍어서 온라인에 포스팅 하는 것이야. (take pictures of)

→ ＿＿＿＿ ＿＿＿＿ ＿＿＿＿ ＿＿＿＿ ＿＿＿＿ food and posting them online.

A ( ) 안에서 어법상 알맞은 것을 모두 고르시오.

1 What about (to order, ordering) food first?

2 Don't forget (to turn off, turning off) the air conditioner in an hour.

3 She dislikes (to tell, telling) her story to other people.

4 They decided (to save, saving) the children in trouble.

5 The little boy keeps (to ask, asking) his mom the same question.

6 She avoided (to drive, driving) in rush hour.

7 He promised (to give, giving) me a ride to school.

B ( ) 안에 주어진 단어를 어법상 알맞게 고쳐 쓰시오.

1 Did you enjoy _____ the roller coaster? (ride)

2 The salesman agreed _____ me a discount. (give)

3 Paula remembers _____ koalas when she was little. (see)

4 Don't be afraid of _____. You can do it! (fail)

5 When did you start _____ kickboxing? (learn)

6 Do you feel like _____ along the coast? (walk)

7 Tina decided _____ her hair cut. (get)

C 보기와 같이 밑줄 친 부분의 의미를 ( ) 안에서 고르시오.

보기 | <u>Stop calling</u> me by that nickname.　　　(∼하는 것을, ∼하기 위해) 멈추다

1 Don't <u>forget to bring</u> your air mattress.　　　(∼했던 것을, ∼할 것을) 잊다

2 Did you <u>forget meeting</u> me last year?　　　(∼했던 것을, ∼할 것을) 잊다

3 I <u>remember buying</u> the same bag.　　　(∼했던 것을, ∼할 것을) 기억하다

4 Please <u>remember to call</u> me at 6 a.m.　　　(∼했던 것을, ∼할 것을) 기억하다

5 He <u>tried to finish</u> his work by noon.　　　(시험 삼아, 열심히 노력) 하다

D 우리말과 의미가 같도록 ( ) 안의 말을 배열하시오.

1 그녀는 과학 수업 보고서 쓰는 것을 끝마쳤어. (finished, a, writing, report)

→ She _____ for science class.

2 그 동물원 사육사는 문을 잠그는 것을 잊었어. (forgot, lock, to, the, gate)

→ The zookeeper _____ .

3 여행객들이 포토존에서 사진을 찍기 위해 멈췄어. (take, stopped, a, to, picture)

→ The tourists _____ in the photo zone.

4 감기 걸리는 것을 피하는 방법을 아세요? (avoid, a, to, how, cold, catching)

→ Do you know _____ ?

5 그녀는 아이스크림 대신에 얼린 바나나를 먹어 봤어. (eating, tried, banana, a, frozen)

→ She _____ instead of ice cream.

6 Jack은 숙제하기 위해 인터넷 검색하느라 바빴어. (the, busy, searching, was, Internet)

→ Jack _____ to do his homework.

7 그 여배우는 그녀의 새로운 영화 촬영을 끝마쳤어. (shooting, finished, her, film, new)

→ The actress _____ .

E 우리말과 의미가 같도록 ( ) 안의 말을 이용하여 문장을 완성하시오.

1 그는 자신의 어린 시절로 돌아가기를 희망했어. (hope, go back)

→ He _____ _____ _____ _____ to his childhood.

2 TV 채널을 바꿔도 될까요? (mind, change)

→ Do you _____ _____ the TV channel?

3 여름에는 익히지 않은 고기나 해산물 먹는 것을 피하세요. (eat, meat, raw)

→ _____ _____ _____ _____ or seafood in the summer.

4 Linda는 컴퓨터를 고치려고 매우 애를 썼어. (fix, hard)

→ Linda _____ _____ _____ _____ the computer.

5 나는 그녀와 같이 불꽃놀이 본 것을 잊지 않을 거야. (watch, the fireworks)

→ I won't _____ _____ _____ _____ with her.

6 너는 왜 네 강아지를 계속 귀찮게 하니? (keep, bother)

→ Why do you _____ _____ _____ _____ ?

▪ 밑줄 친 부분에 대한 설명을 체크하고 틀린 경우엔 바르게 고치시오. (맞으면 'O' 표시)

*가능한 답은 모두 체크

1 <u>Watch</u> musicals is fun.
   (→   )
   '뮤지컬을 보는 것'은
   (주어, 목적어) 역할의 (동사, 동명사)

2 She enjoys <u>to sing</u> loudly.
   (→   )
   '~하는 것을 즐기다'를 의미하는
   enjoy의 목적어는 (동명사, to부정사)

3 I am interested in <u>make</u> robots.
   (→   )
   주어 + 동사 + 전치사 + 목적어
                   (동사, 동명사)

4 His hobby is <u>take</u> pictures.
   (→   )
   '(사진을) 찍는 것이다'는
   (보어, 목적어) 역할의 (동명사, 동사)

5 Using chopsticks <u>are</u> good for the brain.
   (→   )
   '~하는 것'을 의미하는
   동명사 주어는 (단수, 복수) 취급

6 Jane began <u>dancing</u> on the stage.
   (→   )
   '~하는 것을 시작하다'는
   begin + (to부정사, 동명사)

7 I remember <u>to visit</u> the museum before.
   (→   )
   '~했던 것을 기억하다'는
   remember + (to부정사, 동명사)

8 Remember <u>to hand in</u> your report tomorrow.
   (→   )
   '~할 것을 기억하다'는
   remember + (to부정사, 동명사)

9 She forgot <u>to meet</u> you last year.
   (→   )
   '~했던 것을 잊다'는
   forget + (to부정사, 동명사)

10 Don't forget <u>to bring</u> your lunch today.
   (→   )
   '~할 것을 잊다'는
   forget + (to부정사, 동명사)

11 We tried <u>solving</u> the puzzle for fun.
   (→   )
   '(시험 삼아) ~해 보다'는
   try + (to부정사, 동명사)

12 We tried <u>solving</u> the puzzle to win a prize.
   (→   )
   '~하려고 노력하다'는
   try + (to부정사, 동명사)

13 He stopped <u>to drink</u> water.
   (→   )
   '~하는 것을 그만두다'는
   stop + (to부정사, 동명사)

Sentence writing

▪ 주어진 단어를 알맞게 이용하여 우리말과 의미가 같도록 영작하시오.

1	watch, musicals	뮤지컬들을 보는 것은 / 재미있다 →
2	enjoy, loudly	그녀는 / 노래하는 것을 즐긴다 / 시끄럽게 →
3	interested, robots	나는 / ~에 관심 있다 / 로봇을 만드는 것 →
4	take pictures	그의 취미는 / ~이다 / 사진을 찍는 것 →
5	chopsticks, the brain	젓가락을 사용하는 것은 / 좋다 / 두뇌에 →
6	begin, dance	Jane은 / 춤추는 것을 시작했다 / 무대 위에서 →
7	remember, visit	나는 / 방문했던 것을 기억한다 / 그 박물관을 / 이전에 →
8	hand in	기억해라 / 보고서 제출할 것을 / 내일 →
9	forget	그녀는 / 잊었다 / 너를 만났던 것을 / 작년에 →
10	bring	잊지 마라 / 너의 점심을 가져올 것을 / 오늘 →
11	try, for fun	우리는 / (시험 삼아) 해 봤다 / 퍼즐을 푸는 것을 / 재미로 →
12	try, win	우리는 / 노력했다 / 퍼즐을 푸는 것을 / 상을 타기 위해 →
13	stop, drink	그는 / 멈췄다 / 물을 마시던 것을 →

GP 25 현재분사와 과거분사

[_____] 형태의 현재분사는 _____, _____의 의미를 갖고,
[_____] 형태의 과거분사는 _____, _____의 의미를 갖는다.

종류	형태	의미	
현재분사	_____	진행: ~하고 있는	boiling water
		능동: ~하는, 하게 하는	shocking news
과거분사	_____	완료: ~된	boiled eggs
		수동: ~되는, ~당하는	shocked people

• Upgrade •

분사는 be동사나 have 동사와 결합하여 _____, _____, _____를 만든다.

He **is writing** a letter. (진행형)

He **has written** a letter. (완료형)

The letter **was written** by him. (수동태)

GP 26 분사의 형용사적 쓰임

❶ **명사 수식**: 명사 _____이나 _____에서 명사를 수식한다.

✰ a **moving** robot
✰ a **used** bike

✰ a robot **moving** underwater
a bike **used** for 7 years

❷ **보어 역할**: 주어나 목적어의 상태를 보충 설명한다.

_____	동사		
The plan	was	amazing.	현재분사
She	looked	amazed.	과거분사

주어	동사	_____		
We	saw	Henry	cleaning ~.	현재분사
He	kept	the rooms	cleaned.	과거분사

She sat **listening** to music. (들으면서: _____)

He designed a dress **made** out of chocolate. (만들어진: _____)

GP 27 감정을 나타내는 분사

현재분사는 '〜한 감정을 _____', 과거분사는 '〜한 감정을 _____'을 의미한다.

동사	현재분사	과거분사
excite / shock	exciting / shocking	excited / shocked
_____ (흥미롭게 하다)	_____ (흥미로운)	_____ (흥미를 가진)
_____ (놀라게 하다)	_____ (놀라운)	_____ (놀란)
satisfy (만족하게 하다)	satisfying (만족스러운)	satisfied (만족한)
bore (지루하게 하다)	boring (지루한)	bored (지루해 하는)

☆ The book *bores* him.
☆ The book *is* **boring** to him.
☆ He *is* **bored** with the book.

○ **Tip** ○
감정을 유발하는 주어는 보통 _____ 이고 감정을 느끼는 주어는 일반적으로 _____ 이다.

GP 28 현재분사와 동명사

[동사원형 + -ing]가 현재분사로 쓰이면 _____ 역할이고, 동명사로 쓰이면 _____ 역할이다.

	be동사		동사원형 + -ing		동사원형 + -ing	명사
현재분사	She	is	playing the piano.	☆ a	sleeping	lion
		≠	_____			
동명사	My hobby	is	playing the piano.	☆ a	sleeping	bag
		=	_____			

Jack *is* **wrapping** birthday gifts.　　(포장하고 있는 중: _____)
My role *is* **wrapping** birthday gifts.　　(포장하는 것: _____)

• Upgrade •

용도나 목적을 나타내는 동명사는 [for + 동사원형 + -ing] 형태로 바꿀 수 있다.
a sleeping bag = a bag _____ sleeping
running shoes = shoes _____ running

분사구문은 [_____]로 이루어진 부사절을 [_____]의 부사구로 줄여 쓴 것을 말하고, 문맥에 따라 시간, 이유, 양보, 조건 등의 의미를 가진다.

부사절　　　　　　　　　주절

| 접속사 | 주어 + 동사 | 주어 + 동사 | When he reads a book, he puts on his glasses. |
| ❶ | ❷　❸ | | |

❶ 부사절의 _____ 생략　　　　　~~When~~ he reads a book, he puts on his glasses.

❷ 부사절의 _____ (주절 주어와 같을 때)　　he reads a book, he puts on his glasses.

❸ 부사절의 동사를 _____로 바꾸기　　read + ing a book, he puts on his glasses.

| 동사원형 + -ing | 주어 + 동사 | ☆ Reading a book, he puts on his glasses. |

분사구문

❶ 시간: _____, _____(~할 때), _____(~하는 동안), before, after(~하기 전에, 후에)

When butterflies taste food, they use their feet.

→ _____ food, butterflies use their feet.

❷ 이유: _____, _____, _____(~ 때문에, ~이므로)

Because I didn't hear the alarm, I kept sleeping.

→ ☆ _____ _____ the alarm, I kept sleeping.

❸ 양보: _____, _____(~일지라도)

Although Emily has a driver's license, she never drives.

→ ☆ **Although having** a driver's license, Emily never drives.

> ○ Tip ○
> 양보, 조건을 나타내는 접속사는 뜻을 분명하게 하기 위해 생략되지 않을 수도 있다.

❹ 조건: _____(만약 ~한다면)

If you read this book, you will find the answer.

→ ☆ _____ this book, you will find the answer.

> ○ Tip ○
> being으로 시작하는 분사구문에서 being은 _____ 가능하다.

❺ 동시동작: _____, as(~하면서)

While he was listening to music, he searched the Internet.

→ ☆ **(Being)** _____ to music, he searched the Internet.

• Upgrade •

분사구문의 부정은 분사구문 앞에 not이나 never를 쓴다.

_____ **feeling** good, he didn't say a word.

A ( ) 안에서 알맞은 것을 고르시오.

1 There was a (talking, talked) bird in the cage.

2 Betty ironed her shirts while (listening, listened) to music.

3 The door was (locking, locked) from the inside.

4 We ordered some (frying, fried) chicken.

5 She didn't hear her phone (ringing, rung).

6 There are two cars (parking, parked) there from yesterday.

B ( ) 안에 주어진 단어를 어법상 알맞게 고쳐 쓰시오.

1 He loves any food _____ by his mom. (cook)

2 Why is your voice _____ ? (shake)

3 Watch out for the truck _____ closer. (get)

4 Her room was _____ with the smell of roses. (fill)

5 You are an _____ person. (amaze)

6 The guests _____ to the party began to arrive. (invite)

C 두 문장을 같은 의미의 한 문장으로 보기처럼 바꿔 쓰시오.

> 보기 | We got on the plane. It was leaving for Turkey.
> → We got on the plane leaving for Turkey.

1 I bought a hat. It was made of silk.

→ I bought a hat _____ _____ _____ .

2 I am looking for a boy. He is named Jack.

→ I am looking for a boy _____ _____ .

3 Look at the kids. They are playing hide-and-seek.

→ Look at the kids _____ hide-and-seek.

4 I like the picture. It was taken by my uncle.

→ I like the picture _____ _____ _____ .

D 우리말과 의미가 같도록 ( ) 안의 말을 배열하시오.

1 그 비둘기는 Adam이 쓴 메시지를 배달했어. (a message, by, Adam, written)

→ The dove delivered _____.

2 경찰은 창문에 남겨진 지문을 하나 발견했어. (left, a, fingerprint, the, on, window)

→ The police found _____.

3 파란색 스웨터를 입고 있는 그 남자는 우리 선생님이셔. (sweater, wearing, blue, the)

→ The man _____ is my teacher.

4 V 형태로 날아가고 있는 저 기러기들을 봐! (geese, flying, in a V-formation)

→ Look at the _____.

5 식사를 제공하고 있는 저 승무원은 매우 친절해. (serving, the, flight attendant, meals)

→ _____ is very kind.

6 그녀는 동물센터에서 입양된 고양이를 길렀다. (from, adopted, animal center, the)

→ She raised a cat _____.

7 그녀는 초콜릿으로 덮인 케이크를 샀어. (covered, with, chocolate)

→ She bought a cake _____.

E 우리말과 의미가 같도록 ( ) 안의 말을 이용하여 문장을 완성하시오.

1 그는 그녀의 웃고 있는 얼굴을 좋아해. (smile)

→ He loves _____ _____ _____.

2 저기 날고 있는 저 드론은 미래에 피자를 배달할 거야. (fly, over there)

→ The drone _____ _____ _____ will deliver pizza in the future.

3 나는 튀김감자보다 구운 감자가 더 좋아. (bake, potatoes)

→ I like _____ _____ better than french fries.

4 그녀는 지붕 위로 떨어지는 빗소리를 좋아했어. (fall, the roof)

→ She liked the sound of rain _____ _____ _____ _____.

5 그는 누군가가 그의 어깨를 만지는 것을 느꼈어. (touch, shoulder)

→ He felt someone _____ _____ _____.

6 아이들에 의해 만들어진 눈사람이 햇빛에 녹고 있어. (make, the kids)

→ The snowman _____ _____ _____ _____

is melting in the sun.

A ( ) 안에서 알맞은 것을 고르시오.

1 The ocean view was (amazing, amazed).

We were (amazing, amazed) by the ocean view.

2 The food at the restaurant was (satisfying, satisfied).

She was (satisfying, satisfied) with the food at the restaurant.

3 The test results were (disappointing, disappointed).

My mom looked (disappointing, disappointed) by the test results.

4 I am (interesting, interested) in your ideas.

Your ideas sound (interesting, interested).

5 The bedtime story by his dad was very (boring, bored).

The kid became (boring, bored) with the bedtime story by his dad.

B 밑줄 친 부분의 해석을 쓰고, 해당 용법을 보기에서 골라 번호를 쓰시오.

보기 ㅣ ① ~감정을 갖게 하는 ② 감정을 느낀	해석	용법
1 His secret was shocking.		
2 Her new film is very boring.		
3 The dog was interested in the cat.		
4 Why do you look so excited?		
5 We were surprised at the news.		

C 두 문장이 같은 의미를 갖도록 보기처럼 바꿔 쓰시오.

보기 ㅣ   She bought a robot for cleaning. → She bought a cleaning robot.

1 They spent two hours in a room for singing.

→ They spent two hours in a _____.

2 The old lady needs a stick for walking.

→ The old lady needs a _____.

3 Don't forget to bring your bag for sleeping tomorrow.

→ Don't forget to bring your _____ tomorrow.

4 How about this paper for wrapping?

→ How about this _____?

D 밑줄 친 부분의 해석을 쓰고, 용법을 ( ) 안에서 고르시오.

> 보기 | We need a new <u>washing</u> machine.　(<u>용도</u>, 진행)　해석 세탁기

1 She bought a new <u>sleeping</u> bag.　(용도, 진행)　해석 _____

2 Don't wake up the <u>sleeping</u> baby.　(용도, 진행)　해석 _____

3 He was <u>driving</u> on the highway.　(용도, 진행)　해석 _____

4 When did you get your <u>driver's</u> license?　(용도, 진행)　해석 _____

5 Please wait in the <u>waiting</u> room.　(용도, 진행)　해석 _____

6 I am <u>waiting</u> in a line to buy a ticket.　(용도, 진행)　해석 _____

E 우리말과 의미가 같도록 ( ) 안의 말을 이용하여 문장을 완성하시오.

1 선생님께서 내 리포트를 맘에 들어 하셨어. (please, with)

→ My teacher _____ _____ _____ my report.

2 우리는 자기의 먹이를 씻고 있는 너구리 사진을 찍었어. (wash, a raccoon)

→ We took a picture of _____ _____ _____ its food.

3 그녀는 선거 결과에 실망했었어. (disappoint)

→ She _____ _____ with the election results.

4 우리는 새로운 세탁기를 구입할 예정이야. (wash, machine)

→ We are going to buy a _____ _____ _____.

5 그녀는 얼어붙은 호수에서 아이스 스케이팅을 하러 갔다. (freeze, lake)

→ She went ice skating on _____ _____.

6 이 역사책은 매우 흥미로워. (interest)

→ This history book is very _____.

7 애완동물을 위한 수영장은 저쪽에 있습니다. (swim, pool)

→ The _____ _____ for pets is over there.

8 연을 날리는 것은 내가 좋아하는 활동이지. (fly, a kite)

→ _____ _____ _____ is my favorite activity.

9 둥지에서 엄마를 기다리는 새끼 새들 좀 봐. (baby birds, wait for)

→ Look at the _____ _____ _____ _____

_____ in the nest.

A ( ) 안에서 알맞은 것을 고르시오.

1 (Chatted, Chatting) with my friend, I saw Grace.

2 (Being, Be) kind to his friends, Austin is popular.

3 (Although, As) loving meat, I can't eat any more today.

4 (You visiting, Visiting) the website, you will find more about history.

B 분사구문을 이용하여 두 문장의 의미가 같도록 문장을 완성하시오.

1 When she got married, she traveled to Europe.

→ _____ _____ , she traveled to Europe.

2 If you take this bus, you will get to the stadium.

→ _____ _____ _____ , you will get to the stadium.

3 After he waved goodbye, he got on the train.

→ _____ _____ , he got on the train.

4 Because I lived next door to Fred, I know him very well.

→ _____ _____ _____ _____ _____ ,

I know him very well.

5 While we flew over the island, we looked down.

→ _____ _____ _____ , we looked down.

C ( ) 안의 접속사를 이용하여 분사구문을 부사절로 고쳐 쓰시오.

*S: 주어, V: 동사

분사구문	**1** Staying in Korea, he taught English. (when)
[접속사 + S + V]	→ _____ , he taught English.
분사구문	**2** Waiting for you, I checked my messages. (while)
[접속사 + S + V]	→ _____ , I checked my messages.
분사구문	**3** Not having a seat, she went out. (as)
[접속사 + S + V]	→ _____ , she went out.
분사구문	**4** Wearing this coat, you will look younger. (if)
[접속사 + S + V]	→ _____ , you will look younger.
분사구문	**5** Although looking tough, Henry is very kind. (although)
[접속사 + S + V]	→ _____ , Henry is very kind.

D 밑줄 친 부분의 해석을 쓰고, 부사절로 고칠 때 필요한 접속사의 번호를 쓰시오.

보기 I	① because	② when	③ if	④ although		
예시 I	Having no money, I can't buy it.		해석 <u>돈이 없어서</u>		접속사	①
1 <u>Eating a lot</u>, he is slim.			해석 _____		접속사	___
2 <u>Leaving now</u>, you can catch the bus.			해석 _____		접속사	___
3 <u>Reading a lot</u>, she is clever.			해석 _____		접속사	___
4 <u>Cleaning my room</u>, I listened to music.			해석 _____		접속사	___

E 우리말과 의미가 같도록 ( ) 안의 말을 배열하시오.

1 같은 우산을 쓰고 걸으면서, 우린 같이 노래했어. (under, the, umbrella, walking, same)

→ _____, we sang together.

2 열심히 연습한다면, 너는 대단한 가수가 될 거야. (hard, practicing)

→ _____, you will become a great singer.

3 미안하다고 말한 후, 그는 내게 초콜릿 한 상자를 주었다. (sorry, saying)

→ _____, he gave me a box of chocolate.

4 중국음식을 좋아해서, 그녀는 중국집을 자주 가. (Chinese, loving, food)

→ _____, she visits Chinese restaurants often.

F 우리말과 의미가 같도록 ( ) 안의 말을 이용하여 문장을 완성하시오.

1 그 파일을 저장한 후에, 나는 컴퓨터를 껐어. (save, file)

→ _____ _____ _____, I turned off the computer.

2 채식주의자여서, George는 고기를 먹지 않아. (be, vegetarian)

→ _____ _____ _____, George doesn't eat meat.

3 스페인에 혼자 살 때, 그는 향수병에 걸렸어. (live, Spain)

→ _____ _____ _____ _____, he felt homesick.

4 버스를 기다리던 중에 나는 옛 친구를 만났어. (wait for)

→ _____ _____ _____ _____, I met my old friend.

5 음식에 만족스러워서, 우리는 종종 이 식당에서 식사를 해. (be satisfied)

→ _____ _____ _____ _____ _____, we often eat

at this restaurant.

• 밑줄 친 부분에 대한 설명을 체크하고 틀린 경우엔 바르게 고치시오. (맞으면 'O', 불필요하면 '삭제' 표시)

1 There is a <u>moved</u> robot.
(→   )

'움직이고 있는'은 (진행, 완료) 의미이므로
(현재, 과거)분사

2 I bought a <u>using</u> bike.
(→   )

'사용된'은 (수동, 능동) 의미이므로
(현재, 과거)분사

3 There is a <u>moving underwater robot.</u>
(→   )

[분사+α]가 명사를 수식할 때,
[분사+α]의 위치는 명사 (앞, 뒤)

4 The book <u>bores</u> him.
(→   )

감정을 (느끼는, 유발하는) 동사이므로
지루함을 (느끼게 하다, 느끼다)

5 The book is <u>bored</u> to him.
(→   )

책이 지루함을 (느끼게 하는, 느낀) 것이므로
(현재, 과거)분사

6 He is <u>boring</u> with the book.
(→   )

그가 지루함을 (느끼게 하는, 느낀) 것이므로
(현재, 과거)분사

7 Look at the <u>sleeping</u> lion.
(→   )

(잠자는 중, 잠자는 용도)인 사자이므로
(동명사, 현재분사)

8 I have a <u>sleeping</u> bag.
(→   )

(잠자는 중, 잠자는 용도)인 가방이므로
(동명사, 현재분사)

9 <u>He</u> reading a book, he puts on his glasses.
(→   )

주절과 같은 부사절의
(주어, 목적어)는 삭제 (함, 안 함)

10 <u>Don't</u> hearing the alarm, I kept sleeping.
(→   )

분사의 부정은
(don't, not)을 분사 바로 (앞, 뒤)에 씀

11 <u>Although</u> having a driver's license, Emily never
drives. (→   )

명확한 의미를 위해 (접속사, 주어)는
생략하지 않을 수도 있음

12 <u>Read</u> this book, you will find the answer.
(→   )

(부사절, 주절)의 동사는
(동사원형, 동사원형 + -ing) 형태로 씀

13 <u>Listened</u> to music, he searched the Internet.
(→   )

(부사절, 주절)의 동사는
(동사원형, 동사원형 + -ing) 형태로 씀

■ 주어진 단어를 알맞게 이용하여 우리말과 의미가 같도록 영작하시오.

1	There is, move	~가 있다 / 움직이는 / 로봇 →
2	buy, use	나는 / 샀다 / 중고(사용된) / 자전거를 →
3	There is, underwater	~가 있다 / 로봇 / 수중에서 움직이는 →
4	bore	그 책은 / 지루하게 한다 / 그를 →
5	bore, to	그 책은 ~이다 / 지루하게 하는 / 그에게 →
6	bore, with	그는 ~이다 / 지루함을 느낀 / 그 책에 →
7	look at, sleep	~를 봐라 / 자고 있는 / 사자 →
8	sleep, bag	나는 갖고 있다 / 침낭을 →
9	(분사구문) put on, glasses	읽을 때 / 책을, / 그는 안경을 쓴다 →
10	(분사구문) hear, keep sleeping	듣지 않아서 / 알람을, / 나는 계속 잤다 →
11	(분사구문) although, driver's license	갖고 있지만 / 운전면허증을, / Emily는 절대 운전 안 한다 →
12	(분사구문) read	읽으면 / 이 책을, / 너는 답을 찾을 거다 →
13	(분사구문) listen to, search	들으면서 / 음악을, / 그는 검색했다 / 인터넷을 →

GP 30 재귀대명사

재귀대명사는 인칭대명사의 소유격이나 목적격에 -self(단수)나 -selves(복수)를 붙인 형태로 '~자신, ~자체'의 의미이다.

	1인칭	2인칭	3인칭
단수	_____	_____	_____
복수	_____	_____	_____

❶ 재귀용법: 동사와 전치사의 목적어로 사용하고, 생략할 수 _____.

	주어	동사	_____
_____의 목적어	He	loved	_____
_____의 목적어	She	talked to	_____

The teacher introduced **herself** to the class.

☆ *You* must be proud of **yourself**.

❷ 강조용법: 주어나 목적어를 강조하기 위해 사용하고, 생략할 수 _____.

_____ 강조	I	*myself* built	the house.
_____ 강조	I	built	the house *myself.*
_____ 강조	I	built	the house *itself.*

Allen **himself** fixed the broken car.

☆ *Allen* fixed the broken car **himself**.

I want to meet *the doctor* **himself**.

❸ 관용적 표현

by oneself	_____	in itself	_____
for oneself	_____	beside oneself	_____
of itself	_____	between ourselves	_____
enjoy oneself	_____	help oneself to	_____
talk to oneself	_____	make oneself at home	_____

☆ *Young children* should not swim **by themselves**.

☆ *He* always enjoys learning new things **for himself**.

부정대명사는 특정하게 정해지지 않은 사람, 사물, 수량 등을 나타내는 대명사이다.

one	_____ 명사와 같은 종류의 _____ 사람이나 사물을 나타낸다.
	He broke his watch, so he bought a new one.

another	_____ (같은 종류의 다른 하나)	another (+ _____)
	Can I have another piece of pizza?	

other	(그 밖의) 다른	other + _____
	Is there life on other planets?	

☆ This *bag* is too big. I need a smaller _____.

☆ I don't like this *ring*. Could you show me _____?

This *song* is more famous than _____ songs.

• Upgrade •

❶ 부정대명사 one: 앞에 언급한 _____ 명사를 대신하는 대명사

I lost my cell phone, so I have to buy a new one. (one = a cell phone)

❷ 인칭대명사 it: 앞에 나온 _____ 명사를 대신하는 대명사

I lost my cell phone, but I found it. (it = my cell phone)

one ~, the other ~	(_____) 하나는 ~, 나머지 하나는 ~
● ■	Here are *two* dogs. One is mine, and the other is hers.

one ~, another ~, the other ~	(_____) 하나는 ~, _____ 하나는 ~, _____ 하나는 ~
● ■ ▲	☆ I bought *three* pens. One is black, another is red, and the other is blue.

one ~, the others ~	(_____) 하나는 ~, 나머지 전부는 ~
● ■■■■	I have *five* students. One is a boy, and the others are girls.

some ~, the others ~	(여러 개 중) 몇몇은 ~, _____ 는 ~
●●● ■■■■	Some of my guests arrived on time, and the others arrived late.

some ~, others ~	(불특정 다수) 몇몇은 ~, _____ 은 ~
●●● ■■■■ ▲▲	☆ Some like going out, and others like staying at home.

all은 '모든, 모두'의 의미로 _____ 이상의 사람이나 사물을 나타내고 뒤에 오는 명사에 따라 단수나 복수 취급한다.
both는 '_____'의 의미로 항상 _____ 취급한다.

all	모든 모두	all (of) + _____	_____	All (of) my students are diligent.
		all (of) + _____	_____	All (of) the money was stolen.
both	둘 다(의)	both (of) + _____	_____	Both (of) my parents have jobs.

✗ **All (of) the children** *need* care and love.

✗ **All the advice** *was* very helpful.

✗ **Both of them** *are* high school students.

　Both teams *were* ready to win the game.

each는 둘 이상에서 '_____' 의미로 _____ 취급하고 every는 셋 이상에서 '(개개인에 중점을 둔) _____'
의 의미로 _____ 취급한다.

each	각각(의)	each + _____	_____	Each player has seven cards.
		each of + _____	_____	Each of us is special.
every	모든	every + _____	_____	Every dog has its day.

✗ **Each person** *is* important for our team's victory.

　Each of my friends *has* a cell phone.

✗ **Every student** *wants* to get a good grade.

> ○ Tip ○
> [every + 단수명사]: _____
> · I go swimming every Sunday.

• Upgrade •

부정대명사 either / neither

either은 '_____'의 의미이고 neither은 '_____'의 의미이다. [not + either]을 _____ 로
나타낼 수 있다.

I wrote two letters. **Neither** of them was sent to her.

I **don't** want **either** of those caps. (= I want **neither** of those caps.)

Unit 22 재귀대명사

A ( ) 안에서 알맞은 것을 고르시오.

1 Why did she blame (you, yourself)?

2 We watched the fireworks (ourselves, us).

3 You should not be ashamed of (you, yourself).

4 I am teaching (me, myself) how to play the flute.

5 My sister (himself, herself) changed the light bulbs.

6 The young kids can't use the oven (themselves, themself).

B ( ) 안의 주어진 단어를 고쳐 빈칸을 채우고, 알맞은 역할을 고르시오.

1 He started the campaign to save water _____. (he)   (강조, 목적어) 역할

2 Trust _____. You can do it!   (you)   (강조, 목적어) 역할

3 She helped the poor people _____.   (they)   (강조, 목적어) 역할

4 He traveled to India _____ for one month.   (he)   (강조, 목적어) 역할

5 Do you think of _____ as a good son?   (you)   (강조, 목적어) 역할

C 보기의 표현을 이용하여 빈칸을 완성하시오.

보기 | enjoy oneself   talk to oneself   teach oneself   help oneself

1 A: Did you learn how to swim from your sister?

B: No, I _____ how to swim.

2 A: _____ to some apple pie.

B: Thank you. I'd love a piece.

3 A: Do you have any plans for this weekend?

B: Why don't we _____ at the school festival this Saturday?

4 A: Did you say anything to me?

B: Sorry. I was just _____.

D　우리말과 의미가 같도록 ( ) 안의 말을 배열하시오.

1 나는 내 자신에게 실망했다. (with, disappointed, was, myself)

　　→ I _____.

2 그는 거울로 자기 자신에게 웃어 주었다. (at, he, himself, smiled)

　　→ _____ in the mirror.

3 두뇌는 그 자체로는 어떤 통증도 느끼지 않아. (doesn't, pain, in, any, itself, feel)

　　→ The brain _____.

4 할머니는 혼자 있을 때, 자주 혼잣말을 하신다. (to, often, she, herself, talks)

　　→ When my grandmother is alone, _____.

5 아이들은 스스로 그 과제를 끝내야 한다. (for, project, themselves, their)

　　→ Children should finish _____.

6 그 새가 자기의 둥지를 직접 만들었어. (its, itself, built, nest)

　　→ The bird _____.

E　우리말과 의미가 같도록 ( ) 안의 말을 이용하여 문장을 완성하시오.

1 여러분께 저에 대해 소개하겠습니다. (introduce)

　　→ Let me _____ _____ to you.

2 우리 오빠는 사람들에게 자기 자신에 관해 말하기를 좋아한다. (about)

　　→ My brother likes talking _____ _____ to people.

3 우리는 우리의 비행기 티켓을 직접 예약했다. (airline tickets)

　　→ We booked _____ _____ _____ _____.

4 나의 이모는 자신의 머리를 직접 자르신다. (her own hair)

　　→ My aunt _____.

5 나는 그 노래 자체를 좋아하지 않아. (the song)

　　→ I don't like _____ _____ _____.

6 아이들이 직접 집안에 풍선을 달았어. (hang, around the house)

　　→ The kids _____ _____ _____ _____

　　_____ _____.

Unit 23 부정대명사 one, another, other(s)

A ( ) 안에서 알맞은 것을 고르시오.

1 This book is too difficult for me. I want to read an easy (one, it).

2 She made a beautiful necklace. She will give (one, it) to her friend.

3 Some visit the island by ship. (Others, Another) visit by airplane.

4 He bought 20 apples. He ate one and put (others, the others) on the table.

5 I have two dogs. One is a bulldog, and (other, the other) is a retriever.

6 I'd like to view (another, other) paintings.

B 보기에서 알맞은 것을 골라 문장을 완성하시오. (한 번씩만 사용)

보기 | ones   it   another   other   others

1 Look at the baby bear. _____ looks like a doll.

2 Some countries tried to dominate _____ countries.

3 This piece of cake is very delicious. Can I have _____ ?

4 These socks are too small for me. Please give me bigger _____ .

5 Some like horror movies, and _____ like comedy.

C 보기의 표현을 이용하여 빈칸을 완성하시오.

보기 | · another was a circle   · the others weren't
       · others don't   · the other was for her mom

1 Some people like playing golf, but _____ .

2 One of the 20 eggs was broken, but _____ .

3 She bought two scarves. One was for herself, and _____ .

4 He drew three symbols. One was a triangle, _____ ,

and the other was a square.

D 우리말과 의미가 같도록 ( ) 안의 말을 배열하시오.

1 그녀는 세 마리의 강아지가 있는데 하나는 검은색, 나머지는 모두 흰색이다. (white, the, are, others)

→ She has three puppies. One is black, and _____.

2 나는 애완동물 둘이 있는데, 하나는 거북이, 나머지는 햄스터야. (the, a hamster, is, other)

→ I have two pets. One is a turtle, and _____.

3 Cindy는 이미 컴퓨터 한 대가 있는데, 하나 더 사고 싶어 해. (buy, wants, she, another, to)

→ Cindy already has one computer, but _____.

4 열 명의 소녀들 중 몇몇은 라면을 원하고, 나머지 모두는 치킨을 원한다. (want, the, chicken, others)

→ There are ten girls. Some want ramen, and _____.

5 어떤 사람은 집에서 만든 식사를 좋아하고, 다른 몇몇은 즉석음식을 좋아한다. (instant, others, food, like)

→ Some like homemade food, and _____.

E 우리말과 의미가 같도록 ( ) 안의 말과 대명사를 이용하여 문장을 완성하시오.

1 커피 한 잔 더 드시겠어요? (cup of coffee)

→ Would you like _____ _____ _____ _____?

2 이 모자는 너무 커서 더 작은 것을 원해요. (want)

→ This cap is too big. I _____ _____ _____ _____.

3 신발을 찾고 계시군요. 흰색 신발 어떠세요? (how about)

→ Are you looking for shoes? _____ _____ _____

_____ _____?

4 엄마가 김밥을 만들어 주었는데, 내 친구들이 좋아했어. (love)

→ My mom made *kimbab*, and _____ _____ _____.

5 나는 두 명의 사촌이 있는데, 한 명은 서울에, 한 명은 부산에 산다. (live)

→ I have two cousins. _____ _____ in Seoul, and _____

_____ _____ in Busan.

6 어떤 동물들은 무리를 지어 살고, 어떤 동물들은 홀로 살아. (live)

→ _____ _____ _____ in groups, and _____

_____ alone.

A ( ) 안에서 알맞은 것을 고르시오.

1 (Every, All) child likes to get presents.

2 (Each, Every) of us has a nickname.

3 (Every, All) his bags were carried to his hotel room.

4 Neither of us (can, can't) speak English.

5 (All, Both, Every) of these two buses go to Gangnam.

6 (All, Both) of the three passengers were wearing seatbelts.

B 우리말과 의미가 같도록 보기의 단어로 빈칸을 채우시오. (한 번씩만 사용)

보기 | all   both   each   every

1 그 소녀들 각각 자신의 침대를 갖고 있다.

→ _____ of the girls has her own bed.

2 내 여동생은 모든 선물을 열어 보았다.

→ My sister opened _____ gift.

3 이 사진들을 모두 네가 직접 찍은 거니?

→ Did you take _____ these pictures yourself?

4 그녀는 그녀의 부모님 두 분 모두를 위해 아름다운 집을 지었어.

→ She designed the beautiful house for _____ of her parents.

C ( ) 안의 동사를 알맞게 고쳐 빈칸을 채우시오. (현재시제 사용)

1 Every house _____ the same to me. I can't find your house. (look)

2 All of the players _____ the rules of the game. (know)

3 Each of the students _____ a different hobby. (have)

4 Both of his parents _____ from Jeju Island. (be)

5 Each speaker _____ just five minutes. (have)

D 우리말과 의미가 같도록 ( ) 안의 말을 배열하시오.

1 우리 둘 다 비밀을 알고 있다. (us, both, of, know)

→ _____ the secret.

2 나의 두 딸 모두 역사에 관심이 있다. (of, are, both, my, daughters)

→ _____ interested in history.

3 그 방 세 개는 각각 바다 전경을 가지고 있다. (of, three rooms, each, the, has)

→ _____ a sea view.

4 내가 방에 들어갔을 때, 모든 창문이 열려 있었다. (open, all, were, windows, the)

→ _____ when I entered the room.

5 교장 선생님은 매일 아침 학생 모두와 악수하신다. (every, each, morning, student)

→ My principal shakes hands with _____.

6 모든 식물과 동물은 공기, 물, 햇빛이 필요해. (plant, animal, every, and, needs)

→ _____ air, water, and sunlight.

E 우리말과 의미가 같도록 ( ) 안의 말과 대명사를 이용하여 문장을 완성하시오.

1 우리는 매주 일요일에 테니스를 쳤다. (Sunday)

→ We played tennis _____ _____.

2 그는 그의 책들 각각에 이름을 썼어. (his books, of)

→ He wrote his name on _____ _____ _____.

3 네 모든 문제를 나에게 말해 주렴. (your problems)

→ Please tell me _____ _____ _____.

4 각각의 챕터는 재미있는 부제목을 가지고 있다. (chapter)

→ _____ _____ _____ interesting subtitles.

5 유리와 캔 두 가지 모두 해변에서는 금지된다. (glass, cans)

→ _____ _____ _____ _____ are forbidden

on the beach.

6 이 동네 모든 집은 컬러풀한 지붕을 갖고 있어. (house, a colorful roof)

→ In this neighborhood, _____ _____ _____

_____ _____ _____.

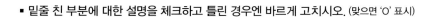

■ 밑줄 친 부분에 대한 설명을 체크하고 틀린 경우엔 바르게 고치시오. (맞으면 'O' 표시)

1	You must be proud of <u>you</u>. (→)	주어와 목적어가 (같음, 다름) 이 경우 (인칭대명사, 재귀대명사) 사용
2	Allen fixed the broken car <u>yourself</u>. (→)	주어를 강조하는 재귀대명사는 (himself, itself)
3	Young children should not swim <u>in themself</u>. (→)	'혼자서(홀로)'라는 의미는 (in, by) + (themself, themselves)
4	He always enjoys learning new things <u>of himself</u>. (→)	'혼자 힘으로(스스로)'라는 의미는 (of, for) + (him, himself)
5	This bag is too big. I need a smaller <u>one</u>. (→)	앞에서 언급한 '가방'과 (같은, 다른) 가방은 (one, it)
6	I don't like this ring. Could you show me <u>other</u>? (→)	앞에서 언급한 '반지'와 (같은, 다른) 종류의 또 다른 하나는 (another, other)
7	I bought three pens. One is black, another is red, and <u>the other</u> is blue. (→)	세 개 중 하나는 one, 다른 하나는 another, 나머지 하나는 (other, the other)
8	Some like going out, and <u>the others</u> like staying at home. (→)	(불특정 다수 중) 몇몇은 some ~, 다른 몇몇은 (others, the others) ~
9	All (of) the children <u>needs</u> care and love. (→)	all(+ 복수명사 + (단수, 복수)동사
10	All the advice <u>were</u> very helpful. (→)	all(+ 단수명사 + (단수, 복수)동사
11	Both of them <u>are</u> high school students. (→)	both of + 복수명사 + (단수, 복수)동사
12	Each person <u>are</u> important for our team's victory. (→)	each + (단수, 복수)명사 + (단수, 복수)동사
13	Every <u>students</u> wants to get a good grade. (→)	every + (단수, 복수)명사 + (단수, 복수)동사

Sentence Writing

**Chapter 08
대명사**

▪ 주어진 단어를 알맞게 이용하여 우리말과 의미가 같도록 영작하시오.

1	must, be proud of	너는 / 자랑스러운 것이 분명하다 / 네 자신이 →
2	fix, broken car	Allen은 / 부서진 차를 고쳤다 / 스스로 →
3	children, should, oneself	어린아이들은 / 수영하면 안 된다 / 혼자서(홀로) →
4	enjoy, learn, new things	그는 / 새로운 것을 배우는 걸 항상 즐긴다 / 혼자 힘으로 →
5	smaller	이 가방은 / 너무 크다. / 나는 / 필요하다 / 더 작은 것이 →
6	ring, show	나는 / 이 반지가 마음에 안 든다. / 보여 줄래요 / 또 다른 것을? →
7	three pens	나는 펜 3개를 샀다. / 하나는 검은색 / 또 다른 하나는 빨간색 / 그리고 나머지는 파란색이다 →
8	going out, staying at home	몇몇은 외출하는 것을 좋아하고 / 다른 몇몇은 집에 있는 것을 좋아한다 →
9	need, care	모든 아이들은 / 필요로 한다 / 돌봄과 사랑을 →
10	the advice, helpful	모든 충고가 / 매우 도움이 되었다 →
11	both, them	그들 둘 다는 / 고등학교 학생이다 →
12	each, person, victory	각각의 사람은 / 중요하다 / 우리 팀의 승리를 위해 →
13	every, get, grade	모든 학생은 / 원한다 / 좋은 점수 얻기를 →

GP 35 원급, 비교급, 최상급

❶ 원급

A [____ 원급 ____] B _____

☆ His speech is **as powerful as** his rival's.

☆ Today is not **as hot as** yesterday.

❷ 비교급

A [비교급 ____] B A가 B보다 ~한(하게)

☆ Hot air is **lighter than** cold air.

☆ Your idea is **more creative than** mine.

❸ 최상급

A [____ 최상급 ____] B A가 B에서 가장 ~한(하게)

☆ The thumb is **the shortest** of all five fingers.

☆ Vatican City is **the smallest** nation in the world.

❹ 비교급과 최상급 만들기

규칙 변화	기본 변화	+ -er / -est	long	long**er**	long**est**
	-e로 끝나는 경우	+ -r / -st	close	_____	_____
	[단모음 + 단자음] 경우	끝자음 하나 더 + -er / -est	big	_____	_____
	[자음 + y]로 끝나는 경우	y → i + -er / -est	busy	_____	_____
	3음절 이상, -ous, -ful	more / most + 원급	famous	_____ famous	_____ famous
	-ly로 끝나는 부사	more / most + 원급	slowly	_____ slowly	_____ slowly
불규칙 변화			_____	_____	best
			bad / ill	_____	_____
			many / much	_____	_____
			little	_____	_____

92

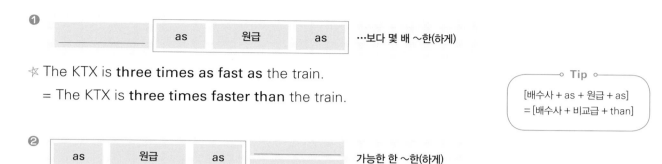

❶

| ____, ____, ____, ____, ____ | 비교급 | than |

훨씬 더 ~한(하게)

☆ I feel **much** *healthier* than before.

❷

점점 더 ~한(하게)

☆ Cell phones are getting **smarter and smarter**.

❸

| ____ ____ (s + v) | , | ____ ____ (s + v) |

~할수록 더 ~하다

☆ **The more** we share, **the happier** we become.

❶

| ____ | of | the | 최상급 | ____ |

가장 ~한 것들 중 하나

☆ The wheel is **one of the greatest inventions** in history.

❷

| the | 최상급 | 명사 | that | ____ |

지금껏 한 것 중 가장 ~한

☆ This is **the worst hairstyle that I have ever had**.

A 주어진 형용사와 부사의 비교급과 최상급을 쓰시오.

원급	비교급	최상급
1 long		
2 bad		
3 big		
4 busy		
5 little		
6 much		
7 good		
8 close		
9 slowly		
10 famous		

B ( ) 안에서 알맞은 것을 고르시오.

1 "Sorry" is the (hard, hardest) word for me to say.

2 This hammock is (not as, as not) comfortable as a bed.

3 I go to the movies (more often, oftener) than Jane.

4 The giraffe doesn't live as (longer than, long as) the chimp.

5 Of all the snacks, my sister likes chocolate the (more, most).

6 The hamburgers in the catalog look (deliciouser, more delicious) than the real ones.

C ( ) 안에 주어진 단어를 이용하여 문장을 완성하시오.

1 This building is as _____ as your school. (big)

2 The Earth is _____ than the sun. (small)

3 It is the _____ tree in my town. (old)

4 I hit the ball as _____ as my dad. (hard)

5 Sophia is the _____ singer of us all. (good)

6 My skirt is _____ than your blouse. (expensive)

D 우리말과 의미가 같도록 ( ) 안의 말을 배열하시오.

1 타조는 사자보다 빨리 뛸 수 있다. (than, run, faster, can, lions)

→ Ostriches _____ .

2 이번 주는 지난주만큼 춥지는 않다. (not, as, as, last, cold, week)

→ This week is _____ .

3 너희 가족 중에서 누가 가장 키가 크니? (in, your, tallest, family, the)

→ Who is _____ ?

4 이 의자는 소파만큼 편안하다. (comfortable, as, as, the, sofa)

→ This chair is _____ .

5 숲에서 걷는 것이 도시에서 걷는 것보다 더 즐겁다. (pleasant, more, than)

→ Walking through a forest is _____ walking through the city.

6 8월은 북반구에서 일 년 중 가장 더운 달이다. (the, the, of, year, month, hottest)

→ August is _____ in the Northern Hemisphere.

E 우리말과 의미가 같도록 ( ) 안의 말을 이용하여 문장을 완성하시오.

1 나는 너만큼 자주 PC방에 가지 않아. (often)

→ I don't go to the Internet café _____ _____ _____ .

2 이 앱이 영어 듣기에 가장 도움이 되었다. (helpful)

→ This app was _____ _____ _____ for English listening.

3 그의 중간고사 성적은 내 성적만큼이나 나빴다. (bad, mine)

→ Her grade on the midterm exam was _____ _____ _____ .

4 내 친구는 때로 선생님보다 학교에 더 늦게 온다. (late)

→ My friend often comes to school _____ _____ his teacher.

5 10번 문제가 문제들 중에서 가장 어려웠어. (difficult)

→ Question number ten was _____ _____ _____ of all the questions.

6 네게는 이 책이 컴퓨터보다 더 유용할 거야. (useful)

→ This book will be _____ _____ the computer to you.

A ( ) 안에서 알맞은 것을 고르시오.

1 Hold your breath (the longest, as long as) possible.

2 The (high, higher) we climbed, the colder it became.

3 The soccer player ran (as two times fast, two times as fast) as I did.

4 As summer passes, the days get shorter and (shorter, more).

5 This lip balm is one of the (popular, most popular) items with girls.

6 Alex is (very, much) taller than Kate.

7 Donald walked as quietly as he (can, could).

8 (The bigger, Bigger) the puppy became, the more it ate.

9 The king's tomb is one of the most mysterious (tomb, tombs) in history.

10 You are (a, the) most wonderful person that I have ever met.

B ( ) 안에 주어진 단어를 이용하여 문장을 완성하시오.

1 I will help you as _____ as possible. (much)

2 _____ _____ he gets, the more often he forgets things. (old)

3 She looked a lot _____ than her sister. (young)

4 My brother usually eats _____ _____ _____ than I do.
(much, two, time)

5 Gyro Drop is the _____ _____ ride that I have ever ridden. (exciting)

6 The store was getting _____ _____ _____ _____.
(crowded)

7 Cathy sang as _____ as a professional singer. (good)

8 When the donkey stood up, the sponges were much _____ than before. (heavy)

9 It was _____ _____ picture that I _____ _____
_____. (good, take)

10 The yellow dust is getting _____ _____ _____ every
year. (bad)

C 우리말과 의미가 같도록 ( ) 안의 말을 배열하시오.

1 어떤 사람들은 가능하면 젊게 보이려고 애쓴다. (as, as, young, possible)

→ Some people try to look _____.

2 이것은 내가 했었던 가장 바보 같은 실수이다. (mistake, the, foolish, most)

→ It is _____ that I have ever made.

3 네가 나를 사랑하는 것보다 내가 너를 훨씬 더 많이 사랑한단다. (than, more, a lot)

→ I love you _____ you love me.

4 많이 걸으면 걸을수록, 더욱 건강해질 것이다. (more, the, healthier, the)

→ _____ you walk, _____ you will become.

5 이 버섯은 고기의 네 배 정도 비싸다. (as, as, four, times, expensive)

→ This mushroom is _____ meat.

6 Tom은 회사에서 가장 부지런한 직원들 중 한 명이다. (of, the, one, most, workers, diligent)

→ Tom is _____ at the company.

D 우리말과 의미가 같도록 ( ) 안의 말을 이용하여 문장을 완성하시오.

1 그는 가능한 주의 깊게 뉴스를 읽었다. (carefully)

→ He read the news _____ _____ _____ _____.

2 이것은 그가 잡아 본 가장 큰 생선이다. (big, catch)

→ This is _____ _____ _____ that he _____ _____
_____.

3 말을 적게 하면 적게 할수록, 우리는 실수를 덜 할 것이다. (little, few)

→ _____ _____ you talk, _____ _____ mistakes you will make.

4 우리 교실이 바깥보다 훨씬 더 추웠다. (cold)

→ My classroom was _____ _____ _____ it was outside.

5 알파고를 이기는 것이 점점 더 어려워질 것이다. (difficult)

→ It is getting _____ _____ _____ _____ to beat AlphaGo.

6 오페라 하우스는 가장 유명한 관광 명소들 중에 하나이다. (popular, tourist attractions)

→ The opera house is one of _____ _____ _____ _____
_____.

■ 밑줄 친 부분에 대한 설명을 체크하고 틀린 경우엔 바르게 고치시오. (맞으면 'O' 표시)

1	His speech is as <u>more powerful</u> as his rival's. (→)	'~만큼 ~한'은 as + (원급, 비교급) + as
2	Today is <u>as not</u> hot as yesterday. (→)	원급 부정은 (as not, not as) + 원급 + as
3	Hot air is <u>lightest</u> than cold air. (→)	'~보다 ~한'은 (비교급, 최상급) + than
4	Your idea is <u>creativer</u> than mine. (→)	3음절 이상인 형용사의 비교급은 (형용사 + er, more + 형용사)
5	The thumb is the <u>shorter</u> of all five fingers. (→)	the + (비교급, 최상급) + of + 복수명사
6	Vatican City is the smallest nation <u>of</u> the world. (→)	'~에서(장소) 가장 ~한'은 the + 최상급 + (in, of) + 단수명사
7	The KTX is <u>as three times</u> fast as the train. (→)	'~보다 몇 배 ~한'은 (as + 배수사, 배수사 + as) + 원급 + as
8	Smile as <u>often</u> as possible. (→)	'가능한 한 ~하게'는 as + (원급, 비교급) + as + possible
9	I feel <u>very</u> healthier than before. (→)	비교급 강조는 (매우, 훨씬) 의미이며 (very, much) + 비교급
10	Cell phones are getting <u>smart and smart</u>. (→)	'점점 더 ~한'은 (원급 + and + 원급, 비교급 + and + 비교급)
11	The more we share, <u>happier</u> we become. (→)	'~할수록 더 ~하다'는 The + 비교급, (비교급, the + 비교급)
12	The wheel is one of the <u>greater</u> inventions in history. (→)	'가장 ~한 것들 중 하나'는 one of (비교급, the + 최상급) + 복수명사
13	This is the worst hairstyle that I <u>ever had</u>. (→)	'지금껏 한 것 중 가장 ~한'은 the + 최상급 + 명사 + 주어 + (과거동사, have ever p.p.)

Sentence writing

▪ 주어진 단어를 알맞게 이용하여 우리말과 의미가 같도록 영작하시오.

1	speech, powerful, rival	그의 연설은 / ~만큼 강하다 / 그의 라이벌의 연설 →
2	today, hot	오늘은 / ~만큼 덥지 않다 / 어제 →
3	air, light	뜨거운 공기는 / 더 가볍다 / 차가운 공기보다
4	idea, creative	너의 아이디어가 / 더 창의적이다 / 내 것보다 →
5	the thumb, finger, short	엄지손가락은 / 가장 짧다 / 다섯 손가락들 모두 중에서 →
6	Vatican City, small	바티칸시티는 / 가장 작은 국가이다 / 세계에서 →
7	three times, as ~ as	KTX는 / ~만큼의 세 배 빠르다 / 그 기차 →
8	smile, possible	웃어라 / 가능한 한 자주 →
9	feel, healthy, before	나는 / 느낀다 / 훨씬 더 건강하다고 / 이전보다 →
10	cell phones, get, smart	휴대폰이 / ~해지고 있다 / 점점 더 똑똑한 →
11	share, become	더 많이 / 우리가 나눌수록 / 더 행복한 / 우리는 된다 →
12	the wheel, inventions, great	바퀴는 / ~ 중 하나다 / 가장 위대한 발명품들 / 역사상 →
13	hairstyle, have, ever	이것은 / 가장 나쁜 헤어스타일이다 / 내가 지금껏 가졌었던 것 중 →

문법패턴 빈칸 채우기

GP 39 시간 접속사

두 문장 사이의 시간 관계를 나타내는 시간 접속사는 when, while, as, until, since 등이 있다. 이런 접속사가 이끄는 문장을 부사절이라고 한다.

	접속사	주어 + 동사		주어 + 동사
~할 때	☆ _____	he goes fishing,		I will join him.
~하기 전에	_____	you take action,		you should think twice.
~한 후에	_____	I packed my school bag,	+	I went to bed.
~하는 동안	_____	kids sleep,		they grow the most.
~할 때까지	☆ _____	she says, "yes,"		her dog won't eat.
~한 이후로	_____	I moved to this city,		I have made many friends.

시간 _____   _____

The movie started **before** Eric arrived.

The old man makes a ho-ho-ho sound **when** he laughs.

• Upgrade •

시간 부사절의 시제

주절이 _____ 일 때에도 시간 부사절의 시제는 미래시제 대신 _____ 를 사용한다.

☆ We will get home *before* it _____ (w̶i̶l̶l̶ ̶g̶e̶t̶) dark.

GP 40 이유 접속사

두 문장 사이의 원인과 결과 관계를 나타내는 이유 접속사는 because, as, since 등이 있다.

	접속사	주어 + 동사		주어 + 동사
	☆ _____	he didn't sleep enough,		he had red eyes.
~하기 때문에	_____	I am under 19,	+	I can't watch the movie.
	_____	my dog has short legs,		it can't run fast.

이유 _____   _____

I don't want to talk to him **because** he is not honest.

The hotel is popular **as** it has a nice view.

GP 41 조건 접속사

두 문장 사이의 조건과 결과의 관계를 나타내는 접속사는 if, unless (= if ~ not) 등이 있다.

	조건			
	접속사	주어 + 동사		주어 + 동사
~한다면	☆＿＿＿＿	you take a walk,		you will feel better.
~하지 않으면	☆＿＿＿＿	we finish the meal,	**+**	we will get hungry soon.
	= If	we don't finish the meal,		we will get hungry soon.

My cat doesn't come to me ＿＿＿＿＿＿ it is hungry.

= My cat doesn't come to me **if** it is **not** hungry.

• Upgrade •

조건 부사절의 시제

주절이 ＿＿＿＿＿＿＿ 일 때에도, 조건 부사절에서는 미래시제 대신 ＿＿＿＿＿＿＿ 를 사용한다.

If she **reads** (~~will read~~) the book, she will find the answer.

GP 42 양보 접속사

두 문장 사이의 내용이 반대이거나 예상하지 못한 결과를 나타낼 때 쓰는 양보 접속사에는 though, although 등이 있다.

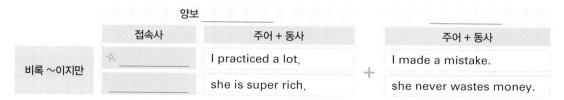

	양보			
	접속사	주어 + 동사		주어 + 동사
비록 ~이지만	☆＿＿＿＿	I practiced a lot,	**+**	I made a mistake.
	＿＿＿＿	she is super rich,		she never wastes money.

Although the cap is not the right size, I will buy it.

GP 43 명령문 and / or

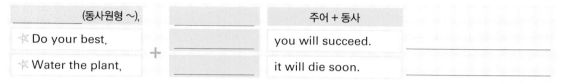

＿＿＿＿ (동사원형 ~),		＿＿＿＿	주어 + 동사	＿＿＿＿
☆ Do your best,	**+**	＿＿＿＿	you will succeed.	
☆ Water the plant,		＿＿＿＿	it will die soon.	

Do your best, ＿＿＿＿＿＿ you will succeed.

= If you do your best, you will succeed.

Water the plant, ＿＿＿＿＿＿ it will die soon.

= Unless you water the plant, it will die soon.

GP 44 접속사 that

접속사 that이 이끄는 문장은 [that 주어 + 동사]의 형태로 '_____'으로 해석하고 문장에서 _____, _____, _____로 쓰인다.

주어	동사	목적어 / 보어
_____ penguins are birds	is	well known.
It	is	well known _____ penguins are birds.
I	know	_____ penguins are birds.
The fact	is	_____ penguins are birds.

☆ _____ is strange _____ it is snowing in May. (주어)

I expect _____ he will marry the woman. (목적어)

The problem is _____ we have too much homework. (보어)

GP 45 상관접속사

상관접속사는 두 개 이상의 어구가 짝을 이루어 문법적으로 동일한 성질의 두 요소를 연결하는 접속사이다.

_____	A	_____	B	A와 B 둘 다
_____	A	_____	B	A와 B 둘 중 하나
_____	A	_____	B	A와 B 둘 다 아닌
_____	A	_____	B	A뿐만 아니라 B도
=	B	_____	A	

Her speech was **both** interesting **and** short.

☆ I will give this ticket to **either** Eric **or** Allen.

☆ He was **neither** rude **nor** unkind.

☆ **Not only** his brothers **but also** Tim has blond hair.

• Upgrade •

상관접속사가 사용된 주어의 동사 일치

[both A and B]는 항상 _____ 취급하며, 나머지는 모두 _____ 에 일치시킨다.

Neither Jane nor *her sisters* **are** shy.

A   ( ) 안에서 알맞은 것을 고르시오.

1 The dog shows its teeth (when, until) it is angry.

2 Please wait here (because, until) we call your name.

3 It is a dry town (if, because) it was built in a desert.

4 Could you look after my dog (while, before) we are away?

5 I will be there for you when you (need, will need) me.

6 Jane has slept by herself (when, since) she was five years old.

7 Andrew got a full-time job (as, unless) he needed money.

8 (Because, Before) I am allergic to milk, I don't eat yogurt.

9 (After, Until) it rained, the street festival got canceled.

B   보기에서 알맞은 접속사를 골라 빈칸을 채우시오. (한 번씩만 사용)

보기 | while   until   since   because   before

1 It has been two years _____ he left Seoul.

2 _____ the sign was written in French, he couldn't read it.

3 The great artist was poor _____ she was alive.

4 She wrote down the idea _____ she forgot it.

5 Bake the bread _____ it turns brown.

C   두 문장이 같도록 보기에서 알맞은 접속사를 골라 문장을 연결하시오.

보기 | while   because   after

1 Your phone was ringing as you were out of the room.

→ Your phone was ringing _____ you were out of the room.

2 He tried on some different shoes before he bought these.

→ _____ he tried on some different shoes, he bought these.

3 The bench is wet, so we shouldn't sit on it.

→ _____ the bench is wet, we shouldn't sit on it.

D ( ) 안의 단어를 알맞은 시제 형태로 고쳐 쓰시오.

1 Let the baby sleep until we _____ home. (arrive)

2 I will turn off the gas when the water _____. (boil)

3 She will leave for Daegu after she _____ her work. (finish)

4 When you _____ home, dinner will be ready. (come)

E 우리말과 의미가 같도록 ( ) 안의 말을 배열하시오.

1 내가 점심을 요리하는 동안 식탁을 차려 주겠니? (I, lunch, while, cook)

→ Can you set the table _____?

2 한국을 마지막 방문한 이후로 6개월이 지났어. (visited, I, since, last, Korea)

→ Six months have passed _____.

3 지구가 자전을 하기 때문에, 두 번의 조수가 매일 발생해. (rotates, the Earth, as)

→ _____, two tides happen every day.

4 우리는 해가 뜰 때까지 텐트에서 잤다. (came up, the sun, until)

→ We slept in a tent _____.

5 나는 온천이 너무 뜨거워서 들어가지 않았어. (it, too, as, was, hot)

→ I didn't get in the hot spring _____.

F 우리말과 의미가 같도록 ( ) 안의 말을 이용하여 문장을 완성하시오.

1 밖이 어두워서, 우리는 안에 머물렀어. (it)

→ We stayed inside _____ _____ _____ outside.

2 너는 음식을 삼키기 전에 잘 씹어야 해. (swallow)

→ You must chew your food well _____ _____.

3 내가 바이올린을 연주하는 동안, 줄이 하나 끊어졌어. (the violin)

→ _____ _____ _____ _____ _____ _____,

a string broke.

4 인생은 미스터리하기 때문에 아름다운 거야. (mysterious)

→ Life is beautiful _____ _____ _____.

5 우리는 많은 실수를 한 후에 마침내 성공했지. (make, mistakes)

→ _____ _____ _____ _____, we finally succeeded.

A ( ) 안에서 알맞은 것을 고르시오.

1 I will do it (if, unless) I have another choice.

2 (If, Unless) you don't like this skirt, I will show you another one.

3 (Although, If) the artist doesn't have hands, he paints great works.

4 Chain your bicycle to the post, (and, or) you may lose it.

5 (And, Even though) they are poor, they look so happy together.

6 Warm up the soup, (and, or) it will taste better.

7 I won't cook for you again unless you (don't finish, finish) the meal.

8 Get some rest, (and, or) you will get too tired.

B 보기에서 알맞은 접속사를 골라 빈칸을 채우시오. (한 번씩만 사용)

보기 | although   if   unless   and

1 I will buy the shoes _____ they are on sale.

2 We can arrive on time _____ there is heavy traffic.

3 _____ the stone looks like a diamond, it is not a real one.

4 Visit us again, _____ you will get one free ticket.

C 두 문장이 같도록 보기에서 알맞은 접속사를 골라 문장을 연결하시오.

보기 | if   unless   and   or

1 Unless I know the answer, I usually stay silent.

→ _____ I don't know the answer, I usually stay silent.

2 I can't keep this puppy if all my family members don't agree.

→ I can't keep this puppy _____ all my family members agree.

3 If you wear the sunglasses, you will look more stylish.

→ Wear the sunglasses, _____ you will look more stylish.

4 If you don't take off your wet shoes, you will catch a cold.

→ Take off your wet shoes, _____ you will catch a cold.

D   ( ) 안의 말을 알맞은 시제 형태로 고쳐 쓰시오.

1 Unless you _____ the alarm, you won't get up early. (set)

2 If you _____ , I will give you this computer. (want)

3 Unless he _____ the book by tomorrow, he will be in trouble. (return)

4 If you _____ the bell, she will answer the door. (ring)

E   우리말과 의미가 같도록 ( ) 안의 말을 배열하시오.

1 기적이 발생하지 않는다면, 그 축구팀은 질 거야. (happens, unless, miracle, a)

→ _____ , the soccer team will lose.

2 네가 혼자 살게 되면, 너는 가족을 그리워하게 될 거야. (live, you, if, alone)

→ _____ , you will miss your family.

3 '고비'는 사막임에도 불구하고 매우 추워. (the Gobi, even though, desert, is, a)

→ _____ , it is very cold.

4 시간 낭비하지 마세요. 그렇지 않으면 후회할 것입니다. (you, or, regret, will, it)

→ Don't waste your time, _____ .

5 높은 곳을 노려라, 그러면 높은 곳을 맞히게 될 거야(목표가 높아야 성과도 높다.) (you, strike, and, will, high)

→ Aim high, _____ .

F   우리말과 의미가 같도록 ( ) 안의 말을 이용하여 문장을 완성하시오.

1 그가 주로 틀리긴 하지만, 이번에는 그가 옳아. (wrong)

→ _____ _____ _____ _____ , he is right this time.

2 네가 이 알약을 복용하면, 기침하는 것을 멈출 거야. (take, pill)

→ _____ _____ _____ _____ _____ , you will stop coughing.

3 찾아라, 그러면 너는 발견할 것이다. (and, find)

→ Seek, _____ _____ _____ _____ .

4 밖이 매우 추운데도 불구하고, 그는 반바지를 입고 나갔어. (it, freezing)

→ _____ _____ _____ _____ outside, he went out in shorts.

5 네가 이 게임기를 사용 안 하면, 내가 이것을 기부할 거야. (game player)

→ _____ _____ _____ _____ _____ _____ , I will

donate it.

A   ( ) 안에서 알맞은 것을 고르시오.

1 (It, That) he likes you is true.

2 Tony as well as you (like, likes) Clara.

3 Cathy is not only cute (also, but also) smart.

4 The movie is both interesting (or, and) moving.

5 The chef hopes (that, if) his guests enjoy the food.

6 We can (either, neither) take the subway or walk there.

B   다음 문장을 가주어(It)와 진주어(that S + V)를 사용한 문장으로 바꿔 쓰시오.

1 That she went to Harvard University is true.

→ _____ is true _____ .

2 That the little girl can sing so well is amazing.

→ _____ is amazing _____ .

3 That he hasn't arrived yet is strange.

→ _____ is strange _____ .

4 That Tom left his homework at home was true.

→ _____ was true _____ .

C   우리말과 의미가 같도록 보기에서 알맞은 상관접속사를 골라 빈칸을 채우시오. (한 번씩만 사용)

보기 | not only ~ but   both ~ and   either ~ or   neither ~ nor

1 아이들은 책에서뿐만 아니라 게임에서도 배운다.

→ Children learn _____ from books _____ also from games.

2 Jane과 나 우리 둘 모두 그의 생일을 기억하지 못했어.

→ _____ Jane _____ I remembered his birthday.

3 당신의 비밀번호는 6자리 또는 9자리 수여야 합니다.

→ Your password must be _____ 6 _____ 9 digits long.

4 우리는 모두 장점과 단점을 갖고 있어.

→ We all have _____ strong _____ weak points.

D 밑줄 친 부분의 해석을 쓰고, 용법을 보기에서 골라 번호를 쓰시오.

보기 | ① 주어(that절의 주어가 ~하는 것은) ② 목적어(that절의 주어가 ~하는 것을) ③ 보어(that절의 주어가 ~하는 것이다)		
예시 | It is true that I like Tom.	해석 내가 Tom을 좋아하는 것은	용법 ①
1 Jane thinks that she is lucky.	해석 _____ 것을	용법
2 The problem is that I am late.	해석 _____ 것이다	용법
3 We hope that you like it.	해석 _____ 것을	용법

E 우리말과 의미가 같도록 ( ) 안의 말을 배열하시오.

1 그뿐만 아니라 나도 당신을 매우 좋아하는 팬입니다. (he, not only, I, but, also)

→ _____ am a big fan of you.

2 그녀의 새 소설은 재미있을 뿐만 아니라 창의적이야. (as, as, well, interesting, creative)

→ Her new novel is _____ .

3 고릴라 한 마리가 동물원을 탈출했다더라. (a, gorilla, that, escaped, from, the, zoo)

→ They said _____ .

4 당신은 전화나 이메일로 저에게 연락할 수 있어요. (by phone, by e-mail, or, either)

→ You can contact me _____ .

5 우리는 경찰이 그 범죄자를 잡기를 바라. (the, police, that, the, criminal, catch)

→ We hope _____ .

F 우리말과 의미가 같도록 ( ) 안의 말을 이용하여 문장을 완성하시오.

1 Tom은 나의 아이디어를 좋아하지도 싫어하지도 않았어. (like, dislike)

→ Tom _____ _____ _____ my idea.

2 너뿐만 아니라 Paula도 그 일자리에 지원했어. (apply)

→ _____ _____ _____ _____ for the job.

3 네가 최선을 다했다는 것이 가장 중요해. (do one's best)

→ It is most important _____ _____ _____ .

4 좋은 소식은 그녀가 그녀의 잃어버린 개를 찾았다는 거야. (find, missing dog)

→ The good news is _____ _____ _____ .

5 아이들뿐만 아니라 그들의 엄마도 아이스크림을 좋아했어. (the kids)

→ _____ _____ _____ liked ice cream.

Error Correction

▪ 밑줄 친 부분에 대한 설명을 체크하고 틀린 경우엔 바르게 고치시오. (맞으면 'O' 표시)

*S: 주어, V: 동사

1	<u>Until</u> he goes fishing, I will join him. (→)	낚시 (갈 때, 갈 때까지) 시간 부사절 접속사 (When, Until)
2	<u>Since</u> she says, "Yes," her dog won't eat. (→)	말(할 때까지, 하기 때문에) 시간 부사절 접속사 (Since, Until)
3	We will get home before it <u>will get</u> dark. (→)	(시간, 조건) 부사절에서는 (현재, 미래)시제 대신 (현재, 미래)시제를 씀
4	<u>Before</u> he didn't sleep enough, he had red eyes. (→)	충분히 못 (자기 전에, 자서) 이유 부사절 접속사 (Before, Because)
5	If you <u>will take</u> a walk, you will feel better. (→)	(시간, 조건) 부사절에서는 (현재, 미래)시제 대신 (현재, 미래)시제를 씀
6	Unless we <u>don't finish</u> the meal, we will get hungry soon. (→)	Unless는 (If, If ~ not)의 의미로 not과 동시 (사용, 사용 불가)
7	<u>Since</u> I practiced a lot, I made a mistake. (→)	열심히 연습(했더라도, 했기 때문에) 양보 부사절 접속사 (Though, Since)
8	Do your best, <u>or</u> you will succeed. (→)	명령문, (and, or) + S + V ~해라, (그러면, 그렇지 않으면) ~할 거다
9	Water the plant, <u>and</u> it will die soon. (→)	명령문, (and, or) + S + V ~해라, (그러면, 그렇지 않으면) ~할 거다
10	<u>This</u> is strange that it is snowing in May. (→)	[that + S + V]가 진주어일 때 문장 앞에 가주어는 (This, It)을·를 씀
11	I will give this ticket to either Eric <u>nor</u> Allen. (→)	상관접속사 either A (or, nor) B A와 B (둘 중 하나, 둘 모두 아닌)의 의미
12	He was neither rude <u>or</u> unkind. (→)	상관접속사 neither A (or, nor) B A와 B (둘 중 하나, 둘 모두 아닌)의 의미
13	Not only his brothers but also Tim <u>have</u> blond hair. (→)	상관접속사 not only A but also B가 (주어, 목적어)일 때 (A, B)에 동사를 일치시킴

Sentence writing

■ 주어진 단어를 알맞게 이용하여 우리말과 의미가 같도록 영작하시오.

1	go fishing, join	그가 낚시를 갈 때 / 나도 같이 갈 거다 →
2	say, "Yes"	그녀가 예스라고 말할 때까지 / 그녀의 개는 안 먹을 거다 →
3	get home, get dark	우리는 집에 도착할 거다 / 어두워지기 전에 →
4	enough, have red eyes	그가 충분히 잠을 못 잤기 때문에 / 그는 눈이 빨갰다 →
5	take a walk, feel	네가 산책을 한다면 / 기분이 좋아질 거다 →
6	unless, the meal	우리가 식사를 마치지 않는다면 / 우리는 곧 배고파질 거다 →
7	practice, make	비록 내가 열심히 연습했지만 / 나는 실수를 하나 했다 →
8	and	최선을 다 하세요, / 그러면 / 당신은 성공할 것입니다 →
9	water, or	그 식물에 물을 줘, / 그렇지 않으면 / 그것은 곧 죽을 거다 →
10	it, that	이상하다 / 5월 달에 눈이 오는 것은 →
11	to, either	나는 줄 거다 / 이 콘서트 티켓을 / ~에게 / Eric이나 Allen →
12	rude, unkind	그는 / ~이지 않았다 / 무례하지도 불친절하지도 →
13	not only, have blond hair	그의 형제들뿐만 아니라 Tim도 / 금발머리를 갖고 있다 →

문법패턴 빈칸 채우기

GP 46 관계대명사의 역할과 종류

관계대명사는 _____와 _____ 역할을 동시에 하고 관계대명사가 이끄는 절은 앞에 나오는 명사(선행사)를 _____ 한다. 관계대명사는 수식을 받는 선행사와 관계대명사의 격에 따라 다음과 같이 나뉜다.

I have	a cat	which	looks like a tiger.
	선행사	관계대명사절: _____ 역할	

선행사	주격 관계대명사	소유격 관계대명사	목적격 관계대명사
사람	_____	_____	_____
동물, 사물	_____	_____	_____
사람, 동물, 사물	_____	-	_____
선행사 없음	_____	-	_____

GP 47 주격 관계대명사 who, which, that

주격 관계대명사는 주어 역할을 하고 바로 뒤에 _____가 온다.

_____	I know	a boy.	+	He	is very kind to everyone.
_____	I know	a boy	_____		is very kind to everyone.

관계대명사가 주어 역할을 하므로, 주격 대명사 _____

My teacher chose *the book*. + It was written in English. <It = _____>
→ ☆ My teacher chose *the book* _____ was written in English.

GP 48 목적격 관계대명사 who(m), which, that

목적격 관계대명사는 목적어 역할을 하고 바로 뒤에 _____와 _____가 온다.

접속사와 대명사	I know	a boy.	+	Everyone likes	him	very much.
관계대명사	I know	a boy	_____	everyone likes very much.		

관계대명사가 목적어 역할을 하므로, 목적격 대명사 _____

He posted *a picture* on his blog. + He took it yesterday. <it = _____>
→ ☆ He posted *a picture* _____ he took yesterday on his blog.

소유격 관계대명사는 소유격 역할을 하며 바로 뒤에 _____가 온다.

접속사와 대명사	I know	a boy.	+	His	voice is soft.
관계대명사	I know	a boy	_____		voice is soft.

관계대명사가 소유격 역할을 하므로, 소유격 대명사 _____

He is from *a country*. + **Its** nature is very beautiful. <Its = _____>

→ ☆ He is from *a country* _____ _____ is very beautiful.

```
○ Tip ○
관계대명사의 격과 어순 관계
① 선행사 + [ _____ + _____ ~]
② 선행사 + [ _____ + _____ + _____ ~]
③ 선행사 + [ _____ + _____ + (주어) + 동사 ~]
```

❶ 관계대명사 that은 _____ 형태가 없으며, 관계대명사 _____, _____ 대신 쓸 수 있다.

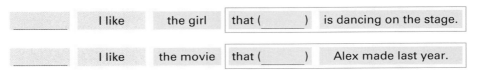

_____	I like	the girl	that (_____) is dancing on the stage.
_____	I like	the movie	that (_____) Alex made last year.

❷ 주로 관계대명사 that을 쓰는 경우

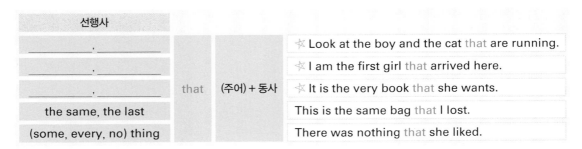

선행사			
_____ , _____			☆ Look at the boy and the cat that are running.
_____ , _____	that	(주어) + 동사	☆ I am the first girl that arrived here.
_____ , _____			☆ It is the very book that she wants.
the same, the last			This is the same bag that I lost.
(some, every, no) thing			There was nothing that she liked.

```
○ Tip ○
[the very + 명사]: _____
[the only + 명사]: _____
```

GP 51 관계대명사 생략

❶ _____ 관계대명사 who(m), which, that은 생략할 수 있다.

선행사	_____ 관계대명사	_____
the book	who(m), which, that	I bought yesterday

❷ 주격 관계대명사는 뒤에 _____ 가 나올 때 _____ 생략할 수 있다.

선행사	____ 관계대명사 ____	~
the boys	who	are	singing a song

The man (_____) I met yesterday is a famous musician.

☆ We have to recycle the cans (_____) we used.

☆ The girl (_____) giving a speech is my sister.

Titanic is a movie (_____) based on a real story.

• Upgrade •

전치사의 목적어로 관계대명사가 쓰일 경우 관계대명사절에 있는 _____ 가 관계대명사 _____ 에 올 수 있다.
이때 관계대명사 _____ 은 쓸 수 _____ 목적격 관계대명사를 _____ 할 수도 _____ .

I know the topic **which (that)** we will talk **about**.
= I know the topic _____ we will talk. (전치사 + 관계대명사)
I know the topic **about that** we will talk. (X)　(전치사 + _____ (X))
I know the topic **about** we will talk. (X)　(전치사 뒤 _____ (X))

GP 52 관계대명사 what

관계대명사 what은 _____ 를 포함해서 the thing which (that)로 나타낼 수 있고 '_____'으로 해석한다.

_____	Tell me	the thing	_____	you are looking for.

_____	Tell me	_____	you are looking for.

Can you show me **the thing which (that)** is in your pocket?
→ ☆ Can you show me _____ _____ ?

관계부사는 _____와 _____ 역할을 동시에 하고 관계부사가 이끄는 절은 앞에 나오는 명사(선행사)를 _____한다. 관계부사는 선행사에 따라 다음과 같이 나누고 [_____ + 관계대명사] 형태로 바꿀 수 있다.

| This is | the place | where | I first met the woman. |

| _____ | 관계부사절: _____ 역할 |

	선행사	관계부사	전치사 + 관계대명사
시간	the time, the day	_____	at / in / on... which
장소	the place, the house	_____	at / in / on... which
이유	_____	_____	_____
방법	_____	_____	_____

| _____ | I remember | the day. | + | You were born | on | the day. |

| _____ | I remember | the day | _____ you were born. |
| | | | _____ you were born. |

❶ _____ : 시간을 나타내는 the time, the day, the year 등이 선행사일 때
9 o'clock is *the time*. + Our class starts **at the time**.
→ ☆ 9 o'clock is *the time* _____ our class starts.

❷ _____ : 장소를 나타내는 the place, the house, the city 등이 선행사일 때
This is *the park*. + I usually exercise **at the park**.
→ ☆ This is *the park* _____ I usually exercise.

❸ _____ : 이유를 나타내는 the reason이 선행사일 때
I don't know *the reason*. + He was absent **for the reason**.
→ ☆ I don't know *the reason* _____ he was absent.

❹ _____ : 방법을 나타내는 the way가 선행사일 때
This is *the way*. + He solved the puzzle **in the way**.
→ This is *the way* **how** he solved the puzzle. (×)
→ This is *the way* _____ he solved the puzzle.
→ ☆ This is _____ he solved the puzzle.

○ Tip ○
선행사 _____와 관계부사
_____는 같이 쓸 수 없다.

A   ( ) 안에서 알맞은 것을 고르시오.

1 Tell me about the girl (which, whom) you met in the park.

2 This is the cake (which, who) my father made for me.

3 I chose the book (which, who) has a yellow cover.

4 Teachers like students (which, who) are interested in learning.

B   보기처럼 선행사와 관계대명사절에 밑줄을 긋고 해석하시오.

> 보기 | He is a <u>pianist</u> <u>whom we want to meet</u>.   해석 내가 좋아하는 (피아니스트)

1 I saved the money which my uncle gave to me.   해석 _____

2 He is a reporter who interviewed the president.   해석 _____

3 Where is the picture which was in my room?   해석 _____

4 The boy who is playing the guitar is my son.   해석 _____

5 The rumor that you heard is not true.   해석 _____

C   관계대명사를 이용하여 다음 두 문장을 한 문장으로 만드시오. (관계대명사 that 제외)

1 This is the song. + Becky made it for me.

→ _____ .

2 The actor is not friendly. + You want to meet him.

→ _____ .

3 Ricky cooked spaghetti. + It smelled really good.

→ _____ .

4 I know a girl. + She can speak four languages.

→ _____ .

5 The Barbie doll is for you. + I bought it yesterday.

→ _____ .

D 보기와 같이 빈칸에 관계대명사, 생략되는 대명사를 쓰고, 관계대명사의 격을 체크하시오.

보기	The picture is the best. And my dad painted it. → The picture which my dad painted is the best.	접속사 + 대명사 and + it	관계대명사의 격 (주격, 목적격)
1 I have a brother. And he can speak three languages. → I have a brother _____ can speak three languages.		and + _____	(주격, 목적격)
2 The students are from China. And we met them. → The students _____ we met are from China.		and + _____	(주격, 목적격)
3 Did you find the cell phone? And you lost it. → Did you find the cell phone _____ you lost?		and + _____	(주격, 목적격)

E 우리말과 의미가 같도록 ( ) 안의 말을 배열하시오.

1 내가 사고 싶은 꽃은 장미가 아니야. (I, to, want, buy, which, the flower)

→ _____ is not a rose.

2 너는 너를 도울 친구들을 찾아야만 한다. (you, will, friends, who, help)

→ You have to find _____.

3 언덕 위에 서 있는 저 건물은 병원이다. (on, hill, which, the, standing, is, the building)

→ _____ is a hospital.

4 내가 정말 좋아하는 작가는 Mark Twain이다. (like, whom, really, I, the writer)

→ _____ is Mark Twain.

F 우리말과 의미가 같도록 ( ) 안의 말을 이용하여 문장을 완성하시오. (관계대명사 that 제외)

1 저것은 내가 보고 싶은 콘서트다. (want, watch)

→ That is a concert _____ _____ _____ _____.

2 그 피아니스트가 연주했던 음악은 멋졌다. (play, the pianist)

→ The music _____ _____ _____ was great.

3 나는 일본에 살았던 친구에게 편지를 보냈다. (live, Japan)

→ I sent a letter to my friend _____ _____ _____.

4 Tom은 마침내 그가 결혼하고 싶었던 여자를 만났다. (want, marry)

→ Tom finally met the woman _____ _____ _____.

A   ( ) 안에서 알맞은 것을 고르시오.

1 My mom is the wisest person (whose, that) I know.

2 I have a friend (whose, that) job is decorating food.

3 We checked everything (which, that) we needed.

4 Tom is the boy (who, whose) voice is very soft.

5 Man is the only animal (which, that) can speak languages.

6 The man (who, whose) car was stolen went to the police.

B   관계대명사를 이용하여 두 문장을 한 문장으로 만드시오.

1 He thanked the girl. + Her dog saved his child.

→ He thanked the girl _____ _____ _____ _____ .

2 All the eggs broke. + My mom bought them.

→ All the eggs _____ _____ _____ _____ broke.

3 I have a friend. + His birthday is the same as mine.

→ I have a friend _____ _____ _____ _____

_____ _____ .

4 The only question is how to get there. + I have it.

→ The only question _____ _____ _____ is how to get there.

5 They saved a sick animal. + Its life was in danger.

→ They saved a sick animal _____ _____ _____ _____ .

C   보기에서 알맞은 표현을 골라 문장을 완성하시오. (한 번씩만 사용)

보기 | · that you've ever seen   · which (that) I am interested in
      | · whose car broke down   · that is good for your health

1 I will cook something _____ .

2 We helped a man _____ .

3 History is the subject _____ .

4 What is the most intelligent animal _____ ?

D 우리말과 의미가 같도록 ( ) 안의 말을 배열하시오.

1 꼬리가 매우 화려한 공작새를 보렴. (very, is, tail, colorful, whose)

→ Look at the peacock _____.

2 나는 네가 나에게 썼던 첫 번째 편지를 가지고 있다. (wrote, that, me, you, to)

→ I have the first letter _____.

3 나는 어제 네가 골라 주었던 마지막 셔츠가 마음에 든다. (yesterday, that, chose, you)

→ I like the last shirt _____.

4 머리가 곱슬머리인 소녀는 곧은 머리를 원한다. (hair, curly, is, whose)

→ The girl _____ wants to have straight hair.

5 오늘 배웠던 모든 것을 제발 기억해라. (you, today, learned, that)

→ Please remember everything _____.

6 작가가 상을 받았던 이 책은 처음에는 인기가 없었다. (the, won, prize, writer, whose)

→ The book _____ wasn't popular at the beginning.

E 우리말과 의미가 같도록 ( ) 안의 말을 이용하여 문장을 완성하시오.

1 그의 개를 잃어버린 저 소년을 도와주자. (dog, missing)

→ Let's help the boy _____ _____ _____.

2 나는 선생님이 가진 것과 같은 펜을 원해. (have)

→ I want the same pen _____ _____ _____ _____.

3 나는 아빠가 한국에서 유명한 디자이너인 친구가 있다. (famous, designer)

→ I have a friend _____ _____ _____ _____

_____ in Korea.

4 취미가 번지점프인 소녀의 이야기는 믿을 수 없다. (hobby, bungee jumping)

→ I can't believe the story of the girl _____ _____ _____

_____ _____.

5 엄마는 내가 원했던 바로 그 코트를 사 주셨다. (want)

→ My mom bought me the very coat _____ _____ _____.

6 네가 그녀로부터 들었던 모든 것을 나에게 말해 줄래? (hear)

→ Could you tell me everything _____ _____ _____

_____ ?

A ( ) 안에서 알맞은 것을 고르시오.

1 I forgot (which, what) my teacher said.

2 I am going to order (which, what) you want to eat.

3 We must do something (that, what) is right for peace.

4 The book (which, what) I borrowed is not easy to read.

5 The country (in which, in that) she lived was very hot.

B 생략할 수 있는 것에 밑줄을 긋고, 생략하는 이유의 번호를 쓰시오. (생략 불가면 X 표시)

보기	① 목적격 관계대명사	② 주격 관계대명사 + be동사	이유

1 Look at the nice chair which my father made himself. _____

2 We like the teacher who teaches science. _____

3 They repaired the building which was damaged by the typhoon. _____

4 He directed the movie which became popular. _____

5 The museum offers special activities that kids can enjoy. _____

6 The boys who are playing baseball are my classmates. _____

C 선행사 여부를 체크하고, 빈칸에 관계대명사 what 또는 that을 써서 문장을 완성하시오.

1 Guess _____ I have in this box. 선행사 (있음, 없음)

2 _____ is important is our effort. 선행사 (있음, 없음)

3 The quiz _____ the teacher gave was not easy. 선행사 (있음, 없음)

4 We saw a film _____ was about modern history. 선행사 (있음, 없음)

5 This book is _____ he wants to read. 선행사 (있음, 없음)

6 We enjoyed the cake _____ you made for the party. 선행사 (있음, 없음)

7 Your smile is _____ makes you beautiful. 선행사 (있음, 없음)

D 우리말과 의미가 같도록 ( ) 안의 말을 배열하시오.

1 Grace는 내가 찍은 사진을 벽에 걸어 두었다. (wall, took, the, I, on)

→ Grace hung the picture _____.

2 백성들을 위해 세종대왕이 했던 일은 기억되어야 한다. (King Sejong, what, did)

→ _____ for his people must be remembered.

3 나는 엄마에 의해 번역된 책이 매우 자랑스럽다. (my mom, by, translated)

→ I am proud of the book _____.

4 내가 작년에 함께 지냈던 룸메이트는 매우 재미있었다. (I, with, last, lived, year)

→ The roommate _____ was very funny.

5 면세점에서 구입한 것을 보여 주세요. (bought, what, you)

→ Show me _____ at the duty-free store.

6 유리로 만들어진 신발을 신는 것은 불가능해. (are, of, which, glass, made)

→ It is not possible to wear shoes _____.

E 우리말과 의미가 같도록 ( ) 안의 말을 이용하여 문장을 완성하시오. (관계사를 생략할 수 있으면 생략)

1 지난달 내가 샀던 모자는 어디에 있니? (buy)

→ Where is the hat _____ _____ _____ _____?

2 내가 점심으로 먹은 것은 단지 사과 하나였다. (eat)

→ _____ _____ _____ for lunch was just one apple.

3 이 웹사이트에 주어진 정보는 사실이 아니다. (given, website)

→ The information _____ _____ _____ _____ is not true.

4 그녀에 대해 내가 알고 있었던 것은 그녀의 이름이었다. (know)

→ _____ _____ _____ about her was her name.

5 내가 어제 빌렸던 책은 읽기에 쉽지 않다. (borrow)

→ The book _____ _____ _____ is not easy to read.

6 나는 Tom에게 그가 가장 원했던 것을 주었다. (want)

→ I gave Tom _____ _____ _____ the most.

A 빈칸에 알맞은 말을 보기에서 골라 쓰시오.

> 보기 |　　　when　　　　　　where　　　　　　why　　　　　　how

1 Please tell me _____ I can use the machine.

2 That is the reason _____ I like him.

3 He didn't remember the time _____ he got home.

4 What is the name of the city _____ we are staying?

B [관계부사]와 [전치사 + 관계대명사]를 이용하여 두 문장을 한 문장으로 만드시오.

1 I know the reason. + She likes Max for the reason.

관계부사　　　→ I know the reason _____ _____ _____.

전치사 + 관계대명사　→ I know the reason _____ _____ she likes Max.

2 Culture shows the way. + People live in the way.

관계부사　　　→ Culture shows _____ _____ _____.

전치사 + 관계대명사　→ Culture shows the way _____ _____ people live.

3 I remember the day. + I first saw you on the day.

관계부사　　　→ I remember the day _____ _____ _____ _____ _____.

전치사 + 관계대명사　→ I remember the day _____ _____ I first saw you.

4 We visited the house. + Mozart lived in the house.

관계부사　　　→ We visited the house _____ _____ _____.

전치사 + 관계대명사　→ We visited the house _____ _____ Mozart lived.

C 앞 문장과 자연스럽게 이어지도록 뒤의 문장을 연결하시오.

1 We all miss the time　　　•　　　　•　ⓐ why Brian is upset?

2 Do you know the reason　　•　　　　•　ⓑ how he saved money.

3 He told me　　　　　　•　　　　•　ⓒ where he was born.

4 He went back to the town　•　　　　•　ⓓ when we were kids.

D 우리말과 의미가 같도록 ( ) 안의 말을 배열하시오.

1 나는 그가 성적을 향상시켰던 방법이 궁금하다. (he, his, how, grades, improved)

→ I wonder _____ .

2 오늘은 우리가 학교를 졸업하는 날이다. (when, from school, graduate, we)

→ Today is the day _____ .

3 우리 오빠가 일하고 있는 건물은 매우 현대적이다. (working, my brother, where, is)

→ The building _____ is very modern.

4 학생들을 야단친 이유가 무엇인가요? (your students, punished, why, you)

→ What is the reason _____ ?

5 이곳은 그의 가족이 휴가 동안 머물렀던 호텔이다. (his family, stayed, where)

→ This is the hotel _____ during his vacation.

6 어떻게 그와 연락할 수 있는지 말해 주시겠어요? (can, him, I, contact, how)

→ Could you tell me _____ ?

E 우리말과 의미가 같도록 ( ) 안의 말을 이용하여 문장을 완성하시오.

1 월요일은 우리가 가장 바쁜 날이다. (the busiest)

→ Monday is the day _____ _____ _____ _____ .

2 나는 그 남자 배우가 인기 있는 이유를 모르겠다. (popular)

→ I don't know the reason _____ _____ _____ _____ .

3 나는 우리가 점심을 먹었던 식당에 핸드폰을 두고 왔다. (have)

→ I left my cell phone in the cafeteria _____ _____ _____ _____ .

4 이 책은 네가 스트레스를 줄일 수 있는 방법을 가르쳐 줄 것이다. (reduce)

→ This book will teach you _____ _____ _____ _____ .

5 너는 그가 부산으로 이사 간 이유를 알고 있니? (move to)

→ Do you know the reason _____ _____ _____ _____ ?

6 나는 연설 대회에서 실수했던 그날을 잊을 수 없다. (make mistakes)

→ I can't forget the day _____ _____ _____ _____ in the
speech contest.

Error Correction

■ 밑줄 친 부분에 대한 설명을 체크하고 틀린 경우엔 바르게 고치시오. (맞으면 'O', 불필요하면 '삭제' 표시)

*S: 주어, V: 동사

1 My teacher chose the book <u>who</u> was written in English. (→   )
선행사 (사람, 사물),
관계대명사 (주격, 목적격) + V

2 He posted a picture <u>who</u> he took yesterday on his blog. (→   )
선행사 (사람, 사물),
관계대명사 (주격, 목적격) + S + V

3 He is from a country <u>which</u> nature is very beautiful. (→   )
선행사 + (주격, 소유격) 관계대명사 + 명사

4 Look at the boy and the cat <u>which</u> are running. (→   )
'사람 + 동물' 포함 선행사는
관계대명사 (that, which)

5 I am the first girl <u>that</u> arrived here. (→   )
서수 포함 선행사는
관계대명사 (that, which)

6 It is the very book <u>which</u> she wants. (→   )
the very 포함 선행사는
관계대명사 (that, which)

7 We have to recycle <u>the cans we used.</u> (→   )
선행사 + [목적격 관계대명사 + 주어 + 동사]에서
목적격 관계대명사 생략 (가능, 불가능)

8 <u>The girl giving</u> a speech is my sister. (→   )
선행사 + [주격 관계대명사 + be동사 + ~]에서
[주격 관계대명사 + be동사] 생략 (가능, 불가능)

9 Can you show me <u>that</u> is in your pocket? (→   )
선행사가 (있으므로, 없으므로)
관계대명사 (what, that)

10 9 o'clock is the time <u>where</u> our class starts. (→   )
선행사 + 관계부사
(장소, 시간)   (where, when)

11 This is the park <u>when</u> I usually exercise. (→   )
선행사 + 관계부사
(장소, 시간)   (where, when)

12 I don't know the reason <u>how</u> he was absent. (→   )
선행사 + 관계부사
(시간, 이유)   (when, why)

13 This is the way <u>how</u> he solved the puzzle. (→   )
선행사 + 관계부사
(방법, 이유)   (how, 없음)

Sentence writing

■ 주어진 단어를 알맞게 이용하여 우리말과 의미가 같도록 영작하시오.

1	choose, write in English	나의 선생님은 / 선택했다 / 책을 / 영어로 쓰여진 →
2	post, take	그는 올렸다 / 사진 한 장을 / 그가 어제 찍은 / 그의 블로그에 →
3	be from, a country	그는 ~출신이다 / 나라 / 그 나라의 자연이 / 매우 아름다운 →
4	look at, run	봐라 / 저 소년과 고양이를 / 달리고 있는 →
5	the first, arrive	나는 / 첫 번째 소녀이다 / 여기에 도착했던 →
6	the very	이것이 / 바로 그 책이다 / 그녀가 원하는 →
7	have to, recycle, cans	우리는 / 재활용해야 한다 / 캔을 / 우리가 사용했던 →
8	give a speech	그 소녀는 / 연설을 하고 있는 / 나의 여동생이다 →
9	show, in your pocket	보여 줄 수 있니 / 나에게 / 네 주머니에 들어 있는 것을? →
10	our class, start	9시는 / 시간이다 / 우리 수업이 시작하는 →
11	the park, exercise	여기는 / 공원이다 / 내가 주로 운동하는 →
12	reason, be absent	나는 / 모른다 / 이유를 / 그가 결석했던 →
13	solve, the puzzle	이것이 / 방법이다 / 그가 퍼즐을 풀었던 →

문법패턴 빈칸 채우기

GP 54 가정법 과거

가정법 과거는 현재 사실과 반대되는 상황을 나타내거나 실현 불가능한 것을 가정할 때 사용한다.

If	주어	_____	+	주어	_____	동사원형
		만약 ~한다면(라면)			~할 텐데	

☆ If my mom _____ how to drive, she _____.

☆ If I _____ you, I _____ the homeless.

❶ 가정법 과거

☆ If he **got up** early, he **would** not **be** late for class.

If you **were** invisible, what **would** you **do**?

○─ Tip ─○
과정법 과거에서 If절의 be동사는
주어의 인칭과 단복수에 상관없이
_____를 사용한다.

❷ 가정법 과거의 직설법 전환: 가정법 과거는 직설법 현재시제로 전환

☆ If I **had** enough time, I **would visit** you.

→ ☆ As I _____ enough time, I _____ you.

• Upgrade •

가정법 과거완료: 과거 사실을 반대로 가정할 때 사용하는 표현

[If + 주어 + had p.p. ~, 주어 + would / could / might + have p.p. ~.]

If I **had hurried**, I **could have taken** the bus.

GP 55 단순 조건문과 가정법 과거

단순 조건문은 말하는 내용이 실현 가능성이 _____ 때 사용하고 가정법 과거는 현재 사실을 반대로 나타내거나 실현 가능성이 _____ 일을 나타낼 때 사용하는 표현이다.

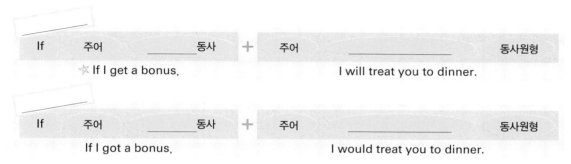

If	주어	_____동사	+	주어	_____	동사원형
	☆ If I get a bonus,				I will treat you to dinner.	

If	주어	_____동사	+	주어	_____	동사원형
	If I got a bonus,				I would treat you to dinner.	

If I **win** the lottery, I **will travel** around the world. (단순 조건문)

If I **won** the lottery, I **would travel** around the world. (가정법 과거)

GP 56 I wish + 가정법 과거

I wish + 가정법 과거는 현재에 이루기 힘든 것을 _____ 할 때 사용한다.

I	_____	+	that	주어	_____
				주어가 ~하면(라면)	

☆ I wish   I lived close to you.
☆ I wish   I were five years younger.

❶ I wish + 가정법 과거

I wish I **could speak** English well.
I wish I **didn't have to go** to school.

❷ I wish + 가정법 과거의 직설법 전환: _____ + 직설법 현재

☆ I wish you **didn't make** so much noise.

→ ☆ _____ you _____ so much noise.

I wish it **stopped** raining.

→ _____ it _____ raining.

GP 57 as if + 가정법 과거

as if + 가정법 과거는 현재 사실의 반대를 가정할 때 사용한다.

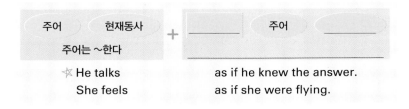

주어	현재동사	+	_____	주어	_____
주어는 ~한다					

☆ He talks   as if he knew the answer.
   She feels   as if she were flying.

❶ as if + 가정법 과거

She acts **as if** she **were** my mother.
He talks **as if** he **had** a girlfriend.

❷ as if + 가정법 과거의 직설법 전환: In fact, + 직설법 현재

☆ She treats me **as if** I **were** a baby.

→ ☆ _____, I _____ a baby.

He talks **as if** he **could fix** the car himself.

→ _____, he _____ the car himself.

A ( ) 안에서 알맞은 것을 고르시오.

1 If you make a mistake, your boss (will, would) get upset.

2 If I were you, I (don't say, wouldn't say) things like that.

3 If she (plays, will play, played) the guitar, she would join a band.

4 What would you do if a ghost (are, were) in front of you?

5 If he is free tomorrow, he (will come, would come, came) here.

B ( ) 안의 단어를 알맞게 고쳐 빈칸을 채우시오.

1 If I _____ the grammar points well, I would teach you. (know)

2 If he gets a second chance, he _____ _____ harder. (study)

3 I _____ _____ her a card if I remembered her address. (send)

4 If she _____ the subway, she will not be late for the meeting. (take)

5 If you _____ a magic wand, what would you do with it? (have)

C 두 문장이 같은 의미를 갖도록 빈칸을 채우시오.

1 As I eat so many sweets, I don't have healthier teeth.

→ If I _____ _____ so many sweets, I _____ _____ healthier teeth.

2 As the TV is so loud, I can't sleep well.

→ If the TV _____ _____ so loud, I _____ _____ well.

3 As he doesn't live in Sydney, he can't visit the Sydney Opera House often.

→ If he _____ in Sydney, he _____ _____ the Sydney Opera House often.

4 As the book isn't easy to read, I won't buy it.

→ If the book _____ easy to read, I _____ _____ it.

5 As I am not a child, I can't learn how to swim quickly.

→ If I _____ a child, I _____ _____ how to swim quickly.

6 This soup isn't tasty as it is not warm.

→ This soup _____ _____ tasty if it _____ warm.

D 우리말과 의미가 같도록 ( ) 안의 말을 배열하시오.

1 그녀가 당근을 더 먹으면, 더 건강할 텐데. (healthier, ate, be, would)

→ If she _____ more carrots, she _____.

2 이 영화가 재미있으면 너에게 추천해 줄게. (will, it, is, recommend)

→ If the movie _____ interesting, I _____ to you.

3 그녀가 사실을 알면, 그녀가 네게 말해 줄 텐데. (she, you, knew, the truth, tell, would)

→ If she _____, _____.

4 이 스커트가 나에게 어울리지 않으면 너에게 줄게. (will, doesn't, give, look good, it)

→ If the skirt _____ on me, I _____ to you.

5 선생님의 말을 들으면, 그들이 실패하지 않을 텐데. (fail, listened to, not, would)

→ If they _____ their teacher, they _____.

6 내가 중국어를 유창하게 하면, 중국을 혼자 여행할 텐데. (would, spoke, travel)

→ If I _____ Chinese fluently, I _____ to China alone.

E 우리말과 의미가 같도록 ( ) 안의 말을 이용하여 문장을 완성하시오.

1 내일 날씨가 좋으면, 우리는 놀이공원에 갈 것이다. (be fine)

→ If it _____ _____ tomorrow, we _____ _____ to the amusement park.

2 네가 만약 외계인을 만난다면 뭐라고 할 거니? (meet)

→ What _____ you say if you _____ an alien?

3 내가 만약 차가 있으면, 집까지 너를 태워 줄 텐데. (will give you a ride)

→ If I _____ a car, I _____ _____ _____ _____ _____ home.

4 그녀가 5분 늦으면, 그녀는 인터뷰에 늦을 텐데. (be, be late)

→ If she _____ five minutes late, she _____ _____ _____ for the interview.

5 내가 영어를 잘하면, 영화를 자막 없이 볼 텐데. (be good at, see)

→ If I _____ _____ _____ English, I _____ _____ _____ _____ without subtitles.

6 네가 다음에 벽을 푸른색으로 칠한다면, 이것은 훨씬 시원해 보일 거야. (paint, look)

→ If you _____ the wall blue next time, it _____ _____ cooler.

A ( ) 안에서 알맞은 것을 고르시오.

1 I wish I (will have, had) a good memory.

2 Jane walks (like, as if) she were a queen.

3 She wishes she (can, could) play tennis.

4 The boy talks as if he (is, were) a famous singer.

5 My dad wishes he (weren't, isn't) busy now.

6 They talk loudly as if there (are, were) nobody around them.

B 두 문장이 같은 의미가 되도록 빈칸에 알맞은 말을 넣어 가정법으로 바꾸시오.

1 I am sorry it rains so much.

→ I wish _____ so much.

2 In fact, he doesn't read many books.

→ He talks as if he _____ many books.

3 I am sorry you have to leave now.

→ I wish you _____ leave now.

4 In fact, my brother doesn't have a fever.

→ My brother acts as if he _____ a fever.

5 In fact, he is not your friend.

→ He talks about you as if he _____ your friend.

C 두 문장이 같은 의미가 되도록 빈칸에 알맞은 말을 넣으시오.

1 I wish I had a twin sister.

→ I am sorry I _____ a twin sister.

2 He cries as if he were a little baby.

→ In fact, he _____ a little baby.

3 I wish it didn't snow so heavily.

→ I am sorry it _____ so heavily.

4 She acts as if she were surprised by the party.

→ In fact, she _____ by the party.

D 우리말과 의미가 같도록 ( ) 안의 말을 배열하시오.

1 그녀가 나를 어떻게 생각하는지 알면 좋을 텐데. (I, knew, wish, I)

→ _____ what she thinks of me.

2 그는 매우 목마른 것처럼 물을 마신다. (very, as, thirsty, he, if, were)

→ He drinks water _____ .

3 내 친구가 나에게 도움을 주면 좋을 텐데. (wish, my friend, I, gave)

→ _____ me a hand.

4 그는 마치 그 팀에 속하지 않은 것처럼 느낀다. (if, were, as, he, not)

→ He feels _____ on the team.

5 그는 땅이 흔들리고 있는 것처럼 느꼈다. (if, shaking, the ground, as, were)

→ He feels _____ .

6 나이가 충분히 많아서 혼자 살 수 있으면 좋을 텐데. (old enough, wish, I, were, I)

→ _____ to live on my own.

E 우리말과 의미가 같도록 ( ) 안의 말을 이용하여 문장을 완성하시오.

1 나만의 방을 갖게 되면 좋을 텐데. (have, own)

→ I wish _____ _____ _____ _____ .

2 그녀는 내 비밀을 아는 것처럼 말한다. (know)

→ She talks _____ _____ _____ _____ my secret.

3 나의 오빠가 자기 방을 매일 청소하면 좋을 텐데. (clean)

→ _____ _____ _____ _____ his room every day.

4 그는 오늘이 가장 행복한 날인 것처럼 말한다. (today, the happiest day)

→ He talks _____ _____ _____ _____

_____ _____ .

5 위층 사람들이 큰 소리로 돌아다니지 않으면 좋을 텐데. (the people upstairs, walk)

→ _____ _____ _____ _____ _____

_____ around so loudly.

6 매일 매일을 당신의 마지막인 것처럼 사세요. (it, be, your last)

→ Live every day _____ _____ _____ _____ .

Error Correction

■ 밑줄 친 부분에 대한 설명을 체크하고 틀린 경우엔 바르게 고치시오. (맞으면 'O' 표시)

*S: 주어

1	If my mom knew how to drive, she <u>can</u> pick me up. (→)	실현 가능성이 (있는, 없는) 가정법은 If + S + 과거동사, S + (can, could) + 동사원형
2	If I <u>am</u> you, I would help the homeless. (→)	실현 가능성이 (있는, 없는) 가정법은 If + S + (과거, 현재)동사, S + would + 동사원형
3	If he got up early, he <u>will</u> not be late for class. (→)	실현 가능성이 (있는, 없는) 가정법은 If + S + 과거동사, S + (will, would) + 동사원형
4	If I <u>had</u> enough time, I would visit you. (→)	실현 가능성이 (있는, 없는) 가정법은 If + S + (과거, 현재)동사, S + would + 동사원형
5	As I <u>didn't have</u> enough time, I won't visit you. (→)	직설법에서는 현재 사실과 (같음, 반대) S + (현재, 과거)시제
6	If I <u>got</u> a bonus, I will treat you to dinner. (→)	실현가능성이 (있는, 없는) 조건문은 if절에 (과거, 현재)시제
7	I wish I <u>lived</u> close to you. (→)	현재에 이루기 힘든 소망은 I wish + S + (현재, 과거)동사
8	I wish I <u>am</u> five years younger. (→)	현재에 이루기 힘든 소망은 I wish + S + (현재, 과거)동사
9	I wish you <u>doesn't make</u> so much noise. (→)	현재에 이루기 힘든 소망은 I wish + S + (현재, 과거)동사
10	I am sorry you <u>make</u> so much noise. (→)	직설법에서는 현재 사실과 (같음, 반대) S + (현재, 과거)시제
11	He talks as if he <u>knows</u> the answer. (→)	현재 (사실, 사실의 반대) 처럼 as if + S + (현재, 과거)동사
12	She treats me as if I <u>am</u> a baby. (→)	현재 (사실, 사실의 반대) 처럼 as if + S + (현재, 과거)동사
13	In fact, I <u>am</u> not a baby. (→)	직설법에서는 현재 사실과 (같음, 반대) S + (현재, 과거)시제

■ 주어진 단어를 알맞게 이용하여 우리말과 의미가 같도록 영작하시오.

1	how to drive, pick me up	만약 엄마가 운전하는 방법을 아신다면 / 나를 데리러 오실 수 있을 텐데 →
2	help, the homeless	만약 내가 너라면 / 집 없는 사람들을 도울 텐데 →
3	get up, be late for	만약 그가 일찍 일어난다면 / 그는 수업에 늦지 않을 텐데 →
4	have, visit	만약 내가 충분한 시간이 있다면 / 나는 너를 방문할 텐데 →
5	have, visit	내가 충분한 시간이 없기 때문에 / 나는 너를 방문하지 않을 거다 →
6	get, treat, to dinner	만약 내가 보너스를 받게 되면 / 너에게 저녁을 한턱낼게 (실현 가능성 있음) →
7	live, close to	나는 좋을 텐데 / 내가 너랑 가까이 살면 →
8	younger	나는 좋을 텐데 / 내가 5살 더 어리다면 →
9	make so much noise	나는 좋을 텐데 / 네가 소음을 많이 내지 않는다면 →
10	make so much noise	나는 유감이다 / 네가 소음을 많이 내서 →
11	talk, know	그는 말한다 / 마치 그가 답을 아는 것처럼 →
12	treat, a baby	그녀는 나를 대한다 / 마치 내가 아기인 것처럼 →
13	in fact	사실상 / 나는 아기가 아니다 →

도전! 필수구문 156

Chapter 01 문장의 형태 통문장 영작

001	그는 스포츠 영웅이 되었다.	→
002	너의 가방은 유행하는 것처럼 보인다.	→
003	Brown 씨가 우리에게 수학을 가르쳤다.	→
004	Mary는 그녀의 아이들에게 약간의 쿠키를 사 주었다.	→
005	그는 그의 의사에게 두 가지 질문을 했다.	→
006	우리는 그를 우리 클럽의 회장으로 선출했다.	→
007	우리는 우리 방을 깨끗하게 유지해야 한다.	→
008	나는 그가 매일 운동하기를 원한다.	→
009	그녀는 그가 침실을 청소하도록 시켰다.	→
010	나는 내 동생이 숙제를 하도록 시켰다.	→
011	엄마는 내가 공포영화 보는 것을 허락하지 않았다.	→
012	나는 그녀가 그림을 그리는 것을 보았다.	→
013	우리는 앵무새 한 마리가 "Hello"라고 말하는 것을 들었다.	→

도전! 필수구문 156 ✏️

Chapter 02 시제 통문장 영작

014	Oliver는 시드니에서 눈을 본 적이 없어.	→
015	너는 움직이는 돌들에 대해 들어 본 적 있니?	→
016	아니, 나는 한 적이 없다. (현재완료 질문에 대한 대답)	→
017	그는 이틀 전에 그 열쇠를 잃어버렸어.	→
018	그는 그 열쇠를 잃어버렸어. (그래서 지금은 없어.)	→
019	나의 언니가 집에 이제 막 돌아왔어.	→
020	너는 배를 타고 여행해 본 적 있니?	→
021	그는 (과거부터 현재까지) 2년 동안 파리에 살아 왔어.	→
022	그녀는 음악에 대한 관심을 잃어버렸어. (그래서 지금도 없어.)	→
023	그녀는 그 영화를 열 번 봐 왔어.	→
024	너는 내가 너를 마지막으로 본 이후로 많이 자랐구나.	→
025	그녀는 런던에 가 본 적이 있어.	→
026	그녀는 런던으로 가버렸어. (그래서 지금 여기 없어.)	→

도전! 필수구문 156

Chapter 03 조동사 통문장 영작

027	그녀는 사람들의 마음을 읽을 수 있어.	→
028	그는 답을 찾을 수 있을 거야.	→
029	그 새는 추하게 보일 수도 있지만, 매우 영리해.	→
030	나는 내 약속을 지키겠다.	→
031	그 소문은 틀림없이 거짓일 거야.	→
032	너는 다른 사람들에게 그 비밀을 말해서는 안 돼.	→
033	너는 서둘러야만 할 거야.	→
034	그녀는 일요일에 일찍 일어날 필요가 없어.	→
035	여러분은 여러분의 휴대폰을 꺼두는 것이 좋을 것입니다.	→
036	Jack은 정크푸드를 먹지 않는 것이 낫겠다.	→
037	우리 오빠는 돌을 수집하곤 했었지.	→
038	그 대통령은 이전에 배우였어.	→
039	나는 유럽으로 여행을 하고 싶습니다.	→

도전! 필수구문 156

Chapter 04 수동태 통문장 영작

040 그 가수는 많은 소녀들에 의해 사랑을 받는다. →

041 그녀의 모든 팬들은 그 여배우에 의해 초대되었다. →

042 이 프로그램은 대학생들에 의해 사용될 것이다. →

043 내 차는 Sam에 의해 세차되고 있다. →

044 저녁식사가 아빠에 의해 부엌에서 준비되고 있었다. →

045 그 책은 그에 의해 쓰여지지 않았다. →

046 그 건물은 Fred에 의해 디자인되었니? →

047 한글은 세종대왕에 의해 언제 창제되었니? →

048 그 규칙들은 사람들에 의해 지켜져야 한다. →

049 그 음악 앱은 그에 의해 켜졌다. →

050 그 알은 엄마 독수리에 의해 돌봐졌다. →

051 우리는 그 영어 수업에 만족하고 있다. →

052 K-pop은 아시아 대부분의 십대들에게 알려져 있다. →

도전! 필수구문 156

Chapter 05 to부정사 통문장 영작

053	날아다니는 차를 발명하는 것은 나의 꿈이야.	→
054	내 친구들은 내 비밀을 지키는 것을 약속했어.	→
055	제발 제게 언제 공부해야 할지를 말하지 말아요.	→
056	그녀는 살 집을 구매했다.	→
057	너는 무언가 차가운 마실 것을 가지고 있니?	→
058	나는 건강을 유지하기 위해서 매일 운동을 해.	→
059	그는 그 소식을 듣게 되어서 놀랐어.	→
060	너는 그렇게 많은 팬을 가졌으니 유명한 것이 틀림없어.	→
061	내가 밤새 공부하기는 어려워.	→
062	소방관이 그 소년을 구한 것은 용감했어.	→
063	그는 나무상자를 들기에 충분히 힘이 세.	→
064	그는 매우 힘이 세서 나무상자를 들 수 있어.	→
065	Cathy는 여섯 시에 일어나기엔 너무 피곤했어.	→

도전! 필수구문 156

Chapter 06 동명사 통문장 영작

066	뮤지컬들을 보는 것은 재미있다.	→
067	그녀는 시끄럽게 노래하는 것을 즐긴다.	→
068	나는 로봇을 만드는 것에 관심 있다.	→
069	그의 취미는 사진을 찍는 것이야.	→
070	젓가락을 사용하는 것은 두뇌에 좋다.	→
071	Jane은 무대 위에서 춤추는 것을 시작했다.	→
072	나는 이전에 그 박물관을 방문했던 것을 기억해.	→
073	내일 보고서 제출할 것을 기억해라.	→
074	그녀는 너를 작년에 만났던 것을 잊었어.	→
075	오늘 네 점심을 가지고 올 것을 잊지 마라.	→
076	우리는 재미로 퍼즐을 (시험 삼아) 풀어 봤어.	→
077	우리는 상을 타기 위해 퍼즐을 풀려고 노력했어.	→
078	그는 물을 마시는 것을 멈췄어.	→

도전! 필수구문 156

Chapter 07 분사 통문장 영작

079 움직이는 로봇이 있어. →

080 나는 중고 자전거를 샀어. →

081 수중에서 움직이는 로봇이 있다. →

082 그 책은 그를 지루하게 한다. →

083 그 책은 그에게 지루하다. →

084 그는 그 책에 지루함을 느낀다. →

085 자고 있는 저 사자를 봐. →

086 나는 침낭을 하나 갖고 있어. →

087 책을 읽을 때, 그는 안경을 쓴다. →

088 알람을 듣지 않아서, 나는 계속 잤어. →

089 운전면허증을 갖고 있지만, Emily는 절대 운전 안 해. →

090 이 책을 읽으면, 너는 답을 찾을 거야. →

091 음악을 들으면서, 그는 인터넷을 검색했어. →

도전! 필수구문 156

Chapter 08 대명사 통문장 영작

092 너는 네 자신이 자랑스러운 것이 분명해. →

093 Allen은 스스로 부서진 차를 고쳤다. →

094 어린아이들은 혼자서(홀로) 수영하면 안 된다. →

095 그는 혼자 힘으로 새로운 것들을 배우는 걸 항상 즐긴다. →

096 이 가방은 너무 커. 나는 더 작은 것이 필요해. →

097 이 반지가 마음에 들지 않아요. 또 다른 것을 보여 줄래요? →

098 나는 펜 3개를 샀다. 하나는 검은색, 또 다른 하나는 빨간색, 그리고 나머지는 파란색이다. →

099 몇몇은 외출하는 것을 좋아하고, 다른 몇몇은 집에 있는 것을 좋아한다. →

100 모든 아이들은 돌봄과 사랑을 필요로 한다. →

101 모든 충고가 매우 도움이 되었다. →

102 그들 둘 모두 고등학교 학생이다. →

103 각각의 사람은 우리 팀의 승리를 위해 중요하다. →

104 모든 학생은 좋은 점수를 얻기를 원한다. →

도전! 필수구문 156

Chapter 09 비교표현 통문장 영작

105	그의 연설은 그의 라이벌의 연설만큼 강하다.	→
106	오늘은 어제만큼 덥지 않다.	→
107	뜨거운 공기는 차가운 공기보다 더 가볍다.	→
108	네 아이디어가 내 것보다 더 창의적이다.	→
109	엄지손가락은 다섯 손가락들 모두 중에서 가장 짧다.	→
110	바티칸시티는 세계에서 가장 작은 국가이다.	→
111	KTX는 그 기차보다 세 배 빠르다. (원급)	→
112	가능한 한 자주 웃어라.	→
113	나는 이전보다 훨씬 더 건강하다고 느낀다.	→
114	휴대폰이 점점 더 똑똑해지고 있다.	→
115	우리가 더 많이 나눌수록, 우리는 더 행복해진다.	→
116	바퀴는 역사상 가장 위대한 발명품들 중 하나이다.	→
117	이것은 내가 지금껏 가졌었던 것 중 가장 나쁜 헤어스타일이다.	→

도전! 필수구문 156

Chapter 10 접속사 통문장 영작

118 그가 낚시를 갈 때, 나도 같이 갈 거야. →

119 그녀가 예스라고 말할 때까지, 그녀의 개는 안 먹을 거야. →

120 어두워지기 전에 우리는 집에 도착할 거야. →

121 그가 충분히 잠을 못 잤기 때문에, 그는 눈이 빨갰어. →

122 네가 산책을 한다면, 너는 기분이 좋아질 거야. →

123 우리가 식사를 마치지 못한다면, 우리는 곧 배고파질 거야. →

124 내가 열심히 연습했음에도 불구하고, 나는 실수를 하나 했어. →

125 최선을 다하세요, 그러면 당신은 성공할 것 입니다. →

126 그 식물에 물을 줘, 그렇지 않으면 그것은 곧 죽을 거야. →

127 5월 달에 눈이 오는 것은 이상해. →

128 나는 이 콘서트 티켓을 Eric 또는 Allen에게 줄 거야. →

129 그는 무례하지도 불친절하지도 않았어. →

130 그의 형제들뿐만 아니라 Tim도 금발머리야. →

도전! 필수구문 156

Chapter 11 관계사 통문장 영작

131	나의 선생님은 영어로 쓰여진 책을 선택했어.	→
132	그는 그가 어제 찍은 사진 한 장을 그의 블로그에 올렸다.	→
133	그는 아름다운 자연을 가진 나라 출신이다.	→
134	달리고 있는 저 소년과 고양이를 봐라.	→
135	나는 여기에 도착했던 첫 번째 소녀이다.	→
136	이것이 그녀가 원하는 바로 그 책이다.	→
137	우리는 우리가 사용했던 캔을 재활용해야 한다.	→
138	연설을 하고 있는 그 소녀는 나의 여동생이다.	→
139	네 주머니에 들어 있는 것을 나에게 보여 줄 수 있니?	→
140	9시는 우리 수업이 시작하는 시간이다.	→
141	여기는 내가 주로 운동하는 공원이다.	→
142	나는 그가 결석했던 이유를 모른다.	→
143	이것이 그가 퍼즐을 풀었던 방법이다.	→

도전! 필수구문 156

Chapter 12 가정법 통문장 영작

144	만약 엄마가 운전하는 방법을 아신다면, 나를 데리러 오실 수 있을 텐데.	→
145	만약 내가 너라면, 집 없는 사람들을 도울 텐데.	→
146	만약 그가 일찍 일어난다면, 그는 수업에 늦지 않을 텐데.	→
147	만약 내가 충분한 시간이 있다면, 나는 너를 방문할 텐데.	→
148	내가 충분한 시간이 없기 때문에 나는 너를 방문하지 않을 거야.	→
149	만약 내가 보너스를 받게 되면, 너에게 저녁을 한턱낼게. (받을 가능성 있음.)	→
150	내가 너랑 가까이 살면 좋을 텐데.	→
151	내가 다섯 살 더 어리다면 좋을 텐데.	→
152	네가 소음을 많이 내지 않는다면 좋을 텐데.	→
153	네가 소음을 많이 내서 유감이야.	→
154	그는 마치 그가 답을 아는 것처럼 말한다.	→
155	그녀는 마치 내가 아기인 것처럼 대한다.	→
156	사실상, 나는 아기가 아니다.	→

Grammar ViSTA

Level **2**

학교 내신시험 대비하기
Practice Tests for School

그래머 맵핑 완성하기
Grammar Mapping

영작 연습하기
Writing Exercises

문법 노트 작성하기
Grammar Note-Taking

문법 개념 스스로 체크하기
Self-Diagnosis Guide

오답 바로잡기
Error Correction

문법 문제 풀어보기
Tests for Grammar

영작 연습하기
Sentence Writing

문법도식 학습하기
Visualization of Grammar

도전! 필수구문 156!
Challenge 156!

눈에 보이는 문법!
능동적인 자기주도 학습!

많은 문법 문제를 풀어 보고 알고 있다고 생각해도 비슷한 문제를 틀리고 실수하는 것은 정확한 문법 체계를 이해하고 있지 못하기 때문입니다. Grammar Vista Series는 문법 개념의 이해를 돕기 위해 체계적인 문법도식을 고안하여 시각적으로 학습할 수 있게 하였습니다. 또한 문법 개념을 명확하게 이해했는지를 학생 스스로 반복 확인할 수 있게 기획하여 자기주도 학습능력을 향상시킬 수 있도록 하였습니다.